THE URBAN PROFILES SERIES

SERIES EDITOR

Marilyn Gittell,

QUEENS COLLEGE OF THE CITY UNIVERSITY
OF NEW YORK

OVER THE PAST DECADE, national concern has increasingly focused on the problems of America's large cities. Yet, despite this growing interest, little is presently available on the political culture of individual cities. It is hoped that the Urban Profiles Series will fill this gap. Each volume is intended to enable the student of urban systems to familiarize himself with the particular characteristics of the city under discussion. At the same time, a common framework connects all of the volumes in the series, making serious comparative study a realistic possibility.

Each profile will select for discussion those characteristics that have been of basic importance to the development of the city and that define its essential quality. Historical information will be summarized briefly, but the emphasis is to be on those phenomena—for example, population growth, industrial development, employment, income, and racial, class, and ethnic distribution—that provide the bases of the city's current political culture. Central to each volume will be a review of the most important sources of city leadership over the years—including both official and informal power holders. In addition to describing existing local institutions and offices, revenue sources, and metropolitan area, state, and federal agencies and programs, each volume will analyze and evaluate the key interest groups and their impact on critical policy areas. Voting behavior, party structure, degrees of centralization or decentralization, the changing role of the bureaucracy in the decision-making process, municipal unions—all will be dealt with so that a complete profile of each city emerges. The contributing authors and the series editor hope that, from these profiles, it will be possible to pinpoint future trends, compare common problems, share innovative solutions, and, in general, provide the basis for a deeper understanding of the urban system in contemporary America.

Autumn, 1971

Milwaukee

A Contemporary Urban Profile

Henry J. Schmandt, John C. Goldbach,
and Donald B. Vogel

PRAEGER PUBLISHERS
New York • Washington • London

309.177
S 347

PRAEGER PUBLISHERS
111 Fourth Avenue, New York, N.Y. 10003, U.S.A.
5, Cromwell Place, London SW7 2JL, England

Published in the United States of America in 1971
by Praeger Publishers, Inc.

Library of Congress Catalog Card Number: 71–167622

Printed in the United States of America

Contents

FIGURES

TABLES

Preface

The swift pace of technological development and population growth in the modern world has, in the opinion of many observers, outrun the adaptive capabilities of existing social and political institutions. Nowhere is this gap more apparent than in the large metropolitan centers of both the industrially mature states and the developing nations. Urban America provides no exception to the universal trend; it exhibits all the symptoms of this disequilibrium. Warning signs are visible in many forms: The unrest and violence of the 1960's, the persistence of poverty amid increasing affluence, the disaffection of youth, the growing political consciousness of minority groups, and the recurring crises in public finance are among the more prominent indicators. Although the problems that underlie these manifestations are predominantly national in character and scope, their impact falls heaviest on the metropolitan communities, where not only people and resources but also social maladies and physical maladjustments are concentrated. As a consequence, the capacity of the cities to function adequately and effectively is being challenged more seriously than at any other time in the nation's history.

Advances in technology, together with the accompanying spatial dispersal of people and resources, have aggravated the social and physical problems of urban agglomerations and given rise to intra-area competition and controversy among the semi-autonomous units that now make up the local political system. What some of the contenders in the resulting game of metro-politics see as so much institutional baggage in the path of good government or social justice is vigorously defended by others committed to more restricted positions. How suburban officials act may irritate City Hall (and vice versa), and how the latter acts may enrage the man in the ghetto. The nature of this environment makes intense demands on the leadership skills of top governmental functionaries, while the realities of urban political life make it difficult for them to perform their role as local statesmen either efficiently or effectively.

The present volume reflects these various trends in the urban world. A profile of a major American city, its primary purpose is to increase understanding of the nature and workings of a local polity as it strives to meet its responsibilities in the last third of the twentieth century. Attention is focused on the institutional structures, roles, and decisional processes through which the community attempts to govern itself and promote the well-being of its citizenry. Although the subject of analysis is a single metropolis, the findings have broader application. Through the treatment of such factors as cultural and political environment, influence patterns, and leadership styles, the book highlights some of the critical and differentiating variables that are relevant to the governance of American urban settlements generally. No attempt has been made to cast the study within a tight conceptual framework, although theoretical constructs are utilized wherever relevant. Implicit in the approach is the concept of the local polity as a system in which individuals and groups seek to protect and enhance their interests and status. More explicit in the analysis is the notion that the environment or context in which local government functions constitutes not only a source of demands and influence-building resources but also a set of constraints on what community decision-makers can do.

The Milwaukee story is not unlike that of many large American metropolises. Confronting the community is the whole array of urban problems, from fiscal imbalances and intergovernmental rivalries to racial unrest and social disorganization. No city can be said to be typical. Although all have many points in common, each has its own personality and style that sets it apart from the others. For Milwaukee, the most distinguishing characteristic is epitomized in its reputation as a "good government" city. The absence of machine politics, emphasis on professional administration, and cautious fiscal policies are among the factors that have contributed to this image. But like its counterparts elsewhere, the Milwaukee polity is today intersected by larger developments and newer demands upon urban life that challenge the long-established patterns of operation and some of the older values as well.

The first chapter of the volume outlines the environmental context—social, economic, cultural, political, and physical—of the Milwaukee community and the second its formal governmental structure. As both suggest, local contests arise as much from resistance keyed to traditional practices and attitudes and to area-wide institutional patterns as from demands for programmatic changes. Chapter 3 examines the roles of two of the key political actors in the system—the central city mayor and the county executive—and the strategies utilized by them in developing and maintaining positions of leadership. Chapter 4 looks at the question of community power more broadly, seeking to determine its configurations and structure. The two chapters that follow concentrate on three of the most critical problems confronting local policy-makers: finances (Chapter 5) and race and housing (Chapter 6). These areas were selected from among others principally to illustrate the community decisional process in operation. The final two chapters extend the problems and issues of the metropolis in place and time: Chapter 7 to the suburban and county governments in the area and to higher levels of public authority in the state and nation; and Chapter 8 to a speculative look at the future of the city and region.

We are indebted to the many public officials and persons in private positions who gave generously of their time and knowledge in providing us with information and insights about the Milwaukee community. The list is far too long for individual acknowledgment. Whatever merit this volume may have is due in major part to their contributions; whatever deficiencies or errors may exist in it are attributable to our fallibility as humans and not to any attempt to impose a preconceived set of notions or conclusions on our subject. No work of this nature, of course, can be entirely free of the authors' biases. We have, however, checked and rechecked our impressions and analyses with knowledgeable Milwaukeeans in both public and private life and with documentary sources whenever available in order to present as accurate and objective a picture as possible. We hope we have succeeded in this effort.

June, 1971

HENRY J. SCHMANDT
JOHN C. GOLDBACH
DONALD B. VOGEL

Milwaukee

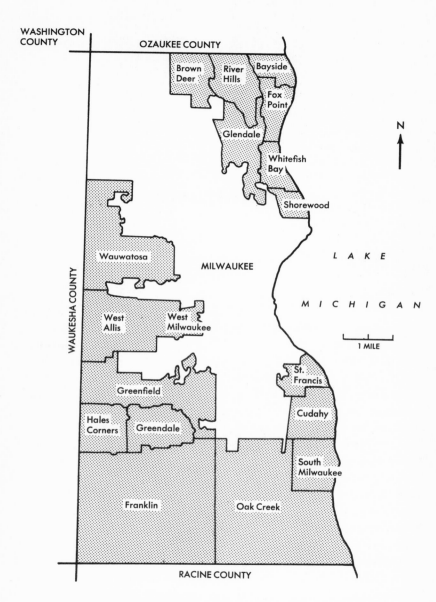

WASHINGTON
COUNTY

OZAUKEE COUNTY

Brown
Deer

River
Hills

Bayside

Fox
Point

Glendale

Whitefish
Bay

Shorewood

MILWAUKEE

N

LAKE

MICHIGAN

Wauwatosa

WAUKESHA COUNTY

1 MILE

West
Allis

West
Milwaukee

St.
Francis

Greenfield

Cudahy

Hales
Corners

Greendale

South
Milwaukee

Franklin

Oak Creek

RACINE COUNTY

MILWAUKEE COUNTY MUNICIPAL SUBDIVISIONS

1

The Village Metropolis

Milwaukee, "the tribal gathering place by the waters," was described by a visitor in 1843 as an uninviting swamp, "intended only for waterfowls and wild beasts, not for the dwellings of man." Today it is an attractive, comfortable, and prosperous community, the twelfth largest city and the nineteenth largest Standard Metropolitan Statistical Area (SMSA) in the nation. Situated on Lake Michigan at the confluence of three rivers— the Milwaukee, the Menomonee, and the Kinnickinnic—it lies eighty miles to the north of Chicago, its one-time rival for regional pre-eminence. Although its architecture is not particularly distinguished, the natural beauty of its lakefront, its outstanding county park system, its obsession for cleanliness and orderliness, its well-maintained homes, the relative lack of congestion, and the absence of extensive areas of residential blight add immeasurably to its attractiveness and appeal. Endowed with the heritage of its Germanic past, in which "a man with a trade is a capitalist already," the area has long been one of the country's top industrial producers, with national and international markets for its output.

Milwaukee's origins as an urban community date back to the end of the eighteenth century, when French-Canadian fur-traders established a post to tap the wealth of its rich hinterland.[1] The first wave of settlers came mainly from the eastern seaboard, lending a distinctly Yankee flavor to the young settlement. Starting in the 1840's, however, German immigrants began to arrive in large numbers, until, by the last quarter of the century, Milwaukee was known as the "most German city in the United States," the German Athens of America. The predominantly Teutonic character of the community began to be diluted well before the end of the century by the stream of newcomers from eastern and southern Europe, with the Polish migrants' far exceeding the others in number. The city early attained major status, reaching the 100,000 mark by 1875 and almost tripling this figure during the next twenty-five years. In this century, overshadowed by Chicago as a regional and lake center, it has grown at a slower pace, thus fulfilling an earlier prophecy that "Milwaukee will grow, perhaps not rapidly, but steadily and solidly, and will become the synonym for thrift, solidity, and mercantile honor."

Milwaukee City today, with its 95.8 square miles of territory, 717,000 residents, and a property-tax base of over $5 billion comprises 40 per cent of the land area, 68 per cent of the population, and 58 per cent of the equalized (market) value of all taxable property in the county. It is the heart of a four-county SMSA that includes the adjacent counties of Waukesha, Ozaukee, and Washington. The total population of Milwaukee county, as reported in the 1970 census, is 1,054,063 and that of the SMSA 1.4 million, with the heaviest growth occurring in the urbanizing ring outside the central county. (See Appendix A.) The city's population followed the pattern common to many of the large core municipalities, showing a loss of almost 25,000 during the decade. Even the county as a whole—much to the surprise of most observers—recorded a gain of only 18,000 for the decennial. A heavy net out-migration of nearly 120,000 residents, many of them moving to the fringe areas, contributed substantially to this result. In contrast to Milwaukee's experience, the other three counties in the SMSA showed an aggregate increase of 107,000 residents, a gain of over 45 per cent.

Geographical decentralization of economic and residential activity began early in the area. Lack of readily available sites for industrial expansion within the city of Milwaukee, together with the proximity of railroad transportation to the cheap land outside its corporate boundaries, led to the exodus of several major plants and the incorporation of four industrial satellites —South Milwaukee, West Milwaukee, Cudahy, and West Allis— around the turn of the present century. By this time also, the "flight" of upper-income families to the suburbs had begun, resulting in the incorporation of three residential enclaves: Shorewood and Whitefish Bay along the lakefront north of the city and Wauwatosa to the west, the last advertised as "the most attractive suburb of Milwaukee with five churches, street lights, transit facilities, and freedom from saloons and heavy industry." No further incorporation occurred until 1926, when the upper-income village of Fox Point was created to accommodate the spill-over from Whitefish Bay. River Hills, the Grosse Point of Milwaukee, and the federally sponsored green-belt community of Greendale followed in the 1930's. The final wave of municipal incorporations occurred during the 1950's, prompted in large part by Milwaukee's vigorous annexation policy, which almost doubled the city's land area during the decade.

Today, as a heritage of these developments, Milwaukee county presents a heterogeneous pattern of social and economic geography. Although there is relatively little poverty in the suburban ring and few members of racial minorities, the spectrum of social classes is wide, with working-class communities existing alongside the villages of white-collar employees and those of the professional and managerial elite. The land-use pattern similarly varies, from exclusively dormitory suburbs to those with substantial concentrations of industry. As the assessment figures reveal, the industrial component of the general property-tax base in the county's eighteen suburbs ranges from none in five to 43 per cent of equalized value in the industrial satellite of West Milwaukee. The comparable figure for Milwaukee city is 16 per cent.[2]

The Community Ethos

Urban communities are complex organisms or systems that defy precise description and analysis. One has to experience them emotionally as well as survey them scientifically in order to achieve a measure of understanding. For each has its own personality, its own flavor and tone, its own history and tradition, its own mores and idiosyncrasies. Each, moreover, is a creature of many forces that can produce such diverse urban complexes as a New York, a San Francisco, a Chicago, and a Miami. It is no easy task to symbolize an individual city such as Milwaukee or give accurate expression to its multifaceted character. As George S. Perry said of Baltimore, "Almost any sweeping statement you make about its character will be wrong."[3]

Each observer sees a community and its qualities in a different light, and each tends to characterize it in ways that reflect his own experiences, attitudes, and need dispositions. Thus, over the years, Milwaukee has been variously called the nation's beer capital, the machine shop of the world, the workingman's city, the Athens of the Midwest, Bushville, and America's cleanest city. Many residents refer to it as the community of *Gemütlichkeit,* the city of good fellowship, but others see it as friendly only to those who are white, wear their hair neatly trimmed, and are orthodox in their behavior and beliefs. Some view it as progressive in dealing with race relations and poverty, while others criticize it as one of the most racially prejudiced cities in the North, a community that has been inordinately slow in meeting housing and other needs of its deprived. Some are proud of its achievements in the performing and fine arts, but others refer to it as a cultural desert with a Lawrence Welk mentality. Contrasting views of this nature run through many other dimensions of the community's life. None are wholly accurate, but each contains enough truth to give it some semblance of credibility.

Despite these divergent images, most Milwaukeeans agree on one aspect of their community's character: its innate conservatism. This quality finds reflection in the area's approach to civic improvements and social problems as well as in the life styles of its inhabitants. Both the relative newcomer and the native constantly refer to the length of time that elapses before projects are brought to completion. No public facility—whether a museum, convention center, or jail—is undertaken without lengthy deliberation, usually stretching over many years. A quarter of a century elapsed, for example, before the recently completed performing arts center was brought from the proposal stage to fruition, and construction of a new jail has just been authorized, almost fifteen years after the question was first placed on the civic agenda.

The same situation prevails in the case of social problems, whether housing, education, or race relations. Ameliorative measures are seldom taken until after long, often controversial debate. The tendency is to deny the existence of such problems or to ascribe their source and solution to factors beyond the locality's pale of responsibility. The racial disorders that struck the city in July, 1967, came as a complete shock to thousands of Milwaukeeans who had believed that "it couldn't happen here." So also a public school boycott a few years earlier had caught many by surprise in the face of the School Board's stubborn insistence that the system was free of racial problems.

This conservative approach is extremely frustrating to a minority of the citizens who feel that the community's problems, unlike those of many other large urban aggregations, are manageable and can be solved by vigorous civic action. On the other hand, it is compatible with the feelings of the overwhelming majority of residents and is stanchly defended by many local officials. Only recently, the president of the Common Council gave expression to the prevalent viewpoint when he insisted that Milwaukee's slowness in acting on projects is beneficial because it avoids hasty decisions that later prove costly. In a similar vein, a *Milwaukee Journal* writer explained that the twenty-five-year gestation period for the performing arts center gave the community "time to develop a true need for one."[4]

The impressions of a representative group of community leaders provide an interesting description of Milwaukee's qualities.

> We have beer and sports and the lake. We have good schools and good government. We may be a little slow but we're careful. We are stolid but not puritanical. We are probably more material minded than we should be, but not irrevocably so. We have more than a subsistence economy and we can and do spend a lot of time looking for our own interpretation of the good life.[5]

Two decades earlier, a veteran newspaperman, Richard Davis, had complained about the community's complacency:

> Small town is the word for Old Lady Thrift ("the plump and smiling city of Milwaukee"). Her hundredth anniversary came in 1946 and found her with a population of about six hundred thousand, but she remains essentially a small town. A great majority of her people want to keep her that way. Everything has been so comfortable, so pleasantly Old World, so free of false pretensions and the travails of ambition that only the vain, the restless, and the conscience-stricken want to change things.[6]

Davis's observation about the city's resistance to change was reiterated in more recent years by Henry W. Maier, the present mayor, in his book on urban leadership. "How to overcome this resistance," he wrote, "was one of the challenges that faced me the day I took office."[7]

The remarks of both Davis and Maier are particularly relevant to an assessment of the community's ethos. Milwaukee's "Old World" qualities have gradually disappeared in the face of continued growth and change, but the city still retains many of the characteristics and mannerisms of a small town. Its deliberateness and caution, its hostility to the nonconformist, its inbred civil service, its repeated stress on being a good place to rear one's family, and its moralistic tone are all reminiscent of a Main Street culture. So also is the nightly pastime of young people driving back and forth on Wisconsin Avenue, downtown's principal "drag."

Bartenders may be suspect as social commentators, but the terse observation of one at Pappy's Tavern comes closer to capturing the community's tone than any learned sociological explication. As he put it, "Milwaukee is where, if an older man walks into a cocktail lounge with a girl young enough to be his daughter, she probably is!" This moralistic orientation has existed almost from the beginning of the city's existence. Early in its history it was pictured as a law-abiding community where children can grow up strong, healthy, and decent. Today, as a reaffirmation of these virtues, it can tolerate and, in fact, strongly laud an autocratic police chief who scoffs at police-community relations programs as "hogwash" and labels his critics "radicals, do-gooders, bleeding hearts, and other dissidents";[8] and a lower-court judge who self-righteously and contemptuously excoriates defendants who come before him on minor disturbance and morals charges.

Like a typical small town also, Milwaukee is inordinately concerned with its image. As the *Milwaukee Magazine,* the official publication of the Association of Commerce, complained several years ago, the city does not have the national image to which it is legitimately entitled.[9] Community leaders were particularly disturbed by the broad press and television coverage given the local civil disruptions of the late 1960's. The July, 1967, riot, the open-housing marches led by Father James Groppi, and the picketing of the homes of public officials who belonged to the Eagles Club (an organization that bans non-Caucasians from membership) appeared to concern many Milwaukeeans more for the damage these activities did to the community's image as a law-abiding people representing *Gemütlichkeit* and good will than for the underlying social maladies they reflected.

Various reasons are given for this conservative, small town orientation: the ethnic composition of the population, with its large German and Polish elements; the predominantly working-class character of the residents (of the twenty largest SMSA's, Milwaukee ranks second in the percentage of the labor force employed in manufacturing); the long-standing dominance of family-owned corporations in the area's economy; and the lack of civic entrepreneurship. Some observers argue that the community's comfortable mode of living, its level of prosperity, and the absence—until recent years—of serious social and physical problems have made it lethargic in responding to the mounting challenges of urban existence. Others maintain that the area's proximity to Chicago has tempered its own enthusiasm for vigorous action—some even refer to Milwaukee as a cultural and economic satellite of Chicago. And still others attribute the slow pace of civic development and public projects to the heritage left by the city's traditional pay-as-you-go policy, which persisted into the post–World War II period.

To speak of Milwaukee's conservatism, however, is to portray only one side of its sturdy character. Despite its drawbacks and problems—the common lot of urban complexes everywhere—it possesses many excellent advantages. Living conditions for all but a relatively small minority of its residents are reasonably good. Its poverty area as a proportion of the total area within the central city is only 9.1 per cent, compared, for example, to 38 per cent in Saint Louis, 25 per cent in Detroit, 22 per cent in Denver, and 45 per cent in Birmingham. Similarly, its percentage of substandard housing and its unemployment rate are lower than in most large metropolises. The central city, moreover, is relatively safe, clean, and orderly, consistently ranking first in traffic safety and lowest in crime rates among municipalities of its size. Public services in the area are generally of superior quality, with the city, county, and suburban governments providing a broad range of well-managed functions.

Milwaukeeans like to live well and comfortably. Their consumption of thirty gallons of beer per person annually—almost twice the national average—is a typical manifestation of their zest for the good life. Over 1,700 bars are scattered throughout the city, the majority of which are, in the local vernacular, "family taverns." The restaurants are excellent and well patronized. As a recent survey revealed, the area ranks second among the twenty largest SMSA's in food sales per household and third in spending at eating and drinking places. (Milwaukeeans place a much higher priority on good eating and drinking than on fashionable dress, with the area ranking only fourteenth in apparel-store sales.)[10] The county park system's 13,000 acres, which include 110 parks, 11 parkways, 10 golf courses, a marina, conservatory, botanical garden, and modern zoo, have few parallels elsewhere in the nation. The Fourth of July circus parade sponsored by the Schlitz Brewing Company, the recently inaugurated Summerfest, and the annual Holiday Folk Fair, featuring the community's many ethnic groups, are among the numerous attractions that Milwaukee regularly offers its residents. Professional sports, badly set back by the departure of the Braves baseball team to Atlanta in 1965, have since been rejuvenated with the acquisition of an expansion franchise in the National Basketball Association (led by Lew Alcindor and Oscar Robertson, the team captured the national championship in 1971, the third year of its existence), and the purchase of the Seattle Pilots baseball team, appropriately renamed the Brewers.

Although Milwaukee has by no means taken full advantage of its cultural potential, it offers an interesting and expanding range of opportunities in this aspect of urban life. The War Memorial on the lakefront, designed by the late Eero Saarinen, houses a growing art collection, and the new $12 million Performing Arts Center on the banks of the Milwaukee River provides a focal point and symbolic stimulus for the community's cultural endeavors. The city can boast of an excellent repertory theatre, a promising symphony orchestra, first-rate library facilities, extensive art and music programs in the public schools, the nation's fourth largest museum of natural history, and a county historical society that has assembled a large collection of local documents and other material. Two major universities, Marquette and the University of Wisconsin-Milwaukee, substantially enhance the area's cultural environment. The latter institution, for example, has a highly regarded School of Fine Arts, with the distinguished

Fine Arts Quartet in residence. The annual Lakefront Festival of Art attracts over 100,000 viewers, and more specialized exhibitions throughout the area are also well attended. Efforts are likewise under way in the black community to develop the artistic potential of inner-city youth and to provide outlets for the creative work of black artists.

Social Dimensions

The ethnological pattern in Milwaukee, like its social structure in general, is heterogeneous in character, drawing on some seventy-five ethnic sources for its composition. This high degree of ethnicity is also reflected in the community's religious mix. Catholics constitute by far the largest denomination, encompassing more than 40 per cent of the county's population; Lutherans are second in number with about 20 per cent; and Baptists, third with 8 per cent. Other Protestant religions with substantial membership include the Presbyterian, Methodist, and Episcopalian sects. Members of the Jewish faith number approximately 35,000, the majority of whom reside in the north shore suburbs.

Although the proportion of foreign-born has declined from 64 per cent a century ago to less than 7 per cent at the present time, more than one person in five, compared to an average of one in six for all SMSA's, are children of foreign-born parents. Residents of German descent predominate, comprising more than one-third of the county's foreign stock (first- and second-generation Americans). However, they no longer form the cohesive and nationality-conscious group they once did. Two world wars against the "mother country," as well as high mobility and rapid social assimilation, have left only minor traces of the community's former Germanism. Swastika-decorated meetings of the Bundists were held in the mid-1930's, and a pro-Nazi training camp was organized north of the city, but these activities were denounced by the overwhelming majority of Milwaukee Germans. Gothic embellishments can still be seen in restaurants and taverns and on some of the older buildings; German surnames

remain commonplace on storefronts and other business establishments; and a few singing societies and *Turnverein* manage to
survive—but the once distinct Germanism of the area's urban
culture is now largely a matter of the past.

Milwaukee is not only about four times as German as the
average metropolis, it is also twice as Polish. The latter ethnic
group, the second largest in the community, constitutes 17 per
cent of the county's foreign stock. Unlike the Germans, the Polish
Americans have closely guarded and retained their national
identity. As a consequence, their impact on the community's
culture and politics has been substantial. The majority of them
reside on the city's southside, with concentrations extending into
the adjacent industrial suburbs of Cudahy and South Milwaukee.
Their solidarity is particularly manifested in the political arena,
where a Polish surname is a prerequisite for election in certain
wards and districts. Five of the six aldermanic seats on the southside, for example, are normally held by people of Polish lineage,
and, since 1890, Polish candidates have had a virtual corner on
the office of city comptroller. In contrast to this prominence in
the political sphere, few Polish surnames are found on the membership rosters of the socially prestigious clubs and organizations
or in the ranks of the top corporate management personnel of
the area.

The towering dome of St. Josaphat's basilica and the beautiful
twin spires of the St. Stanislaus church, which greet the traveler
on Interstate 94 as he approaches downtown Milwaukee from
the south, stand as symbols of the Polish subcommunity's solidarity, while the many fraternal organizations, restaurants, taverns, specialty shops, physicians, and lawyers catering to a Polish
clientele attest to its extensive dimensions. Observations such as
these relative to ethnic identification must, however, be tempered
by an awareness of the signs—the termination of the Polish-lan-
guage newspaper in 1962, after seventy-five years of publication,
is one—that point to the group's increasing assimilation into the
larger community. The shutting-off of immigration from eastern

Europe after World War II and the growing proportion of third- and fourth-generation descendants among the Polish Americans have hastened this process.

Neighborhood enclaves of other ethnic groups, such as the Hungarians, Czechs, Slovaks, Yugoslavs, Greeks, Russians, and Italians, still exist, but their number and sizes are declining. For example, the Italians, the third largest nationality group in the community, were at one time clustered in the old lower Third Ward adjacent to the central business district. Their dispersal, which began in the 1930's, was completed in 1957, when Milwaukee's first redevelopment project dislodged the remaining families. A second Italian section, in the Brady Street area on the city's east side, is now also beginning to disperse because of the influx of "hippies" into the neighborhood. The Irish, never large numerically but always influential in Milwaukee's political life, have long been scattered throughout the county. What has happened, in short, is that spatial segregation by nationality or ethnicity has gradually yielded to residential separation by social or economic class and in more recent years by race.

The latest wave of newcomers to Milwaukee has consisted mainly of blacks and, to a lesser extent, of Spanish-speaking families. Migrants from rural sections of Wisconsin, the victims of agricultural technology, have also moved into the area during recent decades, but the majority in this category have possessed the education and skills, as well as the skin color, conducive to ready assimilation. (An exception is the Indians, of whom there are some 3,300 in the city, largely from the northern Wisconsin tribes.) Appalachian whites constitute another group of relative newcomers to Milwaukee, but their number is small. Most of them have settled on the near southside, where the only low-cost housing outside the black neighborhoods of the inner city can be found. The absence of such housing has probably served as a deterrent to greater migration into the area by deprived southern whites.

Milwaukee's black population in 1940 was less than 9,000, a proportion smaller than that in twenty-two of the nation's twenty-five largest cities. By 1950, this number had increased to about 22,000. The big push came during the following two decades as in-migration accelerated. From 1950 to 1960, the black population almost tripled in size, and, by 1970, the total had reached 105,000, an increase of nearly 70 per cent over the ten-year period. (See Appendix B.) Coupled with the 70,000 loss of white population suffered by Milwaukee during the last decade, this increase has raised the proportion of blacks within the central city from 9 per cent in 1960 to 14.7 per cent at present. The proportion is even greater in the public schools, where Negro pupils now comprise over one-fourth of the city's enrollment. The rate of black movement into the area, however, appears to have slackened somewhat during the last several years, a trend observed elsewhere in the nation. Should the pace continue to diminish, much of the future growth of the black community will result from natural increase rather than in-migration, which has been accounting for more than 50 per cent of the accretion.

Spatially, the blacks are concentrated in highly segregated neighborhoods extending in a northwesterly direction from the central business district. The high degree of this segregation is evidenced in the fact that almost half of the city's Negro students attend schools where blacks make up 95 per cent or more of the total enrollment. Virtually no black family resides south of the industrialized Menomonee River Valley, referred to by some social critics as the local Mason-Dixon line, which cuts an east-west corridor through the heart of the community. Moreover, the white noose around the city is the most pronounced (equaled only by the Minneapolis–Saint Paul pattern) among the sixty-six largest metropolitan areas in the United States. Only 1,444 blacks, or 0.2 per cent of the total suburban population in the four-county SMSA, reside outside the core municipality.

All of the area's public housing projects, except a veterans' development operated by suburban West Allis, are located within the city of Milwaukee, and none of these, except an all-white veterans' project and a just-completed high-rise complex for the elderly, are situated south of the Menomonee

Valley. At the present time, the city operates approximately 2,500 low-rent units for families, 1,000 for veterans (well over 90 per cent of which are occupied by whites) and 2,100 for the elderly (again predominantly white occupied). Fear of Negro penetration has been one of the impelling motives prompting southside aldermen to oppose the location of all public housing, including even that for the aged, in their section of the community. Recently, however, with nudging from some of their elderly constituents, they approved a total of 310 units for the aged on the southside and reluctantly agreed, as part of a larger package insisted on by federal authorities, to permit the construction of a small number of low-income housing units on scattered sites owned by the city in their bailiwicks.

The Spanish-speaking minority, virtually nonexistent in Milwaukee in 1940, has now grown to an estimated 15,000. Mexican Americans began to move into the area shortly after World War II, and during the last fifteen years they have been joined by Puerto Ricans and some Cuban refugees. The majority of them live on the near southside, where industrial and commercial establishments predominate, but those who have managed to succeed economically have had little difficulty in moving to more physically desirable sections of the community.

Milwaukee as a whole enjoys a relatively high level of prosperity, evidencing fewer extremes of wealth and poverty than most metropolises. In 1970, almost one-half of the 435,000 households in the SMSA had incomes of over $10,000, and three out of four had effective buying incomes (after taxes) of over $5,000, the fifth highest proportion among the twenty largest metropolitan areas. About 10 per cent of the families have incomes below the poverty level, as defined by federal guidelines, while, at the other end of the continuum, only about 3 per cent of the households are in the $25,000-and-over category.[11] As the welfare records graphically demonstrate, most of the poverty families in Milwaukee county are located within the central city, where over 95 per cent of the Aid for Dependent Children and general-assistance cases are concentrated. Moreover, the proportion of those deprived among the black population is over three times that of the white residents. Equally revealing is the fact that poverty among the latter is most predominant in the upper age brackets (40 per cent of whites classified as poor are over sixty-five), while the reverse is true in the case of blacks (well over 90 per cent of the impoverished among them are under sixty-five years of age). These ratios, in turn, reflect the younger age structure of the Negro population (50 per cent are under twenty-six years of age) and the fact that almost one-third of the black families are headed by women.

As we have already indicated, the Milwaukee area does not conform to the common stereotype of a central city of low-income and ethnic dimensions surrounded by white-collar and high-income suburbs. Although most of the poor and virtually all of the racial minorities are confined to the core municipality, it also contains an abundance of middle-class neighborhoods and an east side of elegant homes that still house some of the area's influential families and civic leaders. New luxury apartments constructed along the lakefront in this section have also served to retain or attract many upper-income families, while the north-western extremes of the city acquired through the annexations of the postwar decades have provided large areas for middle-class residential development. In recent years, the migration to suburbia has been weighted heavily with working-class and white-collar families, principally from the areas on the north side, where Negro expansion is taking place, and with upper-middle-income families in the child-rearing cycle who are attracted by the college-oriented school systems of the wealthier suburbs. What all this adds up to is that the central city, despite in-migration and exodus and the existence of pockets of poverty, remains essentially a middle-income community with no immediate prospect of any radical change in its basic socio-economic character.

The Economy

Milwaukee county is the industrial heart of the dairyland region. Containing more than one-fourth of the value of all taxable real and personal property in Wisconsin, it accounts for 35 per cent of the state's total industrial employment and a similar percentage of the total value added by manufacturing. When the remainder of the SMSA is included in the computation, these proportions increase to 35, 42, and 43 per cent, respectively. Until 1875 Milwaukee enjoyed the distinction of being the greatest primary wheat market in the world. During the last quarter of the century, however, agricultural operations in the region shifted to dairying and diversified farming. During this period also, the industrial activities that had their origins in the small backyard shops of the German immigrants began to develop into large manufacturing complexes. Beer production, which brought national and international fame to Milwaukee, was the area's first major industry, expanding from an annual output of 108,842 barrels in 1870 to 3.7 million barrels in 1910. Meat-packing, milling, and leather-tanning were next in importance, but all of these activities were displaced in primacy during the early years of the present century by the manufacture of capital or durable goods.

Contrary to popular impression, the beer industry today constitutes only a small portion of Milwaukee's economic base, employing about 2 per cent of the county's labor force. More to the point, the Milwaukee SMSA ranks ninth among American metropolises for industrial output and is among the world leaders in the manufacture of road-building and construction equipment, tractors, cranes, electrical generators, diesel and gasoline engines, motorcycles, and outboard motors. In terms of employment, nonelectrical machinery is the principal activity, represented by such well-known firms as Allis-Chalmers, Bucyrus-Erie, Falk, Kearney and Trecker, Ladish, and Rex Chainbelt. Second in importance is electrical machinery, the most rapidly growing sector of the economy, Allen-Bradley, Cutler-Hammer, Square D, Briggs and Stratton, Louis Allis, and Nordberg being the most prominent corporations in this category. The first three, in fact, account for 40 per cent of all electrical control equipment manufactured in the United States. Transportation equipment is next in line, with American Motors (body plant), Harley-Davidson, and A. O. Smith among the major employers. Food and kindred manufacturing is the largest nondurable-goods industry, followed by printing and publishing. Cudahy Packing, Borden, Schlitz, Pabst, Miller, and Sealtest Foods are representative of the former, and Milprint and Columbian Art Works of the latter.

A mature industrial community, Milwaukee has produced few flamboyant entrepreneurs. Its economy, like its social character, has been stolid, stable, and conservative. Old and well-established firms continue to dominate the area's economic life and set its style. Until recently most of the major enterprises were locally owned and controlled, but the 1960's witnessed heavy inroads on the family-type business through absorption by national corporations and stock offerings to the general public. Since World War II, Milwaukee has had to depend for its growth principally on the expansion of existing firms. Of every 100 new jobs in manufacturing created in the county during the past 25 years, 85 have resulted from this source. Few new branch plants of national corporations have been attracted to the area, the only significant exceptions in recent decades being American Can, Continental Can, AC Electronics Division, General Electric X-Ray, and Hotpoint. As a result of this pattern, less than 20 per cent of the county's export earnings is derived from branch operations, while the remainder originates in locally headquartered companies.

The labor force in Milwaukee county exceeds 425,000, with almost three-fourths of this number working within the central city. Consistent with national trends, employment in the manufacturing sector has remained fairly stable in recent years, while the largest gains have occurred in the retail trade and service sectors. In the competition for tax resources, the central city has moved vigorously to retain existing industrial plants within its boundaries and to attract new enterprises. To pursue this goal, it has created a division of economic development and established an industrial land bank of over 650 acres. For the most part, these efforts have been moderately successful, with the manufacturing component of the city's tax base increasing by almost one-fourth and the commercial component by 45 per cent during the period from 1960 to 1969. Proportionately, however, the city's share of the county tax base declined from 62 per cent to 58 per cent in the manufacturing sector and from 82 per cent to 72 per cent in the commercial category. When all types of property are considered, the ratio drop was from 65 per cent to 59 per cent.

Compatible with the community's corporate base, Milwaukee's labor force is stable and conservatively oriented—qualities that find reflection in the relatively low rate of work stoppages as compared to most other large industrial cities. It is not unusual to see people employed as craftsmen in the same firms where their fathers and grandfathers worked. The area's steady if not dynamic growth owes much to the competence of this labor pool, as well as to the production skills of the managerial elite. It is in many ways reflective of Milwaukee's stolid character that its talents have been devoted to the production side, while relatively little of its total industrial budget has been allocated to research and development (R and D). This orientation may help explain the fact that Wisconsin ranks low in defense contracts despite Milwaukee's huge industrial complex. In 1967, for example, it ranked in the bottom quartile among the states in the proportion of its work force in defense employment, receiving only about 1 per cent of prime contract awards by the Department of Defense. This figure compared to 18 per cent for California, 9 per cent for New York and Texas, and 3 per cent each for Illinois, Michigan, and Indiana.

In the commercial sector, Milwaukee county is served by 8,800 establishments, 80 per cent of which are within the central city. The major department stores are Gimbels, Boston Store (an affiliate of Federated Department Stores), Chapman (locally owned), and Marshall Field. The first three have downtown locations, with branches in a number of the outlying shopping centers; the last, a postwar newcomer to the area, has only a suburban location, a deviation from the common pattern. The number of retail establishments has dropped sharply in recent years, owing to the decline of the small neighborhood store. Well over 2,000 such shops have closed their doors since 1958, and the trend is still continuing. The volume of retail trade within the core municipality showed some increase during the 1960's, but the city's share of total sales in the county dropped from 83 per cent in 1958 to 70 per cent in 1968. This relative decrease is a reflection of the changing city-suburban population ratio as well as the growing popularity of outlying shopping centers.

Milwaukee's commercial decentralization is not a product of recent decades but the continuance of a long-established trend. Deconcentration of commercial activities, as of industry, started around the turn of the present century with the opening of major shopping areas outside the central business district (CBD). Long before department stores in the larger cities were establishing branches to tap the outlying market, Milwaukee had its Mitchell Street, its Upper Third Street, and its Twelfth and Vliet shopping districts, all situated within the core city at trolley-line terminations not more than two or three miles from the principal hub of activity. This early competition between downtown and the outlying clusters of stores restricted the growth of the CBD and hence made it less sensitive to the later effects of the suburban shopping centers. It is these older and intermediate neighborhood areas, however, that are now finding survival difficult in the face of residential changes and the competition from the more modern retail concentrations in the newer sections of the city and beyond.

One final factor should be noted in discussing the area's economy. Despite its size and high level of industrial and commercial activity, Milwaukee is not a regional center enjoying the dominance in business and trade characteristic of such other SMSA's of comparable size as Kansas City, Seattle, Dallas, and Cincinnati. It does not, in other words, perform large-scale business and financial functions for a sizable service hinterland. (Other manufacturing centers in similar positions are Toledo, Syracuse, and Dayton.)[12] One reason for Milwaukee's status in this regard is the nature of its economic base, principally its manufacturing sector. The area is primarily a producer of goods that are not destined for final consumption but are fed into other industries for further processing or for use as fabricating equipment. Thus a large portion of its output is produced for a national or world market rather than for use within the region. A second, and more significant, reason is its geographical location. Its proximity to the giant manufacturing, financial, and trade center of Chicago to the south and to the expanding metropolis of Minneapolis–Saint Paul to the north has circumscribed its potential as a regional hub. Milwaukeeans may at one time have envisioned their community as the "Queen City of the West," but today most of them accept the reality of geography and look upon it as perhaps a blessing in disguise.

The Political Setting

Milwaukee enjoys the distinction of being the first of the small number of American cities that came under Socialist control.[13] Capitalizing on the municipal reform movement that swept across the nation in the early years of this century, and appealing to the "bread and butter" interests of the working class, the Social Democratic Party mustered sufficient strength in 1910 to capture the office of the mayor and obtain a majority on the Common Council. Success was short-lived, however, because Republicans and Democrats joined hands to secure the enactment of legislation providing for nonpartisan elections to city offices. This maneuver destroyed the leverage that the Socialists had enjoyed as a third party and permitted a fusion of supporters of the two major parties for municipal election purposes. Although the change prevented the Social Democrats from again gaining control of the Common Council, they remained a strong minority into the 1930's and held the mayor's office for all but twelve years from 1910 to 1960. (See Appendix C.)

The long mayoralty tenure of the Socialists was due far more to the personalities and administrative policies of the two men— Daniel Hoan and Frank Zeidler—who occupied the office during this time than to any ideological commitment by the electorate to the party's principles.[14] Almost from the beginning the appeal of the party locally was based on a concern for the practical problems of the community and the needs of the workingman. Whenever its candidates got into office, they directed their efforts largely at the establishment of honest and progressive municipal government and the improvement of public services and facilities —so much so, in fact, that Milwaukee's brand of socialism was dubbed "sewer socialism" by party members outside the area. Hoan's principal activities during his twenty-four years in office, for example, were aimed at reforming financial and budgetary procedures, ensuring fiscal solvency, extending services, installing centralized purchasing, strengthening planning and zoning controls, and promoting such commercial projects as harbor development and the Saint Lawrence Seaway. These efforts prompted historian Bayrd Still to write that, if Hoan's was a "sewer socialism," it was "socialism suffused with an Association of Commerce appeal as well."[15]

Milwaukee residents have now enjoyed more than half a century of nonpartisan government at both the municipal and county levels. Only the traditional county administrative officials —clerk, sheriff, treasurer, district attorney, clerk of the circuit court, and register of deeds—are elected on partisan tickets. Moreover, in marked contrast to the situation in some cities, Milwaukee's nonpartisanship has been observed in practice as well as form. Although the Socialist victories were initially responsible for the demise of partisan elections, a tradition of nonpartisanship has developed over the years that no candidate for local public office can afford to disregard. Because of this heritage, party organizations are precluded from playing an active role in municipal and county government politics. One would be hard put, for example, to discover any issues that are decided on clearly partisan lines in either the Common Council or the County Board of Supervisors. Candidates for both bodies find it an advantage to be a known Democrat in some city wards or a Republican in some suburban districts, but this is about as far as party influence extends in the local government realm. Even in this respect, a majority of those who run see fit to list "no political affiliation" in the biographical sketches that are published by the metropolitan press before each election.

In national and state politics, Milwaukee county has long been a stronghold of the Democratic Party, consistently accounting for more than 30 per cent of its total state-wide vote. In the twenty-eight contests for President, governor, and U.S. senator since 1946, Democrats have carried the county handily twenty-five times (President Dwight Eisenhower in 1952 and 1956 and Senator Alexander Wiley in 1956 were the only exceptions).[16] The area's importance to the party is further demonstrated by the fact that six of the eight senate seats within the county and twenty of its twenty-five assembly districts are regularly captured by Democrats. So are all of the partisan county offices; no Republican has been elected to such a post since 1952. Two of the county's three congressional districts are also "safe" Democratic strongholds: the Fourth on the southside, held by Clement Zablocki since 1948, and the Fifth on the northside, by Henry Reuss since 1954. The Ninth District, which includes the northern suburbs and extends into the adjacent counties, is predominantly Republican. Its present incumbent is Glenn Davis, one of the more conservative members of the party.

The bulk of the Democratic strength lies in the central city, where two-thirds of the county's registered voters reside and where majorities of 60 per cent or more are normally recorded for the party's candidates. Since 1956, every Milwaukee ward, with only two exceptions, has favored Democratic candidates for the offices of President, governor, and U.S. senator, and in only two of the wards have the Republicans been able to capture the state assembly seats. Outside the central city the situation is mixed. Republicans hold the advantage in numbers, but Democrats have won a majority of the suburban vote in ten of the twenty-eight contests noted above. (See Appendix D.) The working-class communities in the southern portion of the county return heavy majorities for the latter, while the GOP regularly carries the upper-income suburbs in the northern half by margins as high as four to one.

Although there is a libertarian faction in the majority party, Milwaukee's Democratic orientation, like the community's general tone, is, at best, middle of the road in character. Highly sensitive to its working-class and ethnic constituency, the party tends to be liberal in economic matters but conservative on social issues. As a study of party officers and delegates in the county revealed, Democrats differ strongly from their Republican counterparts with respect to public spending and the role of government but show little variance from them in their attitudes toward racial minorities.[17] Some indication of this disposition could be seen in the presidential preference primary of 1964, in which George Wallace captured 31 per cent of the vote in the central city and 33 per cent in the suburbs. The vote was obviously less pro-Wallace than anti-Reynolds, the incumbent Democratic governor who ran as a favorite son. Cross-over voting by Republicans contributed to the results because there was no contest on their ticket. (A truer test of sentiment occurred in the 1968 Presidential election, in which Wallace polled only 9 per cent of the county total.) Yet the fact that almost one-third of Milwaukee county voters could bring themselves, for whatever reason, to cast a ballot for an avowed segregationist is a revealing commentary on latent community attitudes.

Milwaukee blacks, because they constitute a relatively small percentage of the population, have been unable to become an important force in local partisan politics or, for that matter, in the nonpartisan politics of either the city or the county government. At the present time, they hold only one State Assembly district, two seats on the Milwaukee Common Council, two on the County Board of Supervisors, and one on the Milwaukee School Board. No other elective office—city, county, or suburban—is occupied by a black. Mayoralty appointments to city boards and commissions (much more so than for the county) have given recognition to the minority community, but a black is at a serious disadvantage, as we shall see later, in attaining a managerial position in the administrative bureaucracy of either government.

Governmental Pattern

The governmental pattern of Milwaukee county presents the usual picture of political fragmentation. The 239 square miles within the county, now wholly incorporated, are divided into the central city and eighteen suburban municipalities, the latter ranging in size from the exclusive upper-class village of River Hills, with slightly more than 1,500 inhabitants, to the industrial and residential subcenter of West Allis, with 72,000 people. (See Appendixes E and F.) Outside Milwaukee county in the remainder of the SMSA are an additional thirty-eight incorporated cities and villages, many of them of long standing. Eighteen autonomous school districts, one technical college district, and a metropolitan sewerage commission complete the county's governmental pattern. The "municipalization" of the entire area within its borders, together with the county government's assumption of many area-wide functions—expressways, parks, airports, and welfare, among others—has prevented the proliferation of special districts common to many other metropolitan communities.

The city of Milwaukee has a mayor-council form of government with nineteen aldermen elected by wards for four-year terms. Three other officials—city attorney, comptroller, and treasurer—are also popularly elected. The county is governed by an elected executive (the office was created by state statute in 1959) and twenty-five supervisors chosen by districts for four-year terms. Supervisory districts are coterminous with those for the election of state assemblymen.[18] The thirteen that are entirely within the central city are also coterminous with the aldermanic wards. Six others encompass portions of both the city and suburbs, and six are wholly within the latter. Elections to suburban governments vary according to the municipality's classification as a city or village. Aldermen in the former are chosen by wards, while trustees in the latter are elected at large. Seven of the nine villages within the county have adopted the city-manager form of government; the remaining two and all of the cities operate under the traditional mayor-council arrangement.

The structural pattern for public education in Milwaukee county has become more integrated in recent years as a result of school-district consolidations, which have reduced the number of districts from sixty-seven in 1950 to the present nineteen. Only eight of these, however, are coterminous with municipal boundaries. The boards that administer the districts vary in size from fifteen members in the central city to three in some of the smaller suburban units. All are elected at large, those in the city of Milwaukee for six-year terms and the others for three. The seven-member board for the vocational, technical, and adult education district (Milwaukee Area Technical College) is indirectly selected by a process involving the local school boards. School districts that serve the county are not of a uniform nature but of several types. Those classified as common districts or as union high schools are required by law to present such matters as the budget and tax rate to the electorate at an annual assembly reminiscent of the vestigial New England town meeting. Those classified as city districts, on the other hand, must submit their annual budget to the municipal council for approval (this procedure does not apply to the city of Milwaukee, where the School Board has ultimate authority over the budget and the tax levy).

The local governmental system in Milwaukee county operates with a relatively high degree of effectiveness despite the multiplicity of autonomous units. Overlapping or duplication of functions is not extensive, and no sections of the area have serious service deficiencies.[19] Suburban governments, with only a few exceptions, are generally well administered and possess tax bases adequate to provide a broad range of public services to their residents. Similarly, the county government is a far cry from the stereotype of the "courthouse gang" and the "dark continent of American politics." It is reasonably well organized and professionally staffed, and its jurisdiction over certain critical area-wide functions has been a major factor in alleviating some of the disabilities normally associated with political fragmentation. Serious problems of an intergovernmental and area-wide nature nevertheless continue to exist—that of fiscal inequities between the central city and suburbs is a prominent example—and these are aggravated by the new demands and changing social and ecological conditions accompanying continued urban growth.

A Contemporary Perspective

Small town may be the name for Milwaukee, but its complacency has been badly shaken by the events of recent years. Caught in the turmoil of contemporary social change, its image as a community of friendly and peaceful burghers has faded despite efforts to deny the reality. For Milwaukee, as for its prototypes elsewhere, there has been no escape from the pressures of modern urban society and the concomitant tactics of confrontation politics, crisis precipitation, creative disorder, civil disobedience, and militant activism. Milwaukeeans, to the horror and disbelief of many, have witnessed angry confrontations between blacks and whites, the seizure and burning of draft records, mass protests against the Vietnam war, hunger marches, student disorders in the high schools and local universities, the spread of marijuana smoking among their children and the increased use of drugs, the growth of an extensive "hippie" colony, the publication of underground papers, and a police strike. They have heard their public officials vilified and their police called "pigs," and they have observed the invasion of their state legislative chambers by welfare recipients and the bombing of their university at Madison by "revolutionaries." In the process, also, they have seen the consensus or near-consensus type of politics to which they were accustomed thrust aside as new groups—and some of the old—have begun to challenge the existing power arrangements and established centers of decision-making.

Milwaukee has experienced its baptism of fire. It is hardly the same community today that it was just ten years ago. Its leisurely mode of operation and innate belief in its moral superiority have been seriously challenged. Although the vortex of events into which it has been hurled is largely the result of forces beyond local control, its own actions have helped shape the consequences. The top political figures of the area, the mayor and county executive in particular, have demonstrated an awareness of, and sensitivity to, these forces and the need for the community to adjust to them, but their response has been conditioned by the limitations of their own offices and the reactions of their constituencies. Central city–suburban hostility and intrametropolitan competition for tax resources, moreover, continue to plague the area and prevent unified action vis-à-vis the problems that confront it. It is against this general backdrop that the governmental and political system of the Milwaukee community must be examined and appraised.

Notes

1. An excellent history of Milwaukee is Bayrd Still, *Milwaukee, The History of a City* (Madison: State Historical Society of Wisconsin, 1948). The volume contains an extensive bibliography of all relevant material up to the late 1940's. Robert W. Wells, *This Is Milwaukee* (Garden City, N.Y.: Doubleday, 1970) is a recent popular account of the city's background and distinguishing features. An up-to-date bibliography of studies, surveys, and reports pertaining to the Milwaukee area is Marilyn M. Levin, compiler, *Milwaukee Reports: A Bibliography* (Milwaukee: Milwaukee Urban Observatory, 1970). Frederick I. Olson, *Primary Bibliography for Research in Milwaukee History* (Milwaukee: Milwaukee County Historical Society, 1971) lists major depositories of source materials as well as selective references.

2. Property valuations for Milwaukee county are reported annually by the Bureau of Property Taxation, Wisconsin Department of Revenue, in a publication entitled *Statistical Report of Property Values, Milwaukee County.*

3. *Cities of America* (New York: McGraw-Hill, 1946), p. 45.

4. *Milwaukee Journal,* Sept. 14, 1969.

5. *Milwaukee Magazine* 13 (May, 1968), p. 21.

6. "Milwaukee: Old Lady Thrift," in Robert Allen, ed., *Our Fair City* (New York: Vanguard Press, 1947), p. 189.

7. *Challenge to the Cities: An Approach to a Theory of Urban Leadership* (New York: Random House, 1966), p. 20.

8. *Milwaukee Journal,* Feb. 2, 1971.

9. *Milwaukee Magazine* 13 (Feb., 1968), p. 17.

10. *Sales Management* 100 (June 10, 1968).

11. The Journal Company conducts an annual market survey of the Milwaukee area, in which information is obtained by probability sampling. The survey is a useful data source, particularly during the intercensal periods.

Results of the latest survey are contained in *1971 Consumer Analysis,* 48th annual edition (Milwaukee: The Journal Company, 1971).

12. See in this connection Otis Dudley Duncan *et al., Metropolis and Region* (Baltimore: Johns Hopkins Press, 1960), pp. 233–47.

13. The history of the Socialist Party in Milwaukee is examined in Frederick I. Olson, *The Milwaukee Socialists, 1897–1941* (Madison: State Historical Society of Wisconsin, 1952). On microfilm.

14. For a somewhat laudatory account of Hoan's political career and administrative accomplishments, see Edward S. Kerstein, *Milwaukee's All American Mayor: Portrait of Daniel Webster Hoan* (Englewood Cliffs, N.J.: Prentice-Hall, 1966). Hoan himself wrote a book on Milwaukee government entitled *City Government: The Record of the Milwaukee Experiment* (New York: Harcourt Brace, 1936).

15. Still, *op. cit.,* p. 527.

16. Voting returns in Milwaukee county for the offices of President, governor, U.S. senator, U.S. representative, county executive, and mayor of the city of Milwaukee are compiled in Sarah C. Ettenheim, *How Milwaukee Voted, 1848–1968* (Milwaukee: Institute of Governmental Affairs, University Extension and the University of Wisconsin, 1970).

17. Roger E. Durand, "The Political Socialization of Party Activists in Milwaukee County" (unpublished Master's paper, Department of Urban Affairs, University of Wisconsin-Milwaukee, May, 1966).

18. The decennial redistricting of the State Assembly in 1971 will bring some modifications in this arrangement because several of the assembly districts will have to cross the county line to comply with the "one man–one vote" principle. Supervisor districts, on the other hand, must be contained wholly within the county.

19. See in this regard, "Growth of Governmental Activities in Milwaukee County" (Milwaukee: Citizens' Governmental Research Bureau, 1960). Also Henry J. Schmandt and G. Ross Stephens, "Measuring Municipal Output," *National Tax Journal* 13 (Dec., 1960), pp. 369–75.

2

The Structure of Government

Governmental structure provides the legal mechanism through which public policy is framed and executed. Therefore, it is an appropriate starting point for the examination of the local polity. This structure, however, does not exist in a vacuum; it is strongly influenced by inputs from its environment and conditioned by the demographic, social, and economic factors that characterize the community in which it functions. Nor does it tell the full story, for within this institutional framework are informal mechanisms, arrangements, interrelationships, and procedures that appear on no organization chart but that are basic to an understanding of urban governance.

We have already looked at the general socio-economic and political environment of the Milwaukee community. In this chapter, we turn to the structural context within which political action transpires. While primary emphasis is placed on Milwaukee city proper, attention is also given to the county government and to a lesser extent other local units that impinge on, and are affected by, the city.

Milwaukee City Government

Political scientist Charles R. Adrian gives the following description of what is commonly known as the "weak-mayor" form of municipal government:

> The council is both a legislative and an executive organization under the weak-mayor plan. . . . Members are (except in small cities) ordinarily elected by wards [and] may serve on several ex officio boards and commissions. A committee of the council usually prepares the budget. . . .
>
> The mayor is not "weak" because he lacks policy-making power—he normally has a veto [and] can recommend legislation. . . . He is "weak" because he lacks administrative power. There is, in fact, no single individual charged with the responsibility of seeing to it that the laws and ordinances are properly carried out or that the city administration proceeds in accord with an overall plan. The mayor has very restricted appointive powers; even when he is allowed to make appointments, he may not be able to remove those he places in office, so that he is deprived of any real control over them or responsibility for them.
>
> Ordinarily several of the principal city offices are filled by direct election. . . . There are also likely to be a large number of boards and commissions, some filled by appointment by the council or the mayor, some ex officio, some elected.[1]

Although general descriptions of this nature more often than not miss their target by a wide mark when they are applied to specific cases, the foregoing summation closely depicts the formal structure of Milwaukee city's government as set out in its charter.[2] Taken at face value and judged by generally recognized organizational principles, the weak-mayor–council plan is ill equipped to meet the needs of the modern urban community and poorly constituted to respond promptly to its problems. Structural form, like reality, however, does not always conform to expectations, as we shall see in the case of Milwaukee.

Besides the mayor and Common Council, the city's government is composed of three other elective offices (city attorney, treasurer, and comptroller), eight boards appointed by the mayor without council approval (the most important of these are the

Library Board, Election Commission, Museum Board, and City Service Commission, which administers the personnel program), and nineteen with council approval (including the Fire and Police Commission, City Plan Commission, Housing Authority, Redevelopment Authority, Harbor Commission, and Board of Assessments). In addition, there are a number of other ex-officio and variously appointed bodies such as the Auditorium-Arena Board and the Board of Purchases. In all, forty-three commissions, boards, and committees perform either policy-making, quasi-judicial, or advisory functions within the organizational framework of Milwaukee's municipal government. (Appendix G lists these bodies along with their responsibilities, size and composition of membership, method of appointment, and length of tenure.)

The over-all formal structure of the government of Milwaukee city is depicted in Figure 2.1. Most of the offices, departments, and boards indicated on the organizational chart require little explanation. Several, however, call for a brief description at this point because of either their uniqueness or the roles they play in community issues to be discussed later.[3]

Board of Estimates. Budgeting is of paramount importance to the decisional process of any organization, and the official or unit responsible for its preparation is in a strong position to influence policy. Many municipalities have placed this power in the mayor or city manager through use of the executive budget. In Milwaukee, however, formal control over the preparation of the city's budget is denied the mayor. By state law, this function is vested in the Board of Estimates, an ex-officio body of municipal administrators and lawmakers. The board consists of eleven members: the mayor, comptroller, treasurer, city attorney, commissioner of public works, president of the Common Council, and the five members of the council's Finance Committee. Six of this number—the mayor, comptroller, and four members of the Finance Committee—make up the Budget Examining Committee. It is this smaller group that is central to the budget-making process, because it conducts the extensive hearings that

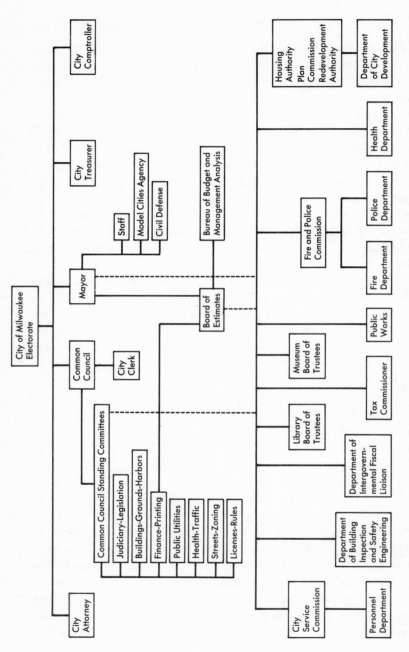

FIGURE 2.1 ORGANIZATION OF THE CITY OF MILWAUKEE

precede consideration of the over-all document by the full board.

The Bureau of Budget and Management Analysis constitutes an important instrumentality in the budgeting process. It serves as the staff agency for the Board of Estimates, providing technical review and recommending allocations for the members' consideration. The director of the bureau, in particular, plays an influential role. Since 1959, he has served as the nonvoting secretary for the board, as well as its principal source of information and advice. All budget requests from the various departments and agencies are directed to his office, where they are examined and analyzed. After holding consultations with the respective units, the bureau adjusts the requests to meet the over-all budgetary requirements it has established on its own initiative. The inauguration of a program budgeting system in recent years has further strengthened the position and influence of the bureau by giving it a more effective means of control over budget preparation.

Although Milwaukee does not have an executive budget, the mayor is provided with several formal points of intervention in the process: at the examining committee level, in the Board of Estimates, and at the legislative stage subsequent to the enactment of the budget by the Common Council. His role at the first two levels is greatly enhanced by the fact that he heads the examining committee and serves as chairman of the full board. His ability to intervene at the third stage is strengthened by his possession of the item veto; that is, he can veto any item in the adopted budget with which he is not in agreement. (Any such action on his part may be overridden by a majority vote of the council.)

In addition to having budget-preparation chores, the Board of Estimates meets regularly throughout the year to administer the current budget and handle any matters pertaining to its implementation. Here again, it must rely heavily on the technical support provided by the Budget Bureau and its director. The board's principal responsibilities in this connection relate primarily to requests from departments and other agencies for changing the level of services, transferring funds from one category to another, and authorizing equipment purchases not previously provided for in the budget document.

Department of City Development. This unit was established in 1961 for the purpose of increasing coordination and improving the operations of the several agencies dealing with renewal and developmental programs. Specifically, the department brought together under the same administrative umbrella three previously separate units: the Housing Authority, Redevelopment Authority, and Plan Commission. Each of the three commissions was retained with its formal powers unchanged (thus obviating the necessity of seeking modification of state enabling legislation under which the three were established), but administration of the programs was vested in a single director and staff. More recently, the Division of Economic Development, previously located in the mayor's office, was transferred to the department.

The Housing Authority is a corporate entity that owns and operates the city's public housing projects. It is composed of five citizen members appointed to five-year staggered terms by the mayor, with council confirmation. It makes major policy decisions in its area of responsibility, while details of operation are performed by the department. The Redevelopment Authority is vested with exclusive power to carry out the city's programs of slum clearance, urban renewal, and blight elimination. It has seven members appointed by the mayor with confirmation by the council. The Plan Commission of seven members, similarly appointed, is charged with the development of a master plan for city growth. It performs an advisory role to the Common Council on matters relating to zoning, platting, street patterns, property transactions, and renewal.

Intergovernmental Fiscal Liaison Department. This unit was created by the council in 1966 at the request of the mayor. Its primary mission is to obtain for the city a larger share of state aid and shared taxes. To this end it seeks to coordinate cooperative efforts with other interested municipalities throughout the state, such as those represented in the Wisconsin Alliance of Cities. It works closely with the Special Council Committee on Taxation and Finance on matters concerning tax redistribution and also serves as an expediting agency for federal and state aid applications originating with other city units and agencies. Since 1966, the department has materially expanded its efforts in seeking additional revenues from county, state, and federal sources.

Fire and Police Commission. Established in 1885, the commission is the oldest civil service authority in Wisconsin. Composed of five citizen members appointed by the mayor with the approval of the council, the board establishes personnel employment policy for the fire and police departments, sets standards for entrance and promotional examinations, and considers candidates seeking original appointment or promotion. It also is the appointing authority for the police and fire chiefs, but, once selected, these officials enjoy life tenure and may only be removed for cause. In major disciplinary actions, the commission serves in a quasi-judicial capacity and conducts appeals hearings. It also investigates and approves state license applications for local private detective agencies and their personnel.

Although the commission structurally appears above the fire and police departments, it lacks any real administrative control over them. Under optional powers provided in state law, policy initiation can be assumed by this body if the local electorate approves.[4] This option, however, has never been exercised in Milwaukee, where it has been traditional for the commission to play a narrow and circumscribed role. Yet, even in those areas where it does have specific power, its actions have been anything but aggressive. The one exception is the recruitment of public safety personnel. Here, following replacement of the chief staff official and an almost complete turnover of members during the past several years, the commission assumed a more active role. Its latest recruitment campaigns have not only filled all vacancies in the police department but also increased the proportion of blacks and other minority group members on the force. Until this success, there was considerable talk at City Hall of divesting the commission of its personnel functions and shifting them to the municipality's regular personnel department.

The commission still remains quiescent in the critical areas of police–minority group relations and in hearing citizen complaints. Its community relations section is manned by one specialist with no secretarial support and no encouragement from the incumbent police chief, Harold A. Brier, who has little sympathy for this activity. Brier's attitude in this respect, however, is beginning to be questioned by some within the system. Recently, an official of the Policemen's Protective Association charged that the chief has shown little interest in programs to ease tensions between police and student and minority groups. The same view was expressed by a black member of the commission, who denied later, however, that his statement was intended to be critical of Brier or the department. The chief's reaction was typical of his response to all such criticism: "We are reaching all the good people in all segments of our community. The lawless we will never reach."[5]

The commission's reluctance to become involved with citizen complaints is classic. It was not until January, 1971, that it held the first hearing in the city's history on a police-brutality charge. In fact, it was not until 1970 that it moved to secure the abolition of the archaic requirement that permitted only freeholders (property-owners) to bring complaints. Despite the contemporary furor over police actions, the commission continues to be apprehensive about entering this field, just as it has been hesitant to assert itself in matters of departmental policy. Its deference to the chief and its reluctance to question his judgment remind one of the position occupied by J. Edgar Hoover at the national level. More recently, however, there are signs of some uneasiness on the part of the members over the essentially passive role they are playing. This feeling manifested itself in a hearing on a citizen's complaint. Although the commission dismissed the charges of brutality, it made it clear that it was unhappy with the officer's action in arresting a young Chicano. As the chairman stated in announcing the decision, "Though the complainant failed to prove the verity of the charges by a preponderance of the evidence, the commission unanimously feels that the accused did not come into this hearing with entirely clean hands."[6]

The limited role played by the Fire and Police Commission has enabled the administrative organizations of the two departments to insulate themselves almost completely from external control over their operations. Except for the budgetary review exercised by the Board of Estimates, the public safety function in Milwaukee is beyond close scrutiny by other parts of the governmental structure or the electorate. Little support appears to exist at the present time for changing this situation.

City Service Commission. Composed of five citizen members selected by the mayor without council approval, the commission establishes personnel policy and handles matters of appeal. Its staff, under a director who is a civil service appointee, administers the city's personnel program. As is the case in most public organizations, entrance into Milwaukee's municipal government is at the lower technical levels and recruitment for management positions is almost entirely from within the organization. Noteworthy in this latter connection is the almost universal practice of recruiting top administrative officials from within the system. Thus, in all but one case (the Public Museum director), the present department heads were not only recruited internally but also from within the unit they now run. The stability of this mode of personnel management is reflected in the average tenure (seventeen years) of departmental directors (excluding those in the most recently created agencies) and in their average age (60).

Division of Labor Relations. The state of Wisconsin has been and continues to be a leader in the field of public employment labor relations. Since the passage of the Wisconsin Employment Peace Act in 1939, the principal agency in this area of concern has been the Employment Relations Board. Consisting of three members appointed for six-year terms by the governor with Senate confirmation, the board deals with the labor relations activities authorized by state law (and which are not prohibited to it by

the National Labor Relations Act or in which the National Labor Relations Board has declined to assert its own jurisdiction).[7]
The Employment Peace Act as amended, together with the
board's actions, establishes the labor relations practices and procedures under which the city as an employer operates.

Consistent with national trends in this area, the union movement of public employees in Milwaukee has been substantial. At
present the city recognizes fifteen separate bargaining units.[8]
Because of the potential threat such organizations pose to unin-
terrupted governmental services and the need to deal with labor
relations issues, such as formal grievances, in a consistent manner
throughout the service, the city established the Division of Labor
Relations in 1965. Administratively attached to the office of city
clerk, this unit is responsible for the over-all coordination of col-
lective bargaining and represents municipal management in
negotiating labor agreements with the various unions recognized
by the city.

Public employee labor organizations in Milwaukee have continued to grow in both size and influence. The high degree of
competition among them for membership has encouraged a militant and hard bargaining posture on their part. Even where such
competition does not exist, as in the case of the police and fire
organizations, the tendency to take noncompromising positions
has become more evident. At the time of this writing, the city
has failed to reach agreement with the police bargaining unit
despite protracted negotiations, and the members have authorized their leadership to prescribe "job actions." This has already led to one work stoppage in the form of the "blue flu,"
and there is strong possibility of similar measures being taken
in the future. Although the same threat prevailed for a time
in the fire department negotiations, settlement was ultimately
reached. As these and similar incidents indicate, the influence
potential of local unions on the structural patterns and policy
determinants of internal governmental operations in the city appears to be increasing. Union demands are no longer being confined to monetary considerations but are directed at management

practices and procedures as well. With these developments, the role of the chief negotiator is becoming more critical in preventing the interruption of governmental operations.

Common Council Standing Committees. The council not only legislates but also participates directly in policy execution, through its permanent standing committees on finance-printing, judiciary-legislation, licenses-rules, streets-zoning, health-traffic, buildings-grounds, harbors, and public utilities; the special committees on economic development, organization and methods, public information, taxation and finance, and water policy; and the Water Pollution and Sewerage Control Board. The division of the city into nineteen wards, the general understanding of proprietary rights of aldermen, and long-established custom permit direct intervention on the part of each council member in administrative matters directly affecting his territory. As the former director of the Department of City Development observed on his retirement, ward politicking has compromised planning and zoning in the city for decades. In his words, "what an alderman wants for his ward, he gets."[9] This practice, together with other aspects of the city's organizational pattern described previously, suggests that whatever degree of integrated leadership and administration currently exists has developed in spite of, and not because of, the formal governmental structure.

County Government

In contrast to the structure of Milwaukee city government, that of the county provides a supportive framework for integrative administration. This situation is the result of a major reorganization effected in 1960. Before that time, the county's organizational setup was an even greater barrier to effective governmental administration than are the existing formal arrangements in the city. The weaknesses and disabilities in the system were in fact so pronounced that they enabled reformers to achieve a more comprehensive reorganization than otherwise would have been possible. Examination of Figure 2.2 will reveal some of the more striking shortcomings inherent in the pre-1960

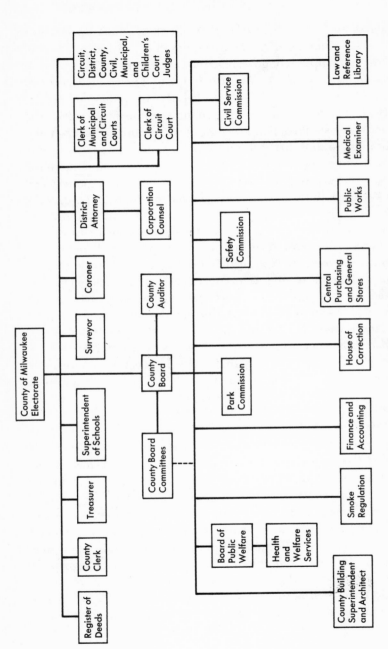

FIGURE 2.2 PRE-1960 COUNTY GOVERNMENT STRUCTURE

structure. Most noteworthy were the complete absence of an executive office, and the proliferation of elective posts and policy-making boards and commissions. In such a system, line departments are left with little or no over-all direction. Not surprisingly, the disjointed framework had proved increasingly inadequate in coping with the growing responsibilities of county government.

Figure 2.3 depicts the structure of Milwaukee county government since its major reorganization in 1960. In addition to the creation of the executive position, changes included the elimination of the elective posts of county superintendent of schools, surveyor, and coroner, shifting the corporation counsel from the district attorney's office to the executive branch, creation of a Department of Administration, and consolidation of the finance and accounting and the central purchasing and general stores departments into the new unit. Although not all changes represented in the chart took place immediately after adoption of the basic reforms, most can be traced from this initial action. (Another major reorganization effort in 1962 revamped the county judicial system, streamlining the structure and increasing the organizational efficiency of the courts.) The trend since 1960 has been toward a greater concentration of administrative control, including departmental consolidation, particularly in the staff areas. Action along these lines, however, has come slowly and hesitantly, indicating the strength of entrenched agencies and officials and the inevitable bureaucratic and legislative resistance to change.

As presently constituted, the county government includes six elective offices (register of deeds, clerk, treasurer, sheriff, district attorney, and clerk of circuit courts) in addition to the county executive, the Board of Supervisors, and the judiciary; four functional policy boards or commissions appointed by the executive (the Board of Public Welfare and the Park, Safety, and Civil Service Commissions); thirteen other special boards, commissions, and citizen committees that are in most cases also appointed by the executive and approved by the board (the most

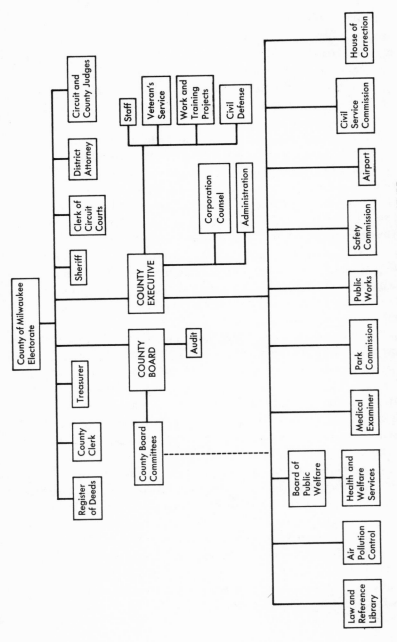

FIGURE 2.3 PRESENT COUNTY GOVERNMENT STRUCTURE

important exceptions to this method of appointment are the Expressway and Transportation Commission appointed by the governor and the Jury Commission appointed by the judges of civil jurisdiction of Milwaukee county).

While significant progress has been made toward enhancing the formal structure of county government so as to make it more amenable to administrative coordination and control, it is clear that there is still much in the framework that militates against the accomplishment of this goal. Again, as is the case with the city, standing committees of the Board of Supervisors and major semi-independent commissions, such as parks and welfare, create a less than ideal situation for the chief administrative official. Consequently, much attention continues to be devoted to bringing about further adjustments in the formal structure. This task, as we shall see in Chapter 3, has been one of the main concerns of the incumbent county executive.

As in the case of the city, no attempt will be made here to describe all of the county administrative offices and agencies indicated on the organizational chart. Most of them exercise the functions normally associated with their counterparts elsewhere. Three units, however, are briefly singled out: the Department of Administration, the Transportation Division of the Department of Public Works, and the Welfare Department. The first is included because of its enhancement of executive control; the second, because of its relation to a community issue of growing concern; and the third, because of its magnitude and the nature of its responsibilities.

Department of Administration. It would be difficult to overstate the importance of the establishment of this unit in 1970. Although substantial progress had been made in improving the county's governmental structure, the creation of the Department of Administration marks the most significant formal reinforcement of the executive function since the reorganization of 1960. The new unit consolidates four separate staff functions—budget, planning, procurement, and administrative services—with each set up as a bureau.

The seeds of the department were sown in 1957, when the County Board authorized the creation of a division of management and budget analysis. Originally, as a staff arm of the lawmakers, it dealt almost exclusively with budget review. When the office of county executive was established in 1960, the division was converted into a department and moved into the executive branch, where it assumed the critical role of assisting in preparation of the budget. Because its concern with management analysis and long-range planning was also expanded, it became a key staff instrumentality with substantial influence of its own.

Under the new organizational arrangement, financial management functions previously carried on by the Department of Management and Budget Analysis have been assigned to the Bureau of Fiscal Affairs and the Bureau of Planning and Research. The first is responsible for budget preparation and analysis, accounting, and pre-auditing; the second for long-range planning and management analysis. The third bureau, Procurement, is charged with the responsibility for centralized purchasing. It encompasses units for administering bids and purchase-order–writing, coordination of procurement standards, and a proposed stores unit. The final unit, the Bureau of Administrative Services, covers the major functions of data-processing, reproduction and mail, and records depository.

Initial planning for the Department of Administration anticipated the inclusion of the personnel function within its purview. This proposed action, however, ran into the strong opposition of the current and longtime director of personnel, who enjoys strong support from within the County Board. The Personnel Council decided, as a temporizing measure, to engage Public Administration Service (a Chicago-based research organization that has done numerous studies for public agencies, including Milwaukee county) to analyze how the existing personnel unit might best be consolidated with the new department. Although such a transfer is unlikely to take place until retirement of the present head, it appears reasonably certain that the function will eventually be moved.

The changes stemming from the creation of the new department have also affected other units in the county governmental structure. The most important by-product in this regard was the reconstitution of the Audit Department, which previously encompassed both pre- and postauditing. Under the new arrangement, it performs only the postaudit function and serves as a staff arm to the Board of Supervisors. Pre-auditing, as previously noted, is now the responsibility of the Budget Bureau, where it can be more effectively employed as a tool of management.

The creation of the new department adds further strength to the formal position of the county executive. It also simplifies the task of over-all management by reducing the number of separate units and by permitting better coordination of central and staff agencies at a lower level than was formerly the case. The step is an important one in the continued refinement of the county's administrative structure. This task has proceeded slowly, hampered by legislative resistance to the expansion of executive powers and by the opposition of officials within the bureaucratic structure who fear a diminution of their own authority. In some cases, this resistance can only be overcome when retirement opens the way to change.

Transportation Division. The Transportation Division of the Department of Public Works, previously known as the Expressway Division, was given the change in name to reflect its growing concern with all modes of moving people and goods in the urban complex. Although administrative control of the division is retained by its parent department, its technical staff (headed by the director of transportation) is under the jurisdiction of the County Expressway and Transportation Commission. That body, consisting of five members appointed by the governor, has the major responsibility of formulating general transportation policy subject to Board of Supervisors approval. It also has the responsibility of coordinating the relevant activities of other governmental agencies that affect the county's transportation program.

Initially there was strong public support for the county's extensive expressway-building program as a means of alleviating the mounting traffic congestion in the area. This enthusiasm has recently been tempered by a growing concern with the problems created for affected residents when such construction takes place and also by environmental considerations. By far, the most serious of these difficulties is the dislocation of families who are often left without any reasonable expectation of securing suitable alternative housing. This burden has fallen most heavily on the low-income families, although it is now beginning to cause considerable inconvenience to those in the higher brackets, who have more political muscle. (The earlier construction went largely through the disadvantaged areas of the central city; the extensions are now going through white middle-class sections as well.) The situation, moreover, has been aggravated by the shortage of housing in the county, particularly for large families of low or moderate income. As a result, there is currently growing opposition to planned expressway extensions, and a demand that such construction be linked with a more comprehensive approach, including mass transit, to the area's transportation problems and needs. Groups as diverse as the Tenants' Union, *ad hoc* suburban neighborhood organizations, and environmentalists have joined forces in this campaign.

Although the county has appointed a relocation administrator and has allocated funds for the activity, an extensive supplementation of the Transportation Division with sufficient staff to deal with all aspects of transportation and relocation is still badly needed. At this juncture, the division has had little success in convincing those who are opposing its activities. As a result, a very real threat exists that even the expressway development might abort without formulation of any alternative approaches. The change in the fortunes of the division vis-à-vis the public at large has been traumatic for its personnel. They feel they are being unfairly blamed for doing what the public originally demanded but has now grown lukewarm, if not hostile, toward. They also feel that, while the people are demanding a new approach, they are also unwilling to modify their automobile-oriented habits to make any other system possible. The division, in short, is faced with a novel situation that is testing in the most severe manner its ability to adjust.

Welfare Department. It was little consolation for Milwaukee county to learn recently that it ranks low nationally in the percentage of its residents on welfare (seventeenth among the twenty-three largest cities and counties in the nation, with approximately 5 people out of every 100 on some form of public assistance).[10] Its relatively good position in this respect does not ease the fact that the welfare function continues to be the most costly responsibility of the county government. Recent cutbacks in state and federal supports, coupled with an increasing case load resulting from unfavorable economic conditions, have caused the proportion of the county's budget devoted to this function to rise sharply from less than 39 per cent in 1966 to over 52 per cent at present.

Organizationally, the Welfare Department comprises four operating divisions: Social Services, Financial Assistance, Medical Services, and the County Children's Home.[11] Following the 1967 amendments to the Social Security Act, the department merged its family and children's services. This consolidation provided a more favorable reimbursement formula for administrative costs. The new Division of Social Services that resulted assists persons who qualify for aid for families with dependent children (AFDC), old age assistance, blind aid, and the county's general relief and veterans' aid programs. It also provides services to children who are separated either temporarily or permanently from their parents. Children are accepted for permanent care upon order of the children's court and placed in adoptive homes. In the case of temporarily separated youngsters, the division arranges for appropriate foster homes. Additionally, it provides assistance to unwed mothers and investigates conditions surrounding dependent and neglected children. The division's total aid for the

AFDC program absorbs approximately 45 per cent of the entire welfare outlays and comprises over 40 per cent of the total welfare case load. (See Table 2.1)

The Division of Financial Assistance encompasses some of the aid tasks formerly included in Social Services. This was made possible by legislative changes in 1967, which permitted the separation of aid and service. Caseworkers and case aides in the division perform tasks related to initial and continuing eligibility and grant-budgeting. The third division, Medical Services, provides medical assistance to individuals who qualify for one of the other types of aid and who live in institutions or nursing homes. The fourth, the Children's Home, provides care for youngsters requiring emergency help when they lack shelter. The home is also used as a residential institution for children whose parents are unable to manage their care and as a treatment center for those whose emotional disturbances preclude them from living in their own homes.

The Welfare Department is governed by a policy-determining board of five members—four private citizens and one county supervisor—appointed by the county executive with confirmation by the Board of Supervisors. This body at present has jurisdiction over health services as well as welfare. However, there is strong feeling that control over these responsibilities should be divided because of both the growing volume of work activity in each sector and, more importantly, the increasing disparity between the clienteles for welfare and health services. The County Board has moved in this direction, and it is seeking a change in the state law to separate the two functions. The county executive, while in basic agreement with the proposed change, has differed with the board over the form such a division should take. His proposal is to create a separate Board of Social Services for the welfare function. The supervisors, on the other hand, have a different notion; they want a standing committee of their own members for this purpose, contending that policy-making functions should be the responsibility of the County Board. The separation is certain to occur in the near future; the unanswered question at this time is that of the specific form it will assume.

TABLE 2.1
WELFARE RECIPIENTS IN MILWAUKEE COUNTY,
BY PROGRAM
(Dec., 1969)

Program	Total (No.) of Persons	Total (No.) of Cases	Racial Distribution (in Per Cent)		
			White	Black	Other
AFDC	40,254	10,670	33.4	62.8	3.8
Child Welfare	4,483	4,483	61.7	24.4	18.9
General Assistance	11,156	4,677	43.2	38.0	18.8
Old Age	3,787	3,787	78.2	20.0	1.8
Disabled	1,366	1,366	80.9	17.1	2.0
Blind	224	224	79.5	18.8	1.8
Total	61,270	25,207	53.0	39.0	8.0

SOURCE: Metropolitan Milwaukee Association of Commerce and Department of Public Welfare, Milwaukee County.

Court System. Although only peripherally related to the administrative structure, the court system is an integral part of county government. Its main features should at least be noted. The state court reorganization, which became effective in Wisconsin in 1962, created essentially a unified judicial system, reducing the number of courts in Milwaukee county to two: circuit and county (see Figure 2.4). The first is a constitutional tribunal with original jurisdiction in all matters and appellate jurisdiction in most cases (except probate) from the county court. It is made up of three divisions—civil, criminal, and family—with a total of seventeen branches. Appeals from it go to the state supreme court.

The county court has jurisdiction over misdemeanors, traffic offenses, civil suits involving a maximum of $25,000, probate, and juvenile cases. It consists of five divisions—civil, traffic, misdemeanor, probate, and children's—with thirteen branches. Judges in the various divisions or branches of each court may be as-

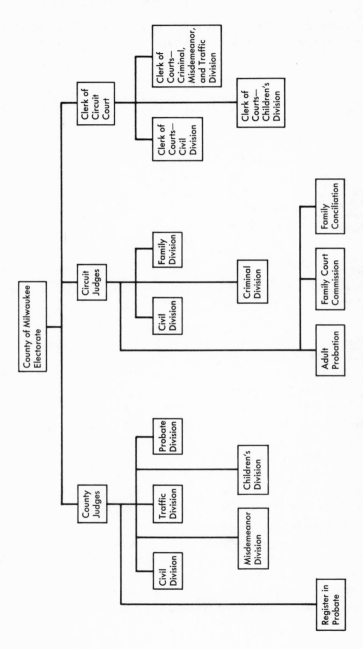

FIGURE 2.4 MILWAUKEE COUNTY COURT SYSTEM

signed to hear cases from any of the others when circumstances such as disqualification, illness, or case load warrant such transfer. Judges of both types of tribunals are elected on nonpartisan ballots for terms of six years. In addition to the circuit and county courts, each of the suburban communities, but not the city of Milwaukee, has its own municipal court to try traffic cases and violations of city or village ordinances.

The clerk of the circuit court is the administrative head of the offices of all courts in the county system, excluding the probate division. He is responsible for the general supervision of the activities of the various clerks of courts, except the register of probate, and his office performs all the clerical work pertaining to the functions of the branches of these courts. The clerk is elected on a partisan ballot for a two-year term and can choose a deputy who is civil service–exempt.

Other Governmental Structures

In addition to the governments of the city of Milwaukee, the county, and the suburban communities, there are several other independent public agencies that function in the area. These include the Metropolitan Sewerage District, the Milwaukee city public schools, and the Milwaukee Area Technical College, the vocational center for the metropolitan area. Beyond these three units, no additional special districts exist within Milwaukee county. In large measure this is the direct result of the significant role played by the county government in providing many area-wide services that are often administered through such districts when no over-all structure with the necessary capability is present.

The Sewerage Commissions. The city of Milwaukee is divided into three drainage areas: the Milwaukee, Menomonee, and Kinnickinnic rivers, which flow through the city from the north, west, and south, respectively, and unite at a point near their combined outlet into Lake Michigan. Before 1925, when the treatment plant was put into operation, the sewage and industrial waste from the city and its suburbs were discharged through combined sewers directly into the three rivers. This discharge would then flow into Lake Michigan. Predictably, the pollution carried by the rivers through the heart of the city created a significant health hazard, to say nothing of the odor nuisance.

The first attempt to remedy the pollution of the rivers and lake caused by the untreated sewage was the construction of flushing tunnels to pump large volumes of lake water into the river outlet. While the flushing did dilute the pollution and reduce the odor nuisance, the more serious problem of water-supply pollution and the consequent health hazard remained. Following state enabling legislation in 1913, the city of Mil-waukee established a sewerage commission empowered to con-struct and develop a sewerage system and treatment facility within its borders.

Proposals were soon made that the plant and intercepting sys-tem handle the sewage from all communities in the immediate tri-river drainage area because upstream pollution by the suburbs could perpetuate the very problem that the proposed facilities were intended to eliminate. The initiative for a metropolitan system came from the suburbs, a number of which were faced with large expenditures for sewerage facilities that exceeded their legal debt limits. The city was receptive to the idea because the construction of the sewer system was also proving more than its own financial resources could bear. With support from both sources, the Metropolitan Sewerage Commission was created by state law in 1921 for the purpose of constructing sewer-line mains outside the central city to connect the various suburban districts to Milwaukee's intercepting sewer system and its dis-posal facilities. The law provided that the city would be reim-bursed over a period of years for the suburban area's proportionate share of the costs of constructing the disposal plant and the intercepting system.[12] The metropolitan district was enlarged in 1959 to include all of Milwaukee county (only the city of South Milwaukee persists in operating its own sewerage system and treatment plant). Its jurisdiction was further expanded the next year, when the two commissions authorized contracts with municipalities outside Milwaukee county for the transmission and treatment of sewage from territory within the drainage area of the district.

The City Sewerage Commission consists of five members appointed by the mayor with council approval for terms of five years; the metropolitan body has three members appointed by the governor for six-year terms. Although the two agencies are organizationally separate, they operate administratively as one unit. At the time the metropolitan commission was created, it was provided that the City Sewerage Commission remain in existence with jurisdiction over all facilities within the Milwaukee city limits. It was also provided that the city's staff and work force become the operating agent for the larger district. Both bodies are thus served by the same chief engineer and general manager, the same secretary, and the same organizational personnel. Moreover, it has been common practice to have one member serve on both commissions so as to provide an additional means of coordination and liaison between the two bodies. This dual arrangement has prevailed up to the present day despite numerous attempts to consolidate the two agencies or transfer the total sewerage function to the county government.

The Milwaukee Public School System. Consistent with other statutory provisions that apply to Milwaukee separately, its school system operates under a special charter. While the city government acts as its tax collector, the system functions in all other respects as an independent governmental unit. Over-all management is vested in a fifteen-member Board of Directors chosen at large for overlapping six-year terms, one-third standing for election every two years. The board president is selected by the directors from their own membership.

Although created by special law, the board of school directors has those powers usually associated with similar bodies throughout the state. It establishes policy relevant to the organization of schools, construction of facilities, textbook selection, instructional employment, and budget. Further, the directors play a significant role in respect to the over-all program for instruction.

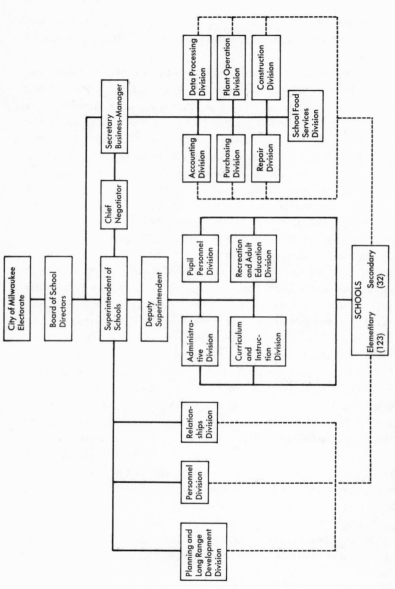

FIGURE 2.5 ORGANIZATION OF MILWAUKEE PUBLIC SCHOOL SYSTEM

Source: Milwaukee Public Schools, *Facts...Figures 1969-1970* (Superintendent's Annual Report), pp. 16-17.

They appoint the superintendent, who is the system's chief administrative officer and whose personnel actions and policy decisions are subject to their confirmation. The board also exercises appointive power over the second key administrative position, that of secretary–business manager. (Figure 2.5 presents the organizational structure of the Milwaukee school system and Table 2.2 gives the distribution of its staff by position.)

The Milwaukee city public schools, with a total enrollment of over 132,000, constitute the eleventh largest school system in the United States.[13] Its 123 elementary schools and thirty-two secondary schools enroll approximately one out of every seven public school children in the state. Like its counterparts in other major northern cities, it has been plagued with the problems of *de facto* segregation, racial unrest, high dropout rates, and inadequate fiscal resources. Its response to these challenges, as seen by the more liberal members of the community, has been timid and partial at best. Conservative members have dominated the board and have been instrumental in preventing it from moving more energetically in the fields of race relations and compensatory education for the disadvantaged. Some critics are now seeking statutory changes to provide for the election of board members by district instead of at large, in order to assure minority group representation. Others are advocating community schools and the use of vouchers to establish a parallel or competing system to the present structure of public education.[14] And still others are calling for decentralization of the system along lines similar to the New York and Detroit plans. The number of Milwaukeeans pushing for these more far-reaching changes is as yet small, but dissatisfaction with the schools and the manner in which they are operated is growing among whites as well as blacks.

In 1968, the superintendent with board approval instituted a reorganization of the system's administrative structure. A deputy superintendent was appointed to direct the ongoing activities of the program operations and development divisions. A new unit was created to consolidate the personnel functions, which had

TABLE 2.2
DISTRIBUTION OF STAFF, BY POSITION,
FOR THE MILWAUKEE PUBLIC SCHOOL SYSTEM

Education Department	
Principals	148
Vice-Principals and Assistants to Principals	110
Teachers, Regularly Assigned	5,000*
Teacher-Aides	1,645
Central Office:	
Administrative Staff	63
Supervisory: Program Service Area Consultants	141
Supportive: Psychologists, Social Workers, Speech Therapists	183
Recreation and Adult Education	
Full-time	97
Hourly Assistants	1,326
Secretarial, Education Department All Locations (Including 173 Part-Time)	679
Business Department	
Administrative Staff, All Divisions	29
Accounting Division:	
Accountants and Auditors	6
Construction Division:	
Inspectors and Draftsmen	11
Data-Processing Division:	
Computer Programmers and Operators	10
Plant Operation Division:	
Engineers, Firemen, Window Cleaners	319
Part-Time: Janitorial Helpers	437
Purchasing Division:	
Buyers, Warehouse Personnel	36
Repair Division: Shop Foremen and Craftsmen	241
School Food Service Division:	
Cook Managers	107
Hourly Workers and Drivers	693
Secretarial, Business Department All Locations (Including 21 Part-Time)	78
Total	12,249†

* Does not include 882 teachers on the substitute list.
† Without part-time positions; the total is 10,736.
SOURCE: Milwaukee Public Schools, *Facts . . . Figures 1969–1970* (Superintendent's Annual Report), p. 13.

previously been scattered among several departments. In addition, two new divisions—relationships and planning and long-range development—were created. The former was established to coordinate internal and external programs of school-community relations, governmental relations, publication activities, and mass-media services; the latter was instituted to give greater emphasis to planning for the future.

The 1968 reorganization also affected the local schools, at least formally. The fourteen district senior high schools and those junior high and elementary schools channeling into them became fourteen cluster units. According to the plan, social workers, psychologists, and curriculum specialists are assigned as teams to "program service areas" consisting of two cluster units from diverse sections of the city. The intended purpose of these areas is to avoid the potential insularity of the cluster arrangement, while at the same time permitting a degree of decentralization that will enable the system to react to specific local problems.[15] The plan is a weak response to those who are demanding decentralization of sufficient scope to give neighborhoods or localities within the city a meaningful measure of control over their schools. Its operation thus far has resulted in no significant deviations from the traditional pattern, either in the degree of centralized administrative control exercised or in the power of the parents.

In recent months, the alignment on the School Board has shifted from the former conservative-liberal split to one based on support of, or opposition to, the superintendent. The new controlling faction, a blend of old-guard and liberal members whose philosophies are far from similar, is bound together only by a shared dislike of the operating head of the schools and the manner in which he functions.[16] Since his appointment in 1967, the present superintendent, Richard Gousha, has moved aggressively to consolidate his control over the administrative structure of the system. This pattern of behavior is in sharp contrast to that of his predecessor, who was scrupulously deferential to the prerogatives and sensitivities of the board. As a result, the superintendent's actions have aroused resentment among some of the veteran members, who feel that they are being bypassed by him and his staff in the management of the schools. They have reacted by hiring an educational consultant responsible directly to the board and by sharply questioning actions of the superintendent, such as administrative reappointments, which they routinely had approved in the past. Part of the problem, of course, lies in personalities, but more fundamentally the local situation is a reflection of the increasing sense of impotence felt by many lay policy-making boards and commissions in the face of incessant bureaucratization and growing dependence on the technicians.

Milwaukee Area Technical College. An independently constituted governmental unit, the Milwaukee Area Technical College (MATC), the largest of its kind in the state, serves as the vocational education center for the city and its environs. Its existence is a reflection of the fact that Wisconsin has long been a leader in the establishment of a comprehensive educational program designed to fill those training gaps or reach those people not covered by the regular schools. As early as 1911, statutory authorization was provided for creating state and local boards of vocational and adult education and giving them the power to levy taxes for their support. By 1967, forty-two municipal vocational schools were offering training programs. Fifteen of the larger schools, including the MATC, had two-year programs (the equivalent of junior colleges) approved by the state, leading to associate degrees for graduates. Although loosely coordinated by the State Board of Vocational, Technical, and Adult Education, the system as a whole was ill equipped to provide relevant training programs on an area-wide basis and ensure a balanced distribution of opportunities throughout the state.

In response to these unfulfilled objectives, major efforts were made starting in the early 1960's to associate the vocational-technical system more clearly with higher education as a part of Wisconsin's effort to provide training beyond that furnished by the regular school system. The most significant change in vocational school organization took place in 1965 when the legislature

directed that the system should be converted from a municipal to an area-wide base. By 1967, this mandate had been formal-
ized by the creation of eighteen Vocational, Technical, and
Adult Education districts throughout the state, most comprising
multicounty areas. The Milwaukee district includes all of Milwaukee county and portions of three adjacent counties.[17]

Each district is governed by a seven-member board and is empowered to levy a tax of up to two mills based on equalized
(market price) valuation.[18] The board appoints a director to
administer the system and sets over-all policy. The reorganization provides that each district is to have at least one major
facility offering a range of two-year associate degree technical
programs. One-year courses, together with part-time day and
evening classes, are also to be included.

As has been the case with the other major independent area-
wide unit in the Milwaukee complex (the Metropolitan Sewerage Commission), suggestions have been made that the county
government assume administrative responsibility for the district
and place it in a status similar to the semi-independent Board of
Public Welfare. However, the state legislature has refused to
amend the law to allow for this option, and no action is currently being taken by those advocating such a change.[19]

Distribution of Governmental Functions

This overview of the formal structure of government in Milwaukee county has concentrated on identifying the various administrative units and describing the hierarchical relations
within them. Nothing, however, has been said about the relative importance of these functional units in comparison with
each other. This importance can be measured in many ways,
depending on one's purpose and the values he holds. Two crude
but objective measures that give some idea of relative emphasis
are the number of personnel committed to the various functions
and the expenditure made for each function. The latter will be
discussed in connection with finances in Chapter 5. Here we

simply call attention to the former as a point of reference for matters treated later in the volume.

Table 2.3 shows the distribution of personnel by major function for the city and county governments. As can be observed, although total employment in the two units is approximately the same, the responsibilities of each as measured by personnel commitment are radically different. The city's principal deployment is in the areas of public works–utilities and public safety, the two accounting for 78 per cent of the total work force. In the county, on the other hand, health and parks are the principal items, utilizing over 69 per cent of the employees. These commitments reflect the responsibility of the county government for the health institutions and medical complex serving Milwaukee area residents and for the park system it operates.

When we take the other governmental units into account (see Table 2.4), we get a fairly clear idea of the allocation of responsibilities among the local public jurisdictions. Education, for example, requires almost 17,000 of the 41,734 local public personnel in Milwaukee county. The central city, with over

TABLE 2.3

COMPARISON OF PERSONNEL DISTRIBUTION (FULL-TIME EQUIVALENT) FOR MILWAUKEE CITY AND COUNTY, BY MAJOR FUNCTION

(In Per Cent)

Functions	City	County	Combined
Public Works and Utilities	48.5	6.4	28.0
Public Safety (All Functions)	29.5	4.9	17.6
General Services	9.4	1.4	5.6
Health (Including Hospitals)	5.9	45.0	24.9
Staff Agencies	3.2	1.9	2.6
City Development	2.4	—	1.2
Legislative	.8	.3	.3
Executive	.3	.1	.2
Parks	—	24.3	11.8
Courts and Judiciary	—	4.9	2.4
Public Welfare	—	10.8	5.4
	100.0	100.0	100.0
	N = 11,383	N = 10,818	N = 22,201

SOURCES: City of Milwaukee, *1969 Budget,* pp. 108–32; County of Milwaukee, *1969 Summary of Budget and Personnel,* pp. 103–59.

TABLE 2.4
MILWAUKEE AREA LOCAL GOVERNMENT EMPLOYMENT

Jurisdiction	Number of Employees	Per Cent
City of Milwaukee	11,383	27.3
County of Milwaukee	10,818	25.9
Milwaukee School District	10,736	25.7
Suburban School Districts	5,367	12.9
Suburban Governments	2,184	5.2
Vocational and Adult Education District	796	1.9
Milwaukee Metropolitan Sewerage District	450	1.1
Totals	41,734	100.0

SOURCES: City of Milwaukee, *1969 Budget*, pp. 108–32; County of Milwaukee, *1969 Summary of Budget and Personnel*, pp. 103–59; Milwaukee Public Schools, *Facts . . . Figures 1969–1970*, p. 13; and administrative officials of these respective units. Personnel totals for the city and county have been calculated for full-time equivalents. Inadequate data prevented similar calculations for the other units.

11,000 municipal employees, dwarfs the combined total of the suburban governments by a five-to-one ratio. The latter, with 2,200 employees, serves a population of 337,000, a proportion of one worker to 154 residents. This ratio contrasts sharply with that in the city of Milwaukee, where there is one municipal employee for every 63 residents. The situation, however, is reversed in the case of education. Here suburban school districts with a complement one-half the size of the city system's serve a student enrollment only 43 per cent as large. When municipal and school district employment are considered together, the city has one public employee to thirty-three residents and the suburbs have one to forty-five.

These proportions provide only gross perspectives; yet they are significant for their implications. From the standpoint of areas of functional responsibility, they indicate the important urban role that the county government has come to play in the Milwaukee polity. Even more significantly, they show a division of welfare-type responsibilities between the county and city, with the former handling most of the traditional social services and the latter physical redevelopment and public housing. The big burdens of the central city, as the figures illustrate, are the maintenance of the physical plant and the preservation of order. From another aspect, the tables show the extent of bureaucratization of the various public sectors, as measured by the number of employees in each. Correlative to this, they also indicate the stakes that substantial numbers of civil employees have in present organizational arrangements. Although they seldom, if ever, act as a collectivity, the more than 41,000 local public personnel in Milwaukee county constitute a potentially influential force in the governmental system of the area. The increased activism—even militancy in some cases—of the unions representing this sector of the population attests to their growing power. More and more, political and administrative officials are finding themselves caught between the demands of public employees and the reactions of angry taxpayers. The impact of this development on the structure and processes of local government could be substantial.

Notes

1. Charles R. Adrian, *State and Local Governments,* 2d ed. (New York: McGraw-Hill, 1967) pp. 218–19.

2. The city of Milwaukee, since its original incorporation on January 31, 1846, has been governed by and under a special charter. The last general revision of this charter was accomplished by the state legislature in 1874. In 1892 a constitutional amendment was adopted prohibiting the legislature from passing any special legislation to amend, alter, or repeal any special charter. The city can amend the charter by a two-thirds vote of the Common Council. Such amendments take effect sixty days after adoption unless referenda petitions are filed in the intervening period.

3. Brief descriptions of the various departments and units are included in City of Milwaukee, *1969 Directory and Report of Milwaukee's Progress in 1968.*

4. Chapter 62.13 of the *Wisconsin Statutes* reads in part:

(6) OPTIONAL POWERS OF THE BOARD. (a) The board of fire and police commissioners shall have the further power: 1. To organize and supervise the fire and police departments and to prescribe rules and regulations for their control and management. 2. To contract for and purchase all necessary apparatus and supplies for the use of the departments under their supervision, exclusive of the erection and control of police and fire station

buildings. 3. To audit all bills, claims and expenses of the fire and police departments before the same are paid by the city treasurer. (b) The provisions of this subsection shall apply only if adopted by the electors.

5. *Milwaukee Sentinel,* March 11, 1971; *Milwaukee Journal,* March 11, 1971. The commission member was also quoted as saying that there would be little improvement in relations between the police department and student and minority groups as long as Brier is chief. The next day the mayor, in his weekly televised news conference, said that the commission member had been misquoted and had denied the statement. Others present at the time, however, said that he had been correctly quoted (*Milwaukee Journal,* March 12, 1971). The incident further underscores the invulnerable position of the chief and his virtual immunity to criticism from city officials.

6. *Milwaukee Journal,* Feb. 18, 1971.

7. Arvid Anderson, "The State and Labor Relations," *Wisconsin Blue Book 1956,* p. 136.

8. The following list indicates those local employee groups officially recognized by the city of Milwaukee as bargaining units:

Local 195 International Brotherhood of Electrical Workers, AFL–CIO;
Municipal Truck Drivers Local Union 242 (affiliated with the International Brotherhood of Teamsters, Chauffeurs, Warehousemen, and Helpers of America);
Local 125B International Brotherhood of Firemen and Oilers, AFL–CIO;
Local 17, Building Service Employees' International Union, AFL–CIO;
International Brotherhood of Electrical Workers, Local 494, AFL–CIO (Fire Alarm Dispatchers and Machine Shop);
Association of Physicians and Dentists;
Team and Staff Nurses Council;
District Council 48, American Federation of State, County and Municipal Employees AFL–CIO (a confederation of unions), Local 17;
Milwaukee Professional Fire Fighters Association, Local 215, International Association of Fire Fighters, AFL–CIO;
Technicians, Engineers and Architects of Milwaukee;
Professional Policemen's Protective Association;
Association of Scientific Personnel;
Uniformed Pilots and Marine Engineers Association, Local 1037, IAFF, AFL–CIO;
Local 75, Journeymen Plumbers and Gasfitters;
Local 317, IUOE, AFL–CIO.

9. *Milwaukee Journal,* February 5, 1971.

10. This ranking was recently announced by the Department of Health, Education and Welfare. See *Milwaukee Journal,* March 10, 1971.

11. The following description is based on information contained in *1971 Executive Budget,* Milwaukee County, vol. V, pp. 8100–8103.

12. For a more detailed description of the historical development of the Sewerage Commission of the City of Milwaukee and the Metropolitan Sewer-

age District of Milwaukee County, together with the technical aspects of their operation, see City of Milwaukee Sewerage Commission, *Milwaukee Waste Water Treatment Facilities, 1968.*

13. Milwaukee Public Schools, *Facts . . . Figures 1969–1970* (Superintendent's Annual Report), p. 5.

14. Seven community schools were formed by neighborhood residents in the late 1960's out of Catholic parochial schools in the inner city. With a total current enrollment of 1,700 students, mostly black, they have struggled through one financial crisis after another. Most of them may soon be forced to close unless new funding sources are found.

15. City of Milwaukee, *1969 Directory and Report of Milwaukee's Progress in 1968,* pp. 57–58.

16. The new coalition has drawn the fire of some civil rights leaders, who are highly critical of the liberally oriented members of the board for participating in it. As one of them commented, "You liberals are going to rue the day you pulled this little caper, aligning with bigots and reactionaries" (*Milwaukee Sentinel,* Feb. 12, 1971).

17. The new consolidated districts, especially the one in the Milwaukee area, shifted part of the burden of vocational education from the central cities (which provide the bulk of the clientele) to the suburbs. The fiscal impact of the change was apparently not realized by the latter until after the new districts were created. In Milwaukee, most of the suburbs met their vocational education needs by paying the tuition for those among their residents who attended the city's school. This represented a total outlay of approximately $400,000 annually. Under the new arrangement, their share of the district levy exceeds $2 million. This "awakening" has led to legal action by eight of the suburbs to have the consolidation law declared invalid on the grounds that it delegates tax-levying power to a nonelected board.

18. The board of the MATC consists of two employer representatives, two employee representatives, two citizens-at-large, and one school administrator. Appointments are made by the board chairman or presidents of the high school districts that form District 9.

19. James R. Donoghue, "The Local Government System of Wisconsin," in State of Wisconsin, *1968 Blue Book,* pp. 136–38.

3

Executive Leadership Patterns

If one is to gain understanding of the actual, as opposed to the apparent, pattern of governmental operations, he must extend his sights beyond the formal structural context. Regardless of how well the visible framework of organization delineates relationships and assigns authority and responsibility, it does not reveal how the system develops ways of adapting to the realities of its environment. This adjustive behavior is particularly evident in those areas of operation where the formal arrangements are inappropriate or inadequate to serve the basic needs of the system. In the case of Milwaukee city government, the executive function—administrative coordination and control—constitutes one such critical area.

The local situation is ideally suited for looking at the question of executive leadership. Not only has the present mayor been in office for a long time, but his counterpart at the county level has also served over a concurrent time span, thus providing parallel examples of the adjustive process. Additionally, comparison between the executive positions in the two governments is useful because the formal structural contexts in which they operate are essentially different. In the former this context is little supportive of executive leadership, while in the latter it is more amenable to it. In neither case, however, do the structure and specified powers of the two offices provide a clear mandate for a strong executive role.

The present chapter focuses on several matters related to the leadership pattern as manifested in the city and county governments. One is the impact, if any, that the mayor and county executive have had on the formal structural arrangements under which they operate. A second is the extent to which influence has shifted to their respective offices. Still another is the adjustments in organizational influence that may have taken place in other areas of the two governments as a result of such shifts. And the final is the existence of other major factors that might independently alter the influence relationships that currently prevail.

Executive Leadership in Milwaukee City

Milwaukee's Mayor Henry W. Maier has exhibited a clear understanding of the inherent shortcomings of his position in the formal structure and of the alternative courses of action that can best remedy them. During his ten years in office, he has altered the basic influence relationships to the point where his position now encompasses probably as much political power as that of most big-city mayors, except Chicago's Richard J. Daley. In accomplishing this feat, he has been explicit as to why his office required alteration and how it ought to occur. He has also remained remarkably consistent in his public utterances of the underlying rationale for the steps he has taken toward this end.

The mayor has worked hard at creating the image of a public official whose actions are firmly grounded in legitimate concepts of political and administrative behavior. As a result, he has added a marked degree of "class" or "tone" to his role as chief executive. To some extent at least, his educational training in political science—he holds a master's degree in this field—has provided him with the theoretical background and conceptual tools for conferring an academic imprimatur on the conduct of his office. As minority leader in the State Senate, his experience in directing former Governor Gaylord Nelson's legislative proposals was useful in preparing him for a not dissimilar situation in the city.[1] During this earlier period he also ran against the Republican incumbent, Alexander Wiley, for the U.S. Senate, capturing 55 per cent of the Milwaukee vote in a losing effort. Thus, when he assumed the office of mayor in 1960, he brought with him a broad background in the realities of politics and the art and theory of governance.

Some insight into Maier's approach to the role of municipal chief executive can be found in a presentation he gave to the 1962 annual meeting of the U.S. Conference of Mayors on the subject of administrative organization. In his words:

> Somehow the Mayor, if he is to be in truth the chief executive officer, must find the quickest and most direct road to the transformation of policies, ideas and general goals into specific actions to produce governmental services and facilities of real and useful meaning to the people of the city. Otherwise, either one of two things is likely to happen: the Mayor's programs will become meaningless because of a lack of implementation; or there will be no time for executive creativity producing new programs, because the Mayor and his staff will be bogged down in the interminable details of follow-through.
>
> Where no device already exists, it is up to the Mayor to construct the administrative machinery to carry programs into effect. Depending upon the powers given him, the machinery can be centered within his own office or within the general administrative procedures of the city government.
>
> In Milwaukee, where strong powers are vested in the Common Council, I have found that the most effective route to efficient execution of city programs is through proper organization of the city government itself, making use of line departments. The department heads must be made to feel that they are part of the team. The Mayor's staff then functions as an extension of the Mayor's own presence—making sure that operating department heads are aware of what the Mayor's goals are and that they are working in harmony with them.
>
> On occasions, the Mayor may find that it is necessary to make changes in departmental organization to achieve the coordination required to forward a major program. A case in point is our experi-

ence in Milwaukee in the field of planning, housing and redevelopment.[2]

It is abundantly clear that the mayor possesses an astute awareness of what is necessary to acquire and maintain power. That he has put this knowledge to effective use is clear from the record of the past ten years. At the outset of his first term of office, he saw the necessity of taking several organizational assumptions into consideration. One was the need to avoid giving any appearance of undermining aldermanic prerogatives, because of the strong position of the council. The other was the relative autonomy of many of the line departments, resulting chiefly from the structural impediments to strong administrative leadership built into Milwaukee's system of government. Here too he saw the importance of proceeding in such a manner that existing relationships would not appear to be threatened. In short, to avoid strong resistance, it was necessary for him to adopt an approach that would not appear threatening either to the council or the line departments. If these considerations were not in fact foremost in the mind of the mayor, at least the actions he chose to take closely followed this format.

To a large extent, the situation at the time Maier came into office was favorable for the changes that would be necessary to enhance his position. Not the least important in this respect was the tenure of his predecessor, Frank Zeidler, who had chosen not to run after completing three terms in office. Generally low-keyed and anything but flamboyant, Zeidler projected the image of the scholar and intellectual more than that of the politician. Although the record clearly indicates that he sought to strengthen the position of mayor both formally and informally, he had been less than successful in doing so. The strong resistance of the Common Council, coupled with Zeidler's personal style and his philosophical aversion to executive domination, resulted in an emphasis on the rules established by the formal structure. This emphasis notwithstanding, the former mayor did establish a foundation for organizational change in several areas affecting the executive function, on which his successor could build.

The national scene was also conducive to a strengthening of the office. With a new Democratic administration in Washington and a new emphasis on the urban scene, a mayor of a major city with a well-known Democratic background was in a strategic position to capitalize on the advantages that such a situation offered. All things considered, the organizational environment was favorable for change when the new mayor took office in the spring of 1960. Although he would be dealing with a council that had shown little inclination to cooperate with his predecessor on matters that appeared to challenge aldermanic pre-eminence, the obstacles to enhancing the powers of his office through administrative and organizational changes and informal mechanisms did not appear insurmountable.

Since the beginning of his tenure as mayor, Maier's principal efforts have been focused on four major categories of concern. Three relate to the problem areas of community renewal, economic development, and city finances, and the fourth involves greater governmental efficiency. If, incidentally, the last objective requires increasing the chief executive's power, such enlargement is readily justified as a means of enabling the city to deal more effectively with the key problem areas. Beyond the enunciation of these focal categories, the mayor has also presented a plan of action. As first stated in his 1960 campaign and inauguration address, this consists of the formulation of detailed plans to meet the city's needs, provision of the necessary organizational tools and authority to enable implementation by the chief executive's office and the council, and coordination of Milwaukee's efforts with those of other governmental units at all levels.[3] Examination of the mayor's efforts in these areas of concern and the strategy he followed will serve to illustrate the manner in which the pattern of influence within city government was modified.

Economic Development. Mayor Zeidler, during his tenure, had established a Division of Industrial Development in his office. Its functions were generally oriented to the expansion of industry in the city, although it also performed minor public relations tasks. Using this unit as a point of departure, Maier, soon after his initial election, proposed the creation of a new Division of Economic Development, which would serve essentially in the same capacity as its predecessor but would have an enlarged role. One major addition was the creation of a land bank for industrial use, to be underwritten by the council. Although the mayor was proposing an expansion of influence for an existing function, he was not seeking a new area of activity for his office or posing a threat of encroachment on other departments or agencies in the government. He succeeded in winning council approval for the creation of the division and for a $1 million fund to finance the industrial land bank program.

Initially a two-man operation, the division continuously increased in importance. As an adjunct to it, an Economic Growth Council and an Industrial Office Development Committee were created in 1963. Three years later, the division established the city's first industrial renewal project. In addition to its economic concerns, the division also has a public relations function. Along with the preparation and dissemination of various promotional tracts, brochures, and advertisements appropriate to this activity, it was given the task in 1963 of studying the feasibility of a Milwaukee world festival to increase tourism and publicity for the city. Summerfest, which was first held in 1968, grew out of these efforts. Designed to accomplish the aims of the initially planned festival, it combines some pre-existing cultural and entertainment activities with new events spread out over a ten-day period.

The establishment and expansion of the Division of Economic Development point out a characteristic pattern regarding the mayor's method of operation. As he has stated, his initial task in office was to determine what gaps existed in the operation of the city government. By the term "gap" he means a basic problem area where there is no instrumentation in the structure that can effectively work toward its solution. Once such identification is made, the next step is to create a center of intelligence or mechanism for eliminating the gap.⁴ Economic Development is an example of such an instrumentality. It enables the mayor to have more information relevant to this area of concern than any other unit in city government has, particularly the Common Council. Because of this knowledge base, his office is placed in the strongest position to suggest appropriate responses and to influence generally the treatment given the problem area.

Not all potential gaps, however, are to be dealt with in this manner. In reality, only those areas vulnerable to this treatment have been given priority. Vulnerability in this sense applies to those areas not under the specific control of the council, either collectively or through individual aldermen, and those controlled by administrative units that are formally under the mayor. Examples of nonvulnerable structures are the Police Department and the city attorney's office. In short, the mayor has been quite selective in filling the gaps as he has defined them. This selectivity in choosing appropriate areas for "instrumentation" has enabled him to augment the informal powers of his office without seriously rupturing those cooperating networks necessary for exercising influence.

Securing Resources. The mayor's major priority, as he sees it, is "foreign policy" generally and the resource problems facing the city specifically. He does not argue that internal operations in the city government are without problems, but he feels that difficulties relevant to intergovernmental concerns are more critical (and also, one might add, more vulnerable). To a great extent the economic development instrumentation deals with this area. A more direct relationship can be found in another "center of intelligence" created by the mayor in 1966 with the approval of the council—the Department of Intergovernmental Fiscal Liaison. Essentially, this unit was established to "make studies and investigations with respect to fiscal matters related to the securing of a greater share of state and federal funds and to do whatever may be required in promoting for the City a greater share of state and federal fund contributions."⁵ Its role has since been expanded to include the processing of all grants-in-aid applications from any department. This centralization gives the mayor potential control over this aspect of departmental operations, a point not overlooked at the time the function was shifted to fiscal liaison.

In addition to using its lobbying function, the mayor draws on the department (which now has five professional staff members) to coordinate and stimulate the efforts of other municipalities in the state seeking similar objectives. It was through this unit that he organized a state-wide group of "have-not" cities to press for tax distribution reforms favorable to the municipalities. This has been part of his highly visible campaign to alter the state tax redistribution policies. Like the Division of Economic Development, the Department of Intergovernmental Fiscal Liaison has provided additional staff support and image enhancement for the mayor in a politically advantageous area.

Recently, the mayor initiated still another intelligence center to deal with resource problems: a Ways and Means Committee, consisting of himself as chairman and six aldermen. This was followed by the creation of the Urban Committee, actually a staff unit, formally attached to the council but designed to serve primarily the Ways and Means Committee. In each case, substantial funds were appropriated for operating purposes. The stated functions of the new instrumentalities are to recommend tax policies and examine alternative solutions to existing intergovernmental arrangements relative to resource allocations. They are also intended to complement the local Urban Observatory, established in 1969.[6] Their creation further strengthened the intelligence and staff resources available to the mayor.

City Renewal. When Maier became the city's chief executive in 1960, the Redevelopment Authority, established two years before, during Zeidler's tenure in office, was engaged in three urban renewal projects together with a conservation-and-rehabilitation program. It had become apparent, however, given the growing needs of the city and the prospect of additional federal funds in the offing, that these efforts had to be expanded. It had also become apparent that better coordination among existing city units involved in the redevelopment process was essential if effective operation of the various related programs was to be achieved.

We have already noted that Maier was successful in securing council approval for the creation of the Department of City Development, which consolidated the housing and redevelopment authorities and the City Plan Commission. In this way he was able not only to improve coordination between areas of overlapping concern but also to concentrate the control and administration of these activities in one bureaucratic unit. The combination, moreover, resulted in the shifting of power from the three boards to the departmental head, who was more vulnerable to the direct control of the mayor. It also allowed for an expansion of staff (currently 375) that went well beyond what these units could have developed individually.

The Model Cities program has provided the mayor with an additional opportunity to extend his control over redevelopment activities. From the outset, he was able to establish his leadership in this area as a continuation of the pattern he had set earlier. Although the council initially rejected the city's formal plan for participation in the program because of the control it vested in the mayor, he was able to overcome this opposition in time to have Milwaukee included in the second round of planning grants. Significantly, the administrative unit established for Model Cities was put under the direct control of the mayor, an arrangement that further augments his leadership resources.

Governmental Efficiency. The mayor, at the beginning of his first term, announced his intention to seek changes in city government that would result in greater efficiency. Administratively, he grouped all departments into four development operation (DO) units or "little cabinets": economic, social-cultural, physical, and services. The purpose was to secure increased coordination and cooperation on an informal basis through the vehicle of these units. Although there was some improvement, the impact on departmental operations vis-à-vis the mayor was far weaker than expected.

Of greater significance are the steps he has taken to exercise control over the budget-making process. These, while less visible than the "little cabinet" plan, have been noteworthy. Central to his strategy has been the augmentation of the city's budget-and-management department and the establishment of a close working relationship with its longtime head. This department has experienced a steady expansion of influence in recent years, progressing from the modest Office of the Budget Supervisor to its present status as Bureau of Budget and Management Analysis. A substantial factor in this growth has been the institution of performance-budgeting, a change that Maier successfully pushed. The new form greatly increases the bureau's ability to monitor departmental budget requests and budget administration.

Instead of attempting to create a new instrumentation that would give him more fiscal control—an effort that undoubtedly would have been doomed to failure—the mayor chose to supplement the activities of the existing budget unit. Although the formal structure does not allow him to formulate the budget, his friendly relationship with the bureau director has given him direct access to this process. Without having any formal authority, he has for all practical purposes succeeded in establishing an executive budget. And, because he is an ex-officio member of the Board of Estimates, he is in a position to influence both budget formulation and enactment. In fact, since 1963, he has been giving an annual budget message to the council.

It is interesting to note the procedure the mayor employs to prepare himself for his role as chairman of the Budget Examining Committee (the key subunit of the Board of Estimates). At the budget preparation stage, his office issues a form to all departments soliciting information on those areas of substantial disagreement between them and the Bureau of Budget and Management Analysis. After the receipt of these forms, staff personnel from the mayor's office confer with both the departments and the bureau. If the mayor is convinced of the validity of the department's position, he is often successful in overriding or modifying the bureau's recommendations.

The mayor has also been able to achieve consolidation of all inspection functions, including building, sanitation, fire, and plumbing, within a new Building Inspection Department. As he had in establishing the Department of City Development, he worked closely with the Common Council's Organization and Methods Committee in formulating this change. Previously, Maier had called for a reconstitution of this committee, originally created under Mayor Zeidler, into what he identified as a "little Hoover commission" to keep watch on city government and make recommendations for economies and increased efficiency. This action was in line with the mayor's strategy of establishing or reconstituting council committees in those areas of major concern to him. In this way he could not be accused of ignoring council prerogatives, while at the same time he placed himself in a position to exert influence over the smaller units in contrast to the larger body.

In instances when it has been unlikely that aldermanic committees would support a policy position the mayor desired, he has resorted to the use of select committees of citizens. This was the case in the formation of the Martin-Weber committee, convened in 1968 to study the organization of Milwaukee's government. Predictably, the group recommended, among other things, that the administrative structure be reorganized to strengthen the office of the chief executive.[7] This proposal, in effect, merely gave formal recognition to what already existed in fact.[8] After endorsing the committee's findings, Maier has done little to push for the adoption of the recommendations, and it is not likely that any significant formal enhancement of the mayor's office will occur in the near future.

As the foregoing clearly indicates, the mayor until very recently felt that his influence in the governmental structure was sufficient to give him the necessary degree of control over the system. Hence, he viewed enlargement of the formal powers and responsibilities of his office simply as a means of facilitating and enhancing an already existing ability to control. Developments subsequent to that time, however, appear to have convinced him that the type of reorganization prescribed by the Martin-Weber report is essential if he is to continue to function in an effective manner. As he states, "I, as mayor, had felt up until very recently that I could operate under the system. Now with recent events, I have some doubts."[9] The events to which he refers are councilmanic actions that ran counter to his wishes. On several occasions in recent months, the council has defeated proposals supported by the mayor, indicating that the leadership faction favorable to him is having increasing difficulty in making its will prevail. This was evidenced, for example, by the council's refusal to have the ward lines redrawn by the Judiciary Committee, which is controlled by pro-Maier aldermen; instead, a special committee was created for this purpose, chaired by a member who is frequently in opposition to the mayor. It was also evidenced by its rejection of a mayoral appointment to the Board of Zoning Review and by its persistent refusal to confirm Maier's choice to head the Department of City Development. Although he ultimately prevailed in the latter case, it was only after extensive efforts and maneuvering on his part.

Mayoral Appointive Power. The mayor has consistently employed his appointive power, limited as it is, to extend his control over the formal structure. (Appendixes G and H indicate the method of appointment for all boards, commissions, and departments.) Although he does not have the power to remove appointees from the boards and commissions that have a policy-making role, the fact that he has been in office for ten years has afforded him the opportunity to replace the holders of all positions in these categories. When he has chosen not to replace individual members, it has been largely because either they were supportive of his point of view or the body they were serving on has little influence in the system.

Noteworthy in this connection was the effort the mayor made to extend his influence over the policy boards and commissions. During his first administration, he established the practice of having individuals appointed to such positions submit undated letters of resignation. When the newspapers focused public attention on the letters, Maier indicated that the policy was a normal one designed to deal with "obstructions of programs and corruption by any commission member." Emphasizing that it was simply a means of enabling him to discharge his responsibilities as mayor, he stated that "I believe I should be empowered to issue an executive order and make it stick."[10] Many on the Common Council who had been unaware of this practice were highly critical on learning of it. The unfavorable reaction the letters evoked, coupled with an opinion by the city attorney that they were not valid, led the mayor to discontinue the practice.

The critical point here is the determination as to where control over governmental operations is actually located. In viewing the formal structure of the city, one would infer that most power is centered in the policy-making boards and in the Common Council, with its budget-making and ward influence. A closer examination, however, reveals that this diffused system of influence has tended to enhance the autonomy or degree of independence of the administrative departments themselves. The situation is somewhat analogous to that in the typical council-manager city where a large measure of control is transferred to the chief administrative officer because of his superior knowledge and expertise. It is not surprising, therefore, to find substantial centers of power in Milwaukee's municipal government lodged in the bureaucratic units and certain Common Council subgroups. Maier has recognized this fact, and he has given considerable attention to establishing his own influence in these quarters, particularly through his departmental appointments.

A clearer understanding of the mayor's efforts in this regard can be gained by examining a number of his major nominations. When the Common Council authorized the transfer of the Division of Economic Development from the chief executive's office to the Department of City Development, it also approved the creation of a new position, that of deputy commissioner. This action was accompanied by the clear indication that the council intended this post to be the second in command and that the person appointed to fill it would be the logical successor of the soon-to-retire head of the department. In taking this action, the council understood that the mayor would appoint his economic development director, Kenneth Fry, one of his long-time staff associates, to the new position.

This appointment marked the second occasion when a close associate of Mayor Maier's was moved into the Department of City Development. Previously, one of his staff members who had been serving temporarily as head of the Model Cities Agency had been named as program director, a position just below the top level in the department. A similar practice has been followed with respect to the Model Cities Agency, where several former staff aides to the mayor, including a former economist with Economic Development, have been placed.

The Department of Intergovernmental Fiscal Liaison provides another instance of the extension of mayoral influence through appointment. As previously mentioned, the creation of this unit was largely due to efforts of the mayor, and not unexpectedly his influence over it has been paramount. To head the department, Maier chose an influential alderman who had, before his appointment, narrowly missed being elected council president. Not only did the selection elicit favorable response from the council, but it also recruited to Maier's "team" a potentially strong rival. Finally, two other major departments—Building Inspection and Safety Engineering, and Tax Assessment—are headed by former aldermen who are close allies of the mayor's. The mayor was also able to increase the over-all importance of the first department by locating within its jurisdiction all inspection activities in the city. At the time of this reorganization, the council also approved the new position of department administrator, and this was filled by another former mayoral staff assistant.

Mayor-Council Relations. The steps taken by Mayor Maier to extend his sphere of influence and control required Common Council acquiescence in most instances. A hostile council, therefore, could easily have thwarted his efforts by refusing to confirm his appointments or approve the organizational changes he requested. Before 1968, the mayor had been careful to avoid any overt manifestations of influence exertion over the city's legislative arm. With the exception of the single instance when he had unsuccessfully attempted to bypass the prerogatives of the council through the device of undated letters of resignation, he had moved cautiously in matters clearly within the purview of that body. By assiduously concentrating on those areas that he identified as "vulnerable" (those that do not interfere with the traditionally recognized domain of the lawmakers), he was able in most cases to secure the necessary approval for his proposals.

The election of 1968, in which Maier carried all nineteen wards and received an unprecedented 86 per cent of the vote, marked the beginning of a more visible leadership role on his part vis-à-vis the council. The active backing he gave to several of the successful aldermanic candidates contributed to a power shift within the legislative body from those neutral or unfriendly toward the chief executive to a clearly identifiable, pro-Maier group of six aldermen. The first manifestation of this shift was the defeat of the longtime council president by a member whose allegiance to the mayor was unmistakable. Through his committee assignment powers, the new president proceeded immediately to establish a firm basis for controlling the critical areas of council decision-making. The three most important standing committees in this regard are finance-printing, judiciary-legislation, and buildings-grounds-harbors. Members of the pro-Maier faction were named as chairmen of two of these key units (judiciary and buildings) and as vice-chairmen of two (finance and judiciary). The latter two committees have a majority of three faction members and buildings a majority of four. (All council committees have a membership of five aldermen, which includes a chairman and vice-chairman.)

The same approach has been used in assignments to special committees of the Common Council, particularly those that have been formed to deal with the new organizational adjustments initiated by the mayor, such as the committees on economic development, taxation and finance (fiscal liaison), and urban ways and means. Additionally, the all-important Board of Estimates and its subunit the Budget Examining Committee are dominated by the mayor and his council supporters. Of the six aldermen on the eleven-man board, four belong to the pro-Maier faction, and the mayor and two of the four make up half of the examining committee. Thus, not only does the mayor have the benefit of the faction's support within the council as a whole, but also he is assured through the committee assignments of direct lines of communication and influence to the key points of policy-making within the city government.

The measure of informal control that the mayor has achieved through these various arrangements does not, however, significantly enlarge his influence over substantive policy. Although the council has been willing to accept the leadership function exercised by his supporters, the efforts of the latter have been directed largely to the implementation of already established programs. In fact, no new major program area has been proposed by the mayor since the 1968 election; instead his primary aim has been to consolidate and expand his previous initiatives. It is still abundantly clear that, in the absence of changes in the basic structure of city government that increase the formal powers of the chief executive at the expense of the council, the mayor must continue to remain acutely sensitive to the long-standing prerogatives of the aldermen. As recent events clearly demonstrate, the mayor's position is particularly vulnerable despite skillful use of limited resources. He is meeting increased resistance from the council, and he is finding it more difficult to exert influence in program formation and execution.

The County Executive

Running parallel to the mayor's role in the political system of the city is that of the county executive in the government of Milwaukee county. Both offices preside over complex units administering a broad range of services (the county with almost eleven thousand employees, the city with over eleven thousand,

and the incumbents of both have held their positions since 1960. Although other similarities between the two posts are readily apparent, there are also basic differences in the structural and organizational settings in which they function. These variations have compelled the incumbents to take different approaches in attempting to establish and carry out their leadership roles.

When discussing the organizational setting that prevailed at the time Maier was elected mayor for his first term, we noted that the condition for enlarging executive influence was most favorable. The "weak-mayor" form of government put few formal demands on the office; a sound bureaucratic operation existed; and the retiring holder of the office had initiated several major avenues for the expansion of mayoral influence with little or no visible recognition of these efforts. In short, the new occupant found a situation that demanded little formally but had great potential for expanded control. The state of affairs in county government, on the other hand, was radically different. Here it was not a case of taking over an already established "weak" or "strong" executive post; it was simply a matter of stepping into an entirely novel position that had just been created. Although John Doyne, the only occupant of the office to date, had been chairman of the County Board and a prime mover in the creation of the position, he assumed a quite different role in the change—from a presiding officer to an administering executive. For a board accustomed to the former, the latter was not readily acceptable.

If Maier could initially face a council that understood the role of the mayor's office and had established an understanding of general relationships to it, Doyne enjoyed no such advantage. And, if Maier could focus his attention on those areas most susceptible to his control while knowing he had a strong and well-functioning administrative structure behind him, Doyne could not. Not only was the latter faced with the necessity of working out relations with a County Board that felt it necessary to scrutinize all his actions as potential threats to the group's pre-existing prerogatives; he was also compelled to develop an effective administrative organization to overcome the disabilities inherent in the old unintegrated and "headless" system, in which considerable influence over policy decisions had accumulated in the hands of the various departmental chiefs, boards, and commissions. These were formidable obstacles; and, if the county executive's leadership role in metropolitan affairs has not developed as rapidly as some expected, the answer lies in large part here.

Establishment of the Office. As the Milwaukee area grew in population and became increasingly urbanized, the county government's scope of activity expanded proportionately. Up to a point, its organizational structure was able to cope with the intensified demands put upon it, but, by the middle of the 1950's, the inadequacies of the then existing system had become abundantly clear. For those individuals and groups, both inside and outside the government, who were concerned with this problem, the absence of an executive post in the structure became a major focal point for reform.

As was the case earlier in the city, outside consultants were retained by the Board of Supervisors in 1956 to analyze the government and make recommendations for improving its functional capability. Like the preparers of the Griffenhagen study made in 1950, the county's consultants, the Public Administration Service of Chicago (PAS), unequivocally counseled the creation of a strong executive position. Specifically, it recommended that the government be reorganized into eight major departments —finance, planning, personnel, public works, parks, recreation, health, and welfare—with a county manager as its administrative head.[11] Among the duties assigned to the manager would be major responsibility for preparation of the budget.

The PAS recommendation pertaining to the executive function and departmental reorganization was not followed, but its proposals dealing with the administration of the county's finances were adopted. For many of the same reasons that it argued for a county manager, the PAS advocated the creation of an administrative unit with the primary responsibility of budget review. In conformity to this proposal, the County Board established a

Division of Management and Budget in 1957 to operate under its Finance Committee.[12] Two years later, it authorized the installation of a centralized accounting system. These steps laid a strong foundation for the budgetary control that was essential if an executive head was to have any real effect on county government operations.

Although the worth of these budgetary and fiscal reforms is not to be minimized, their greatest contribution initially was to bring the inadequacy of the existing administrative structure into sharper focus. Even with the additional assistance afforded by these changes, the Board of Supervisors became less and less able to pass intelligently on the growing number of financial requests made on it (the county budget by this time had surpassed $50 million annually) or to oversee the sprawling bureaucracy. The thrust of events, which placed ever increasing responsibilities on the board members, finally convinced them that a county executive was desirable. Using arguments consistent with the PAS report and with general community consensus, the Board of Supervisors sought state enabling legislation in March, 1959, to create the office of county executive in Milwaukee county. Although there had been some support for the manager concept, the view that the position should be elective prevailed within the board.

The final version of the office as approved by the state legislature provided for a county executive with general authority over the administration of county government, including preparation of the budget, and with the powers of the veto and unlimited appointment. To ensure the constitutional validity of the law, a test suit was brought in the state supreme court challenging the statute. While finding the position constitutional, the court ruled that the veto and expanded appointive functions established powers for the executive that would be unique to Milwaukee and thus in violation of the state uniform county law. The ruling left the office with a still wide, albeit not unlimited, range of appointive authority, but it completely eliminated the power to veto acts of the County Board. These restrictions further handicapped the first incumbent of the post in his initial efforts to establish the position on a strong footing.

The Office in Operation. The election of John Doyne proved providential for those concerned with making the office of county executive an important center of control. In a very real sense, Doyne's influence was apparent even before his election. His position as chairman of the County Board had enabled him to generate a large degree of support in the body that actually stood to lose the most in influence if the change was accomplished. Although not the originator of the idea within the board, Doyne had seen the wisdom of the move from his experience as chairman. Because he not only was a strong supporter of the change but also intended to be a candidate for the post if it was created, he eliminated the problems that might otherwise have arisen. For, if the board as a whole had the most to lose under the new arrangement, the position of chairman would suffer the greatest erosion of organizational influence.

Once he had been elected as county executive, Doyne had to face the problem of establishing a working relationship with his successor to the board chairmanship, Eugene Grobschmidt. The loss of the veto and the restrictions on his appointive powers as a result of the court's ruling lessened his ability to shape these relations as he would have liked. Moreover, the imperative task of having the powers lost by the court's action restored was made more difficult now that he was no longer board chairman. Clearly, a Doyne-less board facing a fact rather than a concept would be more difficult to convince that it should yield up these additional items. This became evident as Doyne's first year in office proceeded.

From the very start, it was apparent that, without the veto power, the position of executive was put in an extremely weak status vis-à-vis the board. The problem was crystallized after Doyne presented his first budget. Previously it had been the board that received the major credit for budget trimming and economies. Under the new system, this task was performed by the executive. Because the budget office was now located under him rather than the board, the latter had lost an important staff arm. It was now restricted to endorsing or making minor changes in the budget as submitted to it by Doyne. In the eyes of some of the members, this meant losing the considerable political credit that would have ordinarily accrued to the board but was now shifted to the executive. For the first time, the supervisors began to see clearly that the office of county executive would require a major readjustment in the role and influence patterns that had prevailed before the reorganization and to which they were well accustomed.

Two other facts were also brought home to the County Board members. For one, they saw that the power of appointment, which they formerly enjoyed, was a more valuable prerogative than they had realized. Even though they could delay or reject the executive's appointments, this was a far cry from initiating them. They also faced a considerable diminution of their public visibility. As the county's chief administrator elected by a county-wide constituency, Doyne immediately became its acknowledged spokesman and ceremonial head, proving most attractive and convincing in this role. Because of his strong need for the veto power, he generally sought every possible forum during his early months in office to plead his case and gather support for the necessary constitutional amendment.

Too late the members of the Board of Supervisors realized that, in helping to create the office of county executive, they had effectively contributed to their own demise as the key center of influence within county government. Many of them had become convinced that a hard second look at the position ought to be taken. Although the post of executive was an established fact from which no backing away was possible, many opportunities still remained to stem the flow of influence to it. The first act in this direction was a reconsideration of the previously endorsed veto power. Prompted by Grobschmidt, who had assumed an aggressive leadership role within the body, the board attempted to influence state legislative action on the veto amendment by going on record against it. When faced with this situation,

Doyne unequivocally indicated that he would be forced to press his case for the veto even if such action meant open disagreement with the supervisors.

Unfortunately for the board, its influence did not extend to the Milwaukee county contingent at the state legislature. Representatives from the area felt that they were under an obligation to complete a job they had already begun. They saw no overriding reason for second thoughts after they had taken the initial action of creating the post. To leave it without adequate powers because of a legal technicality made no sense to them. Doyne and those who favored his position were able strongly to reinforce this view at the state capitol and subsequently with the voters who endorsed the amendments in a state-wide referendum.[13]

The negative posture manifested by the board in the early months of Doyne's tenure and the pre-existing arrangements between it and the line departments have continued to impede his efforts to extend and enhance the initial improvements in county government operations brought about by the creation of his office. From the beginning, Doyne has been steadfast in his commitment to streamlining county government and centralizing over-all administrative control in his office in the interest of efficiency and executive effectiveness. His efforts in this regard have closely paralleled the recommendations made in the PAS reports. Success toward this end has been steady if not spectacular. However, because of repeated blocking actions by the board and the resistance of some of the entrenched administrators, the time span required to institute the necessary reforms has been unduly prolonged. It has been Doyne's misfortune to have been constantly faced with a faction on the board led by Grobschmidt that has remained virtually unchanged since the inception of the executive office. Although this situation has not resulted in the defeat of Doyne's over-all goals of administrative reorganization, it has caused him to concentrate most of his energies on internal concerns at the expense of his potential leadership role in metropolitan affairs.

Changing Perspectives. Doyne, like Maier, has exercised a strong degree of executive leadership in the context of the environment within which he must operate. Like Maier also, he has not had at his disposal the full complement of tools that would assure him an unqualified position at the center of power in his government. Although he has had strong formal authority and a governmental structure amenable to centralized control, he has been faced during most of his tenure in office with a legislative body that has been resistant to executive expansion. The persistent opposition of the Board of Supervisors to his reorganization efforts might have caused a weaker personality to take the easy way out and choose not to fight. At the outset, when the supervisors reversed their previous support for the veto, Doyne could have acceded to this view and agreed to what would in effect be a board-directed government. Instead, he chose the much more difficult path of developing an office that would in reality have over-all control of administrative activity.

Doyne's views regarding the role of the executive in county government have changed since he first occupied the post. In a review of his initial year in office, but before the veto fight with the board, Doyne described his role in these terms: "The reason this office was set up in the first place was to see that the mandates of the County Board are carried out. I consider this my major task."[14] Four years later, in reviewing his first term, he admitted to difficulties with the supervisors, commenting that one "couldn't throw things at the county board too fast." He lamented, "I wish I could find someone who has mastered the technique of dealing with legislative bodies."[15] By 1970, his conception of the office had completely reversed itself. When asked for his view on the position of an elected executive versus an administrator or manager appointed by the County Board, he observed that the major difference in the two forms (besides the veto power) was "the independence of being an officer in county government elected by all the people." Then he reflected, "I would and could never be an administrator. I just have resistance to some things the County Board acts on. As an executive

I serve at the will of the people and not the County Board and only the people can fire me if and when they disagree with something I have done."[16]

Politically popular as Doyne has been personally—he ran unopposed in his last two elections in 1964 and 1968—this popularity has not been reflected in the County Board. Unlike Mayor Maier with respect to the Common Council, Doyne has been unable to expand his influence significantly over the lawmaking body. Resistance to the enhancement of his office—even to the enlargement of his small staff—continues. The substantial gains in administrative reorganization that he has achieved have been due to his patience and persistence. So long as the present chairman of the County Board remains in office, executive-legislative relationships as they have existed for the past ten years are not likely to change. The countercenter of power that the chairman has established ensures dual leadership within the internal operations of Milwaukee county government. Whether this arrangement has now become sufficiently institutionalized to survive the present incumbent's tenure is a question for the future.

The efforts of Maier and Doyne to alter the focus of organizational influence closely fit the theoretical construct of political scientist Herbert Kaufman.[17] According to his formulation, administrative structures in government periodically undergo change when the pre-eminence of one of three core values—executive leadership, representativeness, and neutral competence—gives way to one of the other two. Such shifts in dominance occur in cyclical fashion and are largely the result of dissatisfaction with governmental responsiveness to the politically articulate groups in the society at large. Historically, these shifts began with the strong control of executive leadership during the colonial period, followed in succeeding eras by the move to legislative-centered governance and then to neutral competence when the spoils system and general inefficiency resulted in demands for more effective administrative structures. Today, growing dissatisfaction with the insularity and unresponsiveness of massive governmental bureaucracies again provides impetus to continue the cyclical change.

In the case of the Milwaukee city and Milwaukee county governments, the period prior to the elections of Maier and Doyne—a period in which neutral competence became increasingly dominant—clearly demonstrated the inability of the existing structures to deal satisfactorily with the demands made upon them. The formal and informal adjustments described in this chapter represent distinct efforts to alter basic relationship patterns within the two governments in order to establish the core value of executive leadership as pre-eminent. Granting the validity of Kaufman's theory, we might predict that both Maier and Doyne will continue to make progress in establishing the dominance of executive leadership so long as they are able to demonstrate that such a focus will enable their respective governments to meet constituency demands effectively. When this is no longer the case, the dominance of this core value will be displaced by a return to greater representativeness in administration and a de-emphasis in the position of the two chief executive officers.

Notes

1. Interview with Henry W. Maier, mayor of Milwaukee, April 29, 1970.
2. United States Conference of Mayors, *City Problems 1962*, Annual Proceedings, p. 21.
3. *Milwaukee Journal*, April 19, 1960.
4. Interview with Henry Maier, *op. cit.*
5. City of Milwaukee, *Code of Ordinances*, Ordinance 962.
6. Sponsored by the National League of Cities and financed principally by the U.S. Department of Housing and Urban Development, the National Urban Observatory is intended to enlist academic expertise in the analysis of problems designated by municipal officials. A national agenda of such problem areas has been established, although each participating city may also consider other matters of specific local interest. It is important to note that Mayor Maier and Robert C. Wood, formerly Undersecretary of HUD, were the prime movers behind the National Urban Observatory project. The mayor now heads the policy committee for the Milwaukee observatory and has been influential in determining its research priorities.
7. Martin-Weber Committee, "Organization Study of the City of Milwaukee"

(an unpublished report submitted to Henry W. Maier, mayor of Milwaukee, Dec. 16, 1968).

8. City of Milwaukee, Administrative Survey Committee, *Final Report Concerning Administrative Practices Based on Recommendations of Griffenhagen and Associates,* Dec., 1955. (The use of an outside body to assess the administrative structure of the city's government was not without precedent. During Frank Zeidler's tenure, a management-consulting firm, Griffenhagen and Associates, had been employed for this purpose. Of a considerably more extensive nature than the Martin-Weber effort, the survey had focused on procedural and functional changes in the line operations of the city. Among its proposals was a recommendation for a strong chief executive office.)

9. *Milwaukee Journal,* March 5, 1971. In essence, what has been occurring is that those aldermen not part of the pro-Maier leadership faction are significantly increasing their ability to coalesce as an opposition group. See also *Milwaukee Journal,* Feb. 14, 1971.

10. *Milwaukee Sentinel,* Dec. 12, 1962.

11. Public Administration Service, *The Government of Milwaukee County —A Concluding Report,* Jan. 12, 1956, pp. 51–52. Mimeographed.

12. Public Administration Service, *Planning and Financial Administration in the Government of Milwaukee County,* Aug. 1, 1955. Mimeographed.

13. When it became apparent to the board that it would not prevail, it reconsidered its position regarding the amendment and formally endorsed it.

14. *Milwaukee Sentinel,* April 23, 1961.

15. *Milwaukee Journal,* Feb. 9, 1964.

16. *Wisconsin State Journal,* Oct. 23, 1970.

17. See Herbert Kaufman, "Emerging Conflicts in the Doctrines of Public Administration," *American Political Science Review* 50 (Dec., 1956), pp. 1057–73.

4

"Who Governs?"

The legal and administrative structure of local government usually receives considerable attention from political observers because it provides the formal machinery for the making and enforcement of community policy. However, not all matters of civic concern fall within the normal jurisdiction of the public establishment. Other institutional sectors of society—business, labor, private welfare organizations, good-government groups, and the churches, among others—are also involved with projects and issues of community interest. And, even in the case of governmental action or decision-making, charges are sometimes made that the output represents the dictates of private individuals or groups and not the independent judgment of public authorities. In fact, the question of who actually "runs the civic show" has been a favorite topic of the man in the street as well as the social scientist.

Milwaukeeans have been as much intrigued by this question as urbanites elsewhere. Their opinions differ widely as to the extent to which power in the community is concentrated or dispersed and as to who the key actors in the policy-making process are. Some, à la Floyd Hunter, embrace the theory that major community decisions are made by a handful of individuals, largely from financial and industrial circles, who stand at the apex of a stable power hierarchy.[1] Others, in a less sophisticated vein, regard labor as the dominant force in local affairs, and many see the mayor as all powerful. Still others, particularly top businessmen, public officials, and knowledgeable observers, flatly reject the notion that a small and cohesive coterie of influentials controls the decision-making structure. Their view corresponds to the now widely accepted "pluralist" theory, which holds that influence is distributed among competing interest groups, no one of which can marshal sufficient political muscle to impose its will regularly on the larger society through control over government policy-making.[2] As many in this category perceive the situation in Milwaukee, the matrix of power is diffused to the point where vigorous and decisive action in the civic arena is a virtual impossibility.

The query "who governs?" whether asked of Milwaukee, Chicago, New York, Los Angeles, or any of the scores of other large cities and metropolises that span the nation, will never be answered to everyone's satisfaction. The inscrutable character of power and the mythology surrounding it militate against such a likelihood. Yet power in every community, from the rural village to the giant metropolis, is structured in one manner or another. In the daily round of activities that characterize urban life, individuals and groups play different roles, possess varying degrees of influence, and interact with each other. These interactions normally fit into a pattern of more or less regularized behavior that lends itself to at least a modicum of generalization and predictability. For the larger and more heterogeneous urban aggregations, such as Milwaukee, the complexity of this pattern and the decisional network it represents defies accurate description. To believe that it can be cognitively mastered with scientific rigor would be far more presumptuous than realistic. The most the analyst can hope to do is to gain some insight into the over-all configuration of power as it manifests itself in the community and identify the major channels through which it is exercised.

This chapter, therefore, has three broad objectives: to demonstrate the range and extent of participation in local public issues in the Milwaukee area, to identify the principal actors—individuals and organizations—in the decisional process, and to describe the major centers of community power and their relationship to each other. For these purposes, it draws heavily on a recently conducted leadership study of Milwaukee and on supplementary interviews and personal observations. The picture that emerges contains few surprises for those intimately familiar with the community and its institutions.

The Leadership Spectrum

One recognized method of investigating the power structure of a community is through event analysis or case study.[3] Under this approach, a systematic examination is made of the major issues or problems that were dealt with over a recent time period, with attention focused directly on the people who were involved in their resolution. Such a study is designed to reveal whether there is a single and cohesive set of leaders, an elite that is mobilized whenever an important local issue arises, or whether several groups are meaningfully involved in the decisional process. By determining who actually participates in key community decisions, the event-analysis approach seeks to provide a more realistic appraisal of the influence pattern than the traditional methodology, which merely identifies those who are reputed to be the power-wielders.

The Milwaukee leadership study is of the event-analysis type.[4] It deals with forty decisions judged by qualified local informants and evaluators to be the most significant made in the community over a five-year period—from 1959 to 1964. The decisions meet a number of criteria: (1) They are representative of the widest possible range of content and of institutional sectors such as government, private welfare, education, and social; (2) they pertain to the development, use, or distribution of resources and facilities that had an impact on large groups of people in the locality; (3) they are administered rather than market-type decisions—that is, they were made by individuals holding positions in organizations rather than by popular vote or referendum; and (4) they are maximally important in terms of the perceptions of the informants. This pool of issues was subjected to intensive analysis for the purpose of identifying the participants in each case and the roles they played. Equally important, they were examined to determine the extent to which the decision-makers formed groups or clusters that worked together toward the solution of more than one problem.

The study identified approximately 300 people as directly (not simply formally or peripherally) involved in one or more of the forty decisions. Well over one-third of this number consists of public officials (elective, appointive, and administrative), while another 30 per cent are from commercial, industrial, and banking circles. The remainder are divided among many institutional sectors including labor, religion, the professions, higher education, civil rights, and the arts. In terms of social characteristics such as income, education, and occupation, the cadre of leaders as a whole ranks consistently above the general population.

Almost three-fourths of those identified as participants took part in only one of the forty decisions, while at the other end of the spectrum eleven were involved in more than five of the issues. All but one of the eleven are public officials, eight of them elective and two appointive. The Milwaukee mayor leads the list by a wide margin, appearing in fifteen of the decisions. He is followed by the county executive, who was named in nine, and the County Board chairman and two Milwaukee aldermen, who were identified in eight. The only private person included in this top group was a participant in eight of the issues.

When the total stockpile of decisions was statistically clustered in terms of people who were actively involved in their resolution, thirteen discrete sets emerged. This finding indicates that thirteen different groups served as decision-makers in those community issues selected as most significant over a five-year span. No single coterie, in other words, could be identified as influential across a wide range of subject matter. The decisions, moreover, clustered on the basis of common content as well as participants. Those that dealt with the economic development efforts of the central city, for example, shared a common core of personnel. So also did those pertaining to education, race relations, metropolitan integration, civic improvement projects of area-wide import, and other similarly broad fields of local concern.

The cluster of economic development issues covers decisions pertaining to a tax assessment freeze for a new downtown office building, the establishment of an industrial land bank program by the city, the formation of a division of economic development in the mayor's office, and the creation of a department of city development. The key personnel in this category are predominantly city government officials, with the mayor playing the most prominent role. Similarly, the set dealing with educational matters, such as the establishment of public school policy for the inner city and the inauguration of pilot classes for capable children, is limited almost exclusively to school officials, both board members and administrators. The cluster on race relations, which includes decisions on the formation of the Milwaukee Conference on Race and Religion and the organization of a school boycott, drew participants from still other institutional sources, with clergymen and civil rights activists most in evidence.[5]

Other decisional groupings show a somewhat broader spread of participants. That relating to issues of metropolitan integration, such as the creation of the Southeastern Wisconsin Regional Planning Commission, establishment of the United Fund, adoption of the office of county executive, and formation of a joint committee to develop uniform job classification and pay plans for the major governmental units of the area, involves personnel from several institutional sectors, particularly business, labor, and officialdom. In like manner, the cluster pertaining to civic improvement projects—construction of a new union station, downtown post office, and music hall—includes economic notables as well as city and county officials. The former, however, played the more prominent role in pushing these undertakings to a successful conclusion.

These and the other groupings revealed by the study serve to point up several characteristics of Milwaukee's power structure. First of all, they dispel the notion of a single or cohesive clique of elites dominating the local polity and scheming to direct the course of its public affairs. At the same time, however, they also attest to the fact that only a minuscule portion of the adult population of the county, less than 0.1 per cent, participates in a direct way in the making of significant community decisions. Those so involved, moreover, do not constitute a microcosm of the total citizen body. They are drawn disproportionately from the higher socio-economic categories, while few from the ranks of the lower classes and racial minorities are included. These findings are not peculiar to Milwaukee; they are common to most other large urban complexes.

Second, the data demonstrate the predominant role that public officials play in community decision-making. Government personnel figure prominently in more than thirty of the forty issues examined in the study. Again, this situation is not unusual to Milwaukee, as sociologist Claire Gilbert demonstrated in a comparative analysis of 167 community power-structure studies. According to her findings, small cities and towns are dominated by the formally elected officials, but major decisions are postponed indefinitely; middle-sized cities are ruled by nonpolitical people or by a coalition of such individuals and elected officials, and, in the larger communities, such as Milwaukee, the elected officials "are in command of whatever power there is."[6]

This pattern may prevail to a greater extent in Milwaukee than elsewhere, because of the historical tendency of the private sector to relegate the conduct of community affairs to local politics and intervene only on those relatively infrequent occasions when projects of direct concern to them are at stake. Not only has there been widespread reluctance on the part of the economic dominants to become involved in issues of a social or political nature, but the common practice has been for them to encourage the public development of civic projects—whether an art museum, baseball stadium, sports arena, or medical center—rather than undertake such development themselves. This passiveness on the part of economic influentials has led to the defining of most community issues in terms that call for governmental solutions. Twenty-nine of the forty decisions, for example, were of a type that required formal action by local authorities. The inevitable result is that public officials, such as the mayor and county executive, are involved as decision-makers in a far greater range of community concerns than private citizens.

Finally, although the data clearly document the pluralistic nature of the decisional structure and the existence of multiple centers of influence, they also suggest that power in Milwaukee, at least as it is reflected by participation in community issues, is not as broadly dispersed as one might expect in an area of its size and complexity. For example, a similar study in Syracuse, New York, a metropolis half the size of Milwaukee, revealed nineteen different leadership groupings in contrast to the thirteen found in Milwaukee.[7] This less diffused pattern in the latter case may be explained in part by the relative absence from the civic arena of the new and more mobile managers of economic power who seem willing to let the older leaders from the locally or family-owned enterprises handle the community chores.

Power Centers

It is to belabor the obvious to say that the formal structure of local government in the modern urban setting provides no effective institutional machinery for centralized decision-making and control. It is more questionable in the eyes of some power-structure theorists to say that the private repositories of influence that undergird the metropolis likewise fail to constitute an informal mechanism or framework for this purpose. As we have already seen, however, the Milwaukee leadership study furnishes no support for those who may be receptive to the notion of a hidden, or not so hidden, power elite. Neither does an examination of the various influence centers of power and the linkages among them offer any corroboration for this notion. Both, on the contrary, point convincingly to the pluralistic character of the community's decisional structure.

The remainder of this chapter is devoted to an overview of the major centers of influence and civic leadership in Milwaukee that reflect this pluralism. For purposes of simplification, we have categorized most of these as government, business, labor, minority groups, mass media, and religious institutions. None of these sectors are monolithic in nature; each represents a broad range of groups and interests, some of which are loosely linked together by common ties or overlapping memberships. The picture is not one of widespread and incessant competition for the rewards of the local political system. For a few groups and individuals—local officials, public-employee unions, the suburban League of Municipalities, and lately minority group leaders—the governmental arena offers the major stage on which to perform. For the great majority, however, the local polity is far less relevant as a reward-allocating structure than the private sector and higher levels of government. As a result, they enter the community's public amphitheater only infrequently and for special purposes.

Government. At the city government level, the major locus of public power and leadership is the office of the mayor. As noted in the preceding chapter, Mayor Henry Maier has been able to achieve a dominant position in the municipal structure despite the weak formal powers of his office and the historically strong status of the Common Council. He has established a close working relationship with the council president, and his supporters have been placed in control of the three most influential standing committees: finance, buildings, and judiciary. In addition, he has appointed people, principally former aldermen with strong political affiliations or sources of support, to key administrative posts.

The mayor, however, is able to maintain this position of dominance only by being sensitive to the traditional prerogatives of the Common Council and by avoiding public stands on issues that would be certain to alienate members on whom he must rely for support. The location of public housing on scattered sites on the city's southside is a recent example of such an issue. In defending the mayor against newspaper criticism for not injecting himself into the dispute and exercising leadership, Robert Jendusa, the council president, argued, "It would be wrong for the mayor to get his foot in the machinery when the common council was deeply involved in it and trying to resolve it without polarizing the issue." The chief executive's involvement, he said, was informal. "A word here and a word there on the part of the mayor; a word of encouragement I can assure you was there. But it did not come out visibly which in turn could have polarized the issue."[8]

At the county government level, two key points of influence have developed, one revolving around the elected executive and the other around the chairman of the Board of Supervisors. Until the creation of the office of county executive in 1959, both legislative and administrative leadership, weak as the latter was, centered in the board chairman. The traditional importance of this post has not easily been eroded, and, in the hands of Eugene Grobschmidt, who has occupied it since the reorganization, it has remained competitive with that of the county executive. As a consequence, John Doyne, the only occupant of the executive office since its inception, has been handicapped in developing the potential of the position for metropolitan leadership. The high rate of involvement of the County Board chairman in the decision-making process, as shown by the leadership study, is a reflection of this power counterpoise.

Each suburban municipality—or, more properly speaking, its municipal government—constitutes a microcenter of power with the ability to impede and on occasions even veto measures of area-wide import. The influence of these units is felt at both the state and county levels. Suburban representatives in the legislature generally enjoy closer relations with rural and small-town members than do those from the central city. Hence they are often in a position to negate legislation that, in their view, would benefit the central city at the expense of the suburban units or pose a threat to the latter's autonomy. Similarly, suburban representatives on the County Board, although in a definite minority, exert influence that is disproportionate to their numbers.

The League of Suburban Municipalities has long been the spokesman for the so-called iron ring, the communities outside the city of Milwaukee. Established in the late 1920's to combat the "imperialism" of the central city, it has historically constituted an important mechanism in setting the "foreign" policies of the outlying units. Its principal function has been to review state legislative proposals to determine their effect on suburban governments. (According to an unwritten rule, the league will take no stand on an issue if two or more of its members dissent. This practice prevents it at times from supporting legislation that might benefit the majority of the units.) The league has long retained a lobbyist at the state capitol, and it has recently expanded its activities by the employment of a part-time executive director to coordinate its public relations efforts. It has enjoyed considerable success over the years at the legislative level. The organization's opposition to the Tarr tax-redistribution proposals in the 1969 session, for example, was instrumental in defeating a bill strongly supported by the city of Milwaukee and other central cities throughout Wisconsin.

The league is essentially an organization of municipal attorneys, who are in many cases the principal architects of suburban positions, rationales, and strategies vis-à-vis the external world. The anti–central city posture of the group continues to be its major nexus; few positive policy proposals emanate from it. Although the old issues, such as annexation, are now moot, the new rallying points for fringe-area solidarity are tax-redistribution proposals, threats to exclusionary zoning practices, and, more generally, the charges by the Milwaukee mayor, who repeatedly zeroes in on the suburbs for their "hypocritical" attitude toward racial integration and the "abdication" of their responsibility with respect to the social problems of the central city.

It is common to think of the major political offices as centers of community power. Valid as this emphasis may be, the local governmental bureaucracy is an additional and major source of influence that should not be overlooked. The importance of the bureaucrat at the local level, as well as the state and national levels, has been augmented by the growing need for expertise in the conduct of public affairs. With functional activities' becoming ever more dependent on science and technology, political officials have found themselves compelled to rely increasingly on the knowledge and specialized skills of professional administrators and technicians. It is not surprising, therefore, that department heads and other top civil servants constitute approximately 10 per cent of the three hundred people who were identified in the Milwaukee leadership study as participants in the decision-making process. Their involvement was particularly evident in such fields as education, redevelopment, health, and welfare.

Some department and agency heads, moreover, have been able to establish a basis of power beyond what they would normally derive from their official position in the structure. The Milwaukee police chief is the most prominent example of this. Enjoying the reputation of a "tough cop" and benefiting from the prevalent "law-and-order" syndrome among the general populace, he runs his department as a virtual autocrat. He has had extraordinary success, as we have seen previously, in resisting the timorous attempts of the Police and Fire Commission (appointees of the mayor) and the Common Council to impose policy with which he is not in accord. The case of the police chief is obviously an extreme example of bureaucratic independence; no other administrator on the local scene enjoys such a degree of immunity from political control. Yet it dramatizes the power potential of the bureaucracy and makes visible a process that operates universally although in a subtler and less open fashion. Several Milwaukee administrators, for example—the Health Commissioner is one—have been able to achieve positions of substantial invulnerability by establishing strong supporting ties with clientele groups or with key points of power inside the governmental and political structure itself.

Business. The influence of businessmen in community decision-making is aggregated in three generalized groups—the Greater Milwaukee Committee (GMC), the Association of Commerce, and the Citizens' Governmental Research Bureau—and in several more specialized organizations such as the Downtown Association and the various neighborhood merchants' associations. The first of the groups, the GMC, is a select body of some two hundred business and institutional leaders, predominantly representative of the large corporate interests of the area. It was formed originally to push for civic improvements of a physical nature to celebrate the city's centennial in 1948, and its activities have continued to be directed largely at promoting "bricks and mortar" projects such as expressways, a zoo, a sports arena, a stadium, and a music hall. Indicative of the organization's high status is the fact that, of the nine private individuals who were identified in the leadership study as participants in three or more decisions, seven were GMC members.

The Committee of We Milwaukeeans, an offshoot of the GMC in the sense that the same leadership personnel is involved, was formed in 1963 as a mechanism for getting top businessmen to devote some of their time and attention to the critical social problems facing the community. The driving force behind the creation of the committee was Irwin Maier, board chairman of the *Journal* and one of the principal activists on the GMC. With the encouragement of the mayor, who felt it essential that business leaders become involved in the then accelerating civil rights issues, Maier and others first formed what was called the Voluntary Business and Industrial Group. On the assumption that a small committee of prominent businessmen and select Negroes could reach understanding on means to alleviate racial unrest and tension, the new body began to meet jointly with the Committee of 34, a group of concerned blacks, mostly from the professions. The two groups shortly thereafter merged into the Committee of We Milwaukeeans, with Irwin Maier and Thomas Cheeks, a black administrator in the public school system, as cochairmen.

One of the first acts of the committee, and perhaps the most important, was to form the Milwaukee Voluntary Equal Opportunity Council, composed of the major employers of the area, to promote minority employment. At the present time, We Milwaukeeans also has subcommittees in such fields as housing and welfare, but its efforts in these matters have been neither extensive nor impressive. Any hope that the committee would provide a key link between the white "establishment" and the black community, or an instrumentality for arbitrating differences between the two, has not materialized, nor has the anticipation that it would serve as a means for involving the economic notables in social-problem–solving. One reason for the failure to meet these expectations is that a new cadre has since emerged of black leaders who are more representative of the deprived and more militant in their stance than the middle-class doctors, lawyers, and educators who comprised the Committee of 34. Another is the continued reluctance on the part of the industrial and commercial elite to enter the social-problem areas.

The second important business organization, the Metropolitan Milwaukee Association of Commerce, has a membership of approximately 3,500 firms, both large and small, scattered throughout the area. Its major activities have been those traditionally performed by chambers of commerce, such as attracting new industry, promoting better airline service, and lobbying for or against legislation affecting business. The association, however, is far more issue-oriented than the Greater Milwaukee Committee. In recent years, with a change in executive directors, it has begun to concern itself with some of the social problems facing the community and has inaugurated a Milwaukee Improvement Program for this purpose. Since 1970, it has been the principal fund-raiser for Commando Project I, a counseling service for young black parolees, operated by former members of Father Groppi's youth council. It also has established a "human development" division headed by a black and has involved itself with the problems of minority employment. The organization's interest in these matters was precipitated largely by the civil disturbances that struck the community in the late 1960's. The impact of these events on the economic well-being and national reputation of Milwaukee convinced the association that it could no longer afford to detach itself from the social problems of the community

A third business-supported organization, the Citizens' Governmental Research Bureau, has played the role of civic watchdog over the operations of the local governmental system since 1913. Under the guidance of its able executive director, Norman Gill, the bureau serves in effect as a staff arm of the civic community. Its research activities have long provided a valuable source of information on the finances and management of the local units and school districts of the area. Moreover, largely through the efforts of its director, it has succeeded in bringing about various changes in governmental procedures and practices in the interest of more efficient administration.

If multiple memberships in key civic organizations and the prestigious social clubs are taken into consideration, the economic leaders in Milwaukee may be described as more closely knit than other segments of the society. These linkages, for example, are evident among the controlling boards of the GMC, the Metropolitan Association of Commerce, and the Citizens' Governmental Research Bureau. Nine GMC directors currently serve on the board of trustees of the Citizens' Governmental Research Bureau, and fifteen serve on the board of the Metropolitan Association of Commerce. Ten of the board members of the latter are also trustees of the Citizens' Governmental Research Bureau. Socially, a large majority of the GMC members belong to the exclusive Milwaukee Country Club and an impressive number to the still more select Milwaukee Club.

These organizational and social interconnections might be viewed as measures of the cohesiveness of the economic dominants and the degree of control they exercise over local public affairs. Such an interpretation, however, would miss the mark by a wide margin. Although they share in a broad consensus about the community in general and the manner in which they would like to see it function, they make no concerted effort to effectuate their views by intervening in the political life of the city. In this respect, Banfield's observation about big businessmen in Chicago is equally apropos of those in Milwaukee: They are to be criticized less for interfering in local public affairs than for failure to assume their civic responsibilities.[9]

The GMC, for example, is not a beehive of activity designed to influence broad aspects of local policy. Only a very small proportion of its members has been directly engaged in the organization's projects, and these for the most part have been careful to see that the agenda is limited to items unlikely to evoke controversy or divide the group. For the vast majority of the area's top businessmen, involvement in the organization and its projects is at best peripheral. Only in the private welfare sector have the economic notables continued to play influential roles. They dominate the United Fund, and many of them (or their wives) serve on the boards of hospitals, social agencies, colleges, and various charitable institutions. Again, however, the number of top-echelon executives who play more than nominal roles in these activities is small.

The principal activists from the ranks of business are two retired board chairmen of Northwestern Mutual Life Insurance Company, an indigenous Milwaukee firm that has long supplied the community with civic influentials. Both natives of the area, they operate as civic brokers, promoting community projects among their peers, ironing out consensus among the various interests involved, and carrying on the necessary negotiations with public officials. (One of them was identified as a participant in eight of the decisions examined by the leadership study.) Along with them, the board chairman of the Journal Company has played a dominant role in shaping the civic project agenda for the corporate leaders. Several other prominent businessmen—the total number is small—have also devoted considerable time and energy to community concerns, largely through the GMC. Those who are willing to make this commitment place themselves in positions where they are instrumental in determining what activities should be undertaken and the means by which these should be carried out. Their role, however, is that of surrogates of the economic managers more than wielders of power in their own right. They are in no position to dictate to their business colleagues, much less local public officials, or to impose on them courses of action to which they are not sympathetic. Just as the Citizens' Governmental Research Bureau is a product of the businessman's withdrawal from active participation in the local governmental arena and his willingness to delegate the task of keeping check on the machinery to professionals in whom he has confidence, so are the GMC and similar organizations means for him to escape personal involvement in community affairs by passively supporting and lending legitimacy to the efforts of the few active members among them.

The Milwaukee business community is not, as sometimes popularly conceived, a monolithic structure of homogeneous and compatible interests. Although certain concerns, such as the preservation of the free enterprise system and the maintenance of a good business climate, are common to all of its many diversified enterprises, differences in perspective and self-interest exist not only between large and small companies or chain stores and neighborhood merchants but also among the major establishments as well. Differences among the latter seldom come to public attention, as they did several years back when the First Wisconsin Bank vigorously opposed the granting of an assessment freeze to one of its major competitors for the construction of a downtown office building.

The present structure of influence as it pertains to the business and governmental sectors is not likely to be materially altered in the foreseeable future. Local officials will continue to dominate in those matters that require the expenditure of public funds, relate to governmental reorganization, or deal with general community policies. In such cases, the interests of major groups and institutions in the private sector will be carefully considered along with political feasibility. The economic leaders in turn will continue to exercise a controlling voice in those projects that entail the utilization of large sums of money from private sources, such as the construction of a music hall or sports paladium, or in those operations that depend on voluntary funds, such as the nongovernmental welfare services.

Labor. Milwaukee is sometimes referred to as a workingman's town because of its many industrial workers and the strength of its unions. Labor leaders can be found on almost every appointive commission of the city and county governments. The secretary of the Labor Council and the president of the Allied Industrial Workers, to cite two examples, are currently members of the City Planning Commission; the Machinists' Union business manager is chairman of the Fire and Police Commission; the secretary of the Carpenters' District Council serves on the Board of Harbor Commissioners; the business manager of the Meatcutters' Union is on the City Board of Assessments; and the former business manager of the Electrical Workers is a member of the County Park Commission.

The main organizational mechanism for union participation in civic affairs is the Milwaukee County Labor Council AFL-CIO. Through this representative body, labor cooperates with business and other local groups in private welfare activities. It also, in conjunction with the economic notables (the president of the council is a member of the GMC board of directors), supports many community projects, such as school building programs and the construction of civic improvements. Labor regularly endorses candidates for local public office—its endorsement is eagerly sought—and, on rare occasions, it takes public stands on community issues. In all of these matters, its leadership has been moderate and conservative, reflecting the tone of the community in general.

If these various activities seem to paint a picture of widespread community involvement by labor, the impression is erroneous.

Although union leaders serve with prominent businessmen on various civic committees, such as those that conduct the annual United Fund campaign or hospital drives, their representation is often of a token nature. Similarly, although they are appointees on many commissions in the local governmental system, few of them play aggressive or influential roles on such bodies. Their appointment in most cases is in the nature of a reward, a *quid pro quo,* for favors rendered (or to be rendered) in election campaigns. (Some of these appointments carry with them modest remuneration. Members of the Fire and Police Commission, for example, receive a stipend of $1,320 annually.) The lack of extensive involvement by organized labor in the community decision-making process is clearly evident from the leadership study. Few union representatives (only five out of the three hundred) were identified as participants in the forty issues examined.

On those occasions—which are infrequent—when labor actively intervenes and uses its political muscle in the local arena, it usually does so because matters of direct relevance to the economic interests of its members are involved. The construction trade unions, for example, resist building code changes that they perceive as threats to the job potential of their constituents, and the Labor Council generally lends its support to public employees' unions in their disputes with municipal or county authorities over wages and working conditions. Labor, moreover, like business, is not a monolithic aggregation of power. Differences among, and even within, unions militate against unified stands on many controversial community issues. The safest course for the leaders in such cases is to avoid the official involvement of their constituencies.

Beyond the impact of organized labor on elections and "bread-and-butter" issues, its influence on the local political system is indirect and difficult to measure. Social scientists have noted that the businessman's power in community affairs is not so much directly exercised as it is anticipated by local officialdom.[10] The same observation may be made about labor in an industrial city such as Milwaukee. Policy-makers are inevitably conscious of, and sensitive to, the fact that they are operating in an environment where the workingman provides important political and cultural inputs. Just as local authorities will normally do nothing that is detrimental to business interests, they will not take any action that might incense the unions or the workingman in general. This is a far cry, however, from saying that either the economic notables or labor organizations dominate Milwaukee's decisional structure.

Minority Groups. The influence of minority groups in Milwaukee public affairs has increased during the past decade from almost total insignificance to minor impact in some areas of community concern. Today, the interests of the blacks and the Spanish-speaking residents of the city are at least articulated in the public arena and the views of their spokesmen listened to more carefully. The demonstrations, civil disturbances, open-housing marches, and picketing, along with such new federal interventions as the poverty and Model Cities programs, have focused attention on the problems of minority groups to the extent that public officials and the community as a whole can no longer afford to ignore them.

To say, however, that the blacks (and to an even lesser extent the other racial minorities) have any real power other than the potential threat of disruption they pose would be greatly overstating the case. Comprising less than 15 per cent of the city's population, they do not constitute a challenge to white dominance of the political machinery as they do in some urban centers. As a consequence, they have had little success in achieving positions of influence within the established structure. A survey made in 1968 showed that blacks held only 6 of the 121 elected positions (exclusive of suburban offices) in the public sector of Milwaukee county.[11] The situation was similar in the case of boards and commissions, where blacks held 28 of the 387 appointments within the city government and 8 of the 201 in the county. Even more revealing were the statistics on the policy-making posts in the administrative structures of the two governments. Only 1 of 81 such positions in the city and none of 66 in the county were occupied by blacks. Similarly, in the Milwaukee city school system, only 5 of 157 principals and 5 of 80 vice-principals were black, despite the fact that more than one-fourth of the enrollment is black. In the private or business sector, blacks have fared even worse; of 1,867 "policy-type" positions among the major employers of the area, only one was held by a black.

Whatever the power potential of Milwaukee's black community may be, its realization is impeded by the badly fragmented character of that community's own leadership.[12] No individual, group, or organization can legitimately and realistically claim to be the community's spokesman. Widespread competition exists for positions of leadership and for supporting constituencies. Although such competition is inevitable, it results in a dispersion of scarce personnel and material resources and thus weakens the bargaining power of blacks vis-à-vis the larger society. It also permits the established centers of white influence to play off one faction against another.

Until the mid-1960's, those who could be identified as black leaders were affiliated with the traditional black organizations, such as the Urban League, the National Association for the Advancement of Colored People (NAACP), the Congress of Racial Equality (CORE), and the churches. The Milwaukee leadership study, for example, showed that, of the nineteen blacks who were named as participants in important community decisions made during 1960 to 1965, all but three were connected with such organizations. Since then, however, the situation has materially changed. The local chapter of CORE has disbanded, that of the local NAACP is badly disorganized, and both the Urban League and the old-line churches (while retaining their ties with the "white establishment") are generally ignored, if not openly criticized, by the emerging cadre of young black leaders. These leaders are found in such groups as the Afro Urban Institute, an economic development corporation; Triple O (Organization of Organizations), the only serious, although largely unsuccessful, effort to form a viable united front of black groups; the Welfare

Rights Organization; and the various community action program (CAP) agencies.

The extremist organizations, such as the Black Panthers, have thus far made little inroad in Milwaukee. Although the community has experienced its share of confrontation and violence, militancy in the pejorative sense of the term has not been characteristic of its black leadership. Even the new corps of young activists can be described more appropriately as aggressive rather than militant. Many of these have been recruited into the poverty-related agencies and federally funded programs, where their activism must necessarily be tempered. It is an interesting commentary that the leader who was by far the most militant on behalf of black rights was a white man, Father James Groppi, who has since retired to parish work. The top leadership of the NAACP Youth Council, the "Commandos" who comprised his marching legion in the two-hundred-day campaign for open housing, has also largely withdrawn from protest activism to engage in counseling services and job-training programs for young black parolees under a contract with the state government. The absence or low status of militant black organizations in Milwaukee does not mean, however, that the community is immune from major disorder. The potential for spontaneous violence still remains in the ghetto areas, where unemployment is high, police relations are poor, and unrest among youth is common.

The second largest minority group in Milwaukee, the Spanish-speaking population, has only recently begun to evidence signs of social and political activism. It is not as yet well organized, however, with no single individual or leadership clique able to serve as a gravitational force in mobilizing the subcommunity. The lack of interest in community organization—even the suspicion of it—on the part of many Latins makes the task of mobilization difficult. The most politically active among the existing groups is the Latin American Union for Civil Rights, with a membership scarcely exceeding one hundred. At the start of the fall, 1970, semester, the union conducted a successful sit-in at the University of Wisconsin-Milwaukee to demand enlarged educational opportunities for students from the Spanish-speaking community. This was one of the first occasions when an exclusively Latin organization in Milwaukee has resorted to the technique of protest activism. More recently, some two hundred Latins clashed with police after a rally urging clemency for two Chicano youths sentenced to jail in connection with a welfare demonstration.

Leadership among the Spanish Americans is widely diffused. No hierarchical power structure exists; even the individual organizations are not monolithic. Differences among Puerto Ricans, Chicanos, and Cubans, as well as social-class distinctions, would of themselves make such a structure highly improbable. One of the more articulate spokesmen for the interests of the Spanish-speaking population has been Father John R. Maurice, the former executive director of the Spanish Center. However, like Father Groppi, he has retired from this position, believing that "Anglos" should step out of leadership roles so they can be assumed by Latins. The possibility of forming an alliance between the Spanish-speaking organizations and the blacks for the purpose of affecting local public policy of common concern is sometimes mentioned, but its materialization in any stable form is unlikely. While certain socio-economic interests are shared by the two groups, there are also major cultural dissimilarities, as well as different views on resource allocation and control. The most that can be expected is some cooperation between leaders of the two minorities on an *ad hoc* basis; even this is not likely to be extensive.

Mass Media. The Milwaukee community is served by two metropolitan dailies, the evening *Journal* and the morning *Sentinel,* both published by The Journal Company, an employee-owned firm. The circulation of the former is 360,000 (on Sundays, 538,000) and that of the latter 169,000 (no Sunday edition is published). The *Sentinel,* purchased from the Hearst chain in 1962, has its own editorial and reporting staff. In contrast to the liberally oriented *Journal,* it attempts to maintain a conservative posture in its editorials, usually supporting Republican candidates and Republican positions on public issues. Together with the dailies, there are two black-owned weeklies, the *Courier* and the *Greater Milwaukee Star,* the first with approximately 4,500 subscribers and the second with a slightly larger circulation. Suburban weeklies within Milwaukee county total thirteen, with a combined circulation of over 60,000. The most prominent of these in terms of their prosuburban, anti–big city editorial policies are the *Reminder Enterprise* of Cudahy, the West Allis *Star,* and the *Voice Journal* of South Milwaukee. The high proportions of union members and Catholics residing in the area are reflected in the circulation figures of the *AFL-CIO Milwaukee Labor Press* (102,500) and the official archdiocesan paper, the *Catholic Herald-Citizen* (186,400).

Milwaukee is also well supplied with radio and television facilities. Fifteen radio stations, a number of which have both AM and FM outlets, are located within, or adjacent to, the county, and Chicago stations, such as WGN and WBBM, are also heard extensively in the area. There are four commercial television channels: WTMJ, the NBC affiliate owned by the *Journal;* WISN, the CBS affiliate, which the Hearst chain retained when it sold the *Sentinel;* WITI, the ABC affiliate; and WVTV, an unaffiliated UHF station. The fifth TV facility, the educational channel, is operated by the Milwaukee Technical College. All of the commercial stations, with the exception of WVTV, have large news staffs, and two of them, WTMJ and WITI, regularly offer editorials, which deal almost exclusively with local and state issues.

According to American folklore, the mass media—newspapers in particular—exert powerful influence over public opinion and the general course of community affairs. However, as numerous studies show, this notion is greatly exaggerated. Although the mass media undoubtedly exercise influence, in most cases it is less than overwhelming and, in many, inconsequential.[13] For the majority of people, the motivation behind their opinions on

local public issues is weak, and, when they seek help from newspapers or television broadcasts, they generally are looking for
clues that make such issues or events simple and consistent with
their pre-existing values and opinions. The reinforcement effect
of the media, in other words, is greater than the conversion
effect. Most people, moreover, have greater faith in the reliability
and trustworthiness of television and radio news than in the
printed medium, and, since the coverage of the former can only
touch upon the highlights, public impressions tend to become
based on mere snippets of information.

Mayor Maier is among those who hold what might be called
a "conspiracy" theory of the press. For the past several years,
he has repeatedly and vigorously attacked the *Journal* and
Sentinel as a monopoly that conspires to set the civic agenda by
giving undue prominence to insignificant or baseless criticism
of city policies and programs and by failing to report objectively
on the progress and accomplishments of his administration. He
overlooks few public opportunities to emphasize this theme.
The press in turn calls the mayor thin-skinned, charging him
with substituting words for deeds and with failure to exercise
leadership, particularly in the area of social problems. For the
last several years, the mayor has refused to meet with *Journal* or
Sentinel reporters or to release news to them. Instead, he holds
a televised press conference each Friday morning for all the
media.

There is little question that the Milwaukee daily press has
been unfair to the mayor on occasions, and in recent years,
in response to his attacks, it has overlooked few opportunities
to embarrass him. It is true also that its criticism and its treatment of issues and events have caused him to devote valuable
time and energy to matters that are outside the main thrust of
his program. Yet it is doubtful that the posture of the *Journal*
and *Sentinel* toward Maier has damaged him politically—
actually he has used their opposition to good advantage—or
has led to the defeat of any of his proposals. While the press has
made life more difficult for him and may have caused him to

modify his stance on some matters, his policies, whether pertaining to open housing, redevelopment, Model Cities, or city-suburban relations, have remained basically unchanged.

In one important respect, however, the mass media in Milwaukee, as elsewhere in the nation, has assumed new importance with the accelerated use of protest activity as a political resource. As Michael Lipsky shows in a perceptive article, relatively powerless groups in the society are now seeking through such means to activate "third parties" to intervene in their behalf in the political bargaining process.[14] A group of welfare mothers, for example, may conduct a sit-in at the mayor's office to draw attention to their grievances and appeal to the sympathies of a wider public to which the city administration is sensitive. Here the communications media play a crucial role. For, if they do not consider protest activities important, or if television and news editors decide to overlook such tactics—which up to now few of them have elected to do—the strategy of the protest groups is not likely to succeed. It is this aspect of the media's coverage that has most irritated and inconvenienced local officials (and national as well) and prompted them to direct a barrage of criticism at the press and television. It is also this aspect that is at the root of much of Mayor Maier's bitterness toward the Milwaukee metropolitan press. The *Journal,* to cite one cause of the mayor's irritation, has reported extensively on the activities of those in the Model Cities area who oppose the control City Hall exercises over the planning and management of the program. The publicity given them and their cause by the daily press, as some of them frankly admit, has been instrumental in enabling them to achieve visibility in the larger community and maintain positions of leadership in the target area. This publicity in turn has forced the mayor to defend his course of action both to HUD officials and to the citizenry in general and to make some minor concessions to the demands of his opponents.

Religious Institutions. Organized religion provides another source of community power. Its institutional forms, ranging from the ecclesiastical hierarchy itself to the parish societies and clubs, give expression to norms that are instrumental in conditioning societal attitudes and policies. In the past, the intervention of the churches or religious groups in the local sphere was limited mostly to matters of a moral nature, such as opposition to the distribution of birth control information or to the sale of pornographic literature. In more recent years, the churches have been thrust into the social arena—willingly or unwillingly—and challenged to concern themselves with the critical problems facing the urban community.

The two largest religious denominations in Milwaukee, Catholics and Lutherans, along with their less numerous counterparts, have moved slowly and hesitantly in the field of social action. Individual Catholic priests, such as Father Groppi, have prominently concerned themselves with social and racial issues and have sought to involve the institutional church more directly in their solution. Their actions have come under considerable fire from conservative clergymen, as well as from many Catholic laymen who still believe that the place of the priest is in the sacristy not the streets. Despite considerable pressure from members of the church, the archbishop, William Cousins, has not curbed the activities of the more socially militant priests, although he has on occasions expressed disapproval of some of their methods. In 1967, he established the Council on Urban Life as one means of making the church more relevant to the inner city and the deprived who live there. Manned by eight professionals, mostly priests with social science training or community organization experience, the council has engaged in a wide range of undertakings. It provides staff services and facilities to community groups involved in various projects, such as housing rehabilitation and the conversion of parochial schools in the inner city to community schools. It also conducts research relevant to its undertakings and concerns. Among the reports it has issued is one critical of the Milwaukee police department and another highly critical of the mayor's handling of the Model Cities program.

The Lutheran churches, although they also have their cadre

of activist ministers, have on the whole moved even more cautiously than the Catholics in their approach to social problems. This has been particularly true with respect to two of the four branches of the church that function in Milwaukee, the conservative Missouri synod and the highly orthodox Wisconsin synod. The other two, the Lutheran Church of America and the American Lutheran Church, have been more receptive to involvement in the social sphere. Other religious groups, the Jews and Episcopalians in particular, have shown various degrees of concern, but none have displayed a high degree of commitment or action.

In early 1970, the Greater Milwaukee Conference on Religion and Urban Affairs was formed by the merger of the Milwaukee Council of Churches, a Protestant body that was broad in purpose but narrow in membership, and the Greater Milwaukee Conference on Religion and Race, which had broad denominational membership but was limited in purpose to race relations. The new organization, comprising a majority of the churches in the area, was established to marshal the resources of the religious community to address the spectrum of urban problems. The conference has, for example, task forces on low-income housing, minority group education, and ecology, among others. Whether the new group will be any more successful than its predecessors in attracting the support and resources necessary to have a meaningful impact in the social sphere remains to be seen.

Other Groups. Many groups and organizations, other than those already mentioned, attempt on occasion to exert influence on local governmental policies and programs. Some such as the neighborhood improvement associations, are organized on a territorial basis; some—the Lions and Rotary clubs are examples —have both fraternal and community service goals; others, including the legal and medical associations, exist to protect professional interests; and still others, such as Planned Parenthood and the Anti-Defamation League, are formed around specific functions or issues. A few, including the League of Women

Voters and the various taxpayers' alliances, are organized expressly for the purpose of influencing local governmental institutions. The vast majority, however, are mobilized around special concerns of a private or semipublic nature; they intervene in the community's political process only when their interests are at stake or an ideological issue to which they are committed is involved.[15]

The local chapter of the Fraternal Order of Eagles provides a good example of the latter type of intervention in the political sphere by groups formed for essentially nonpublic purposes. A social and fraternal organization of some seven thousand members, basically a working-class constituency, the Eagles have taken public stands on such questions as law and order, rock festivals, and student demonstrations. Despite the notorious clause in its national charter that excluded non-Caucasians from its ranks, many local officeholders and party functionaries have found membership in the club politically advantageous. Few of them, in fact, have resigned since Father Groppi and the Commandos dramatized the organization's exclusionary policy by picketing the suburban home of one of its more prominent members, a circuit court judge. In the turbulent contemporary scene, public stances such as those represented by the Eagles are likely to become more common among groups that heretofore have not concerned themselves with controversial community issues.

Community Power in Perspective

The term "establishment" is commonplace in today's parlance, especially among the young and the deprived. In its broadest sense it refers to the total array of institutions—economic, social, political, educational—that hold predominant power in the society or community. Implicit in the usage of the term is the assumption that these institutions and their managerial elite are somehow bound together by common interests, values, and ideologies. There are obviously elements of truth in this assumption because those who possess power are likely to come from the higher socio-economic classes. They are also likely to be opposed to basic changes in the rules of the game under which they acquired and under which they maintain power. However, as the Milwaukee case well illustrates, numerous "establishments" are found in the local community, each with its own set of interests, ideological predispositions, and reward-generating mechanisms. Access to one is not automatically a ticket of admission to the others.

Even within each "establishment," moreover, the structure of power is seldom monolithic. This can be observed most clearly in the case of organized labor, where such factors as skill, race, and ethnicity constitute elements of division. It can also be seen in the business sector, which is often marked by general disunity and the parochial concerns of its members. This complex pattern means that the points of access to the community's influence structure are many and divergent, with each providing entry to only a special and limited area. To speak of the "establishment," therefore, is to speak in metaphorical rather than empirical terms.

During recent decades, decisions of vital concern to the local community have been made or influenced more and more by outside sources. In Milwaukee's private sector, for example, major economic decisions pertaining to such matters as plant location or expansion have increasingly passed from the hands of locally based and locally controlled enterprises to the corporate boardrooms of national firms. Similarly, in the governmental sector, the ever growing reliance of the city and county on federal and state funds has added a major external factor to the community decision-making process. Paradoxically, this trend has increased the relative influence of local public officials in community affairs while diminishing that of the private elites. For, as more projects and programs are financed by higher levels of government, local authorities assume more prominent roles in the decisional structure as the instrumentalities of communication and negotiation with the funding agencies. Welfare provides a case in point. When the responsibility rested in the hands of the private sector, the economic notables had a controlling voice in policy-making and administration in an important area of community concern. But, as welfare became increasingly a governmental function, the influence of the economic elite over its course correspondingly waned. The shift of functions from the private to the public sector has, in other words, substantially enlarged the decision-making role of public officials in the affairs of the local polity. Their predominance in this sphere, as revealed in the Milwaukee leadership study, should occasion little surprise.

In the current setting, the large urban community will be confronted with a mounting need to mobilize its leadership resources if it is to remain a viable entity. The task is a complex one in metropolises such as Milwaukee, where formal decision-making powers are broadly shared and where the informal structure provides no effective mechanism or web for aggregating and exercising power. Public officials in Milwaukee will continue to play major roles in community issues, but their leadership potential—even that of the central-city mayor—is closely circumscribed by jurisdictional limitation and the political culture of their constituencies. Among the economic notables, no great regeneration of interest in community involvement is evident and none is likely to emerge in the foreseeable future. Under these circumstances, external pressures on community decision-making, particularly from higher levels of government, can be expected to grow in intensity.

Notes

1. The classical expression of this theory is found in Floyd Hunter, *Community Power Structure: A Study of Decision Makers* (Chapel Hill: University of North Carolina Press, 1953).

2. The pluralist theory of community power is supported in Robert Dahl, *Who Governs?* (New Haven, Conn.: Yale University Press, 1961) and in Arnold Rose, *The Power Structure* (New York: Oxford University Press, 1967).

3. The event-analysis approach is described in Linton C. Freeman *et al., Local Community Leadership* (Syracuse, N.Y.: University College of Syracuse University, 1960).

4. For the theoretical and methodological basis of the Milwaukee study,

see Warner Bloomberg, Henry Schmandt, and David Livingston, "Power Structure Research and the Urban Polity: Issues and Irrelevancies," paper presented to the Committee on Community Research and Development, Society for the Study of Social Problems, Montreal, Canada, September, 1964.

5. The survey of issues and participants was completed before the civil disturbances and increased activism of minority groups during the late 1960's and, hence, does not include decisions made in connection with these events.

6. "The City," *Psychology Today* 2 (Aug., 1966), p. 66.

7. Linton C. Freeman *et al., op. cit.*

8. *Milwaukee Journal,* May 3, 1970.

9. Edward Banfield, *Political Influence* (New York: Free Press, 1961).

10. Peter B. Clark, "Civic Leadership: The Symbol of Legitimacy," paper presented at the 1960 annual conference of the American Political Science Association.

11. "Black Powerlessness in Milwaukee Institutions and Decision-Making Structure," report prepared by Community Relations-Social Development Commission and Milwaukee Urban League (March, 1970). See also Wisconsin Department of Industry, Labor and Human Relations, *Equal Employment Opportunity Report, 1968.*

12. Steven I. Pflanczer, "Negro Community Leadership in a Northern Metropolitan Center," Ph.D. diss., Loyola University, 1968).

13. See in this connection Bernard Hennessy, *Public Opinion* (Belmont, Calif.: Wadsworth, 1965), pp. 270–316.

14. Michael Lipsky, "Protest as a Political Resource," *American Political Science Review* 62 (Dec., 1968), 1144–58.

15. Political parties constitute another center of power, but, as pointed out in Chapter 1, they play an insignificant role as an organized group in the affairs of the local polity. The minuscule amount of patronage at this level and the banning of partisan labels in elections for all municipal and county offices (except for six traditional county posts) have not been conducive to the involvement of the political parties in local public affairs. Occasionally, party activity on a small, informal scale may be evidenced in behalf of candidates for local office, but, even in such cases, the commitment is of little more than token nature.

5

Financing Governmental Services

The financial crisis that now confronts most of the nation's older and larger municipalities—and many others as well—is not solely the result of shrinking tax assessments due to obsolescence and blight; it is also attributable in important part to the inexorable movement of income and resources outward as metropolitan expansion continues undiminished. Along with, and largely as a result of, this latter development, vast differences have arisen among the local jurisdictions within urban areas in their ability to support municipal and school services. These disparities are most evident between the core city and its more affluent fringe communities, but they also are present in varying measure among the suburban units themselves. What is even more significant than the existence of such fiscal inequities is the fact that they have persisted, and in some cases actually increased, despite the growing interdependence of the localities within SMSA's. In few areas has there been any significant adjustment in the differential abilities of the individual communities to bear the costs of public services.

The Milwaukee situation differs little from the national picture. The government of the central city, like its counterparts elsewhere, is faced with costs that exceed its annual tax levy and supplemental income. The other four taxing units within the city—school board, county, Technical College, and metropolitan sewer district—are similarly confronted with soaring budgets and unmet needs. With the exception of the first, however, they are in a more favorable position than the core municipality because they draw upon a larger revenue base. The money problem, curiously enough, is related more to the maintenance of traditional services than to the undertaking of the newer social programs. One of the major factors in boosting the budgets of the local units has been mounting personnel costs. In 1970, for example, the Milwaukee city government was faced with a $12 million deficit because of wage increases granted the previous year; current negotiations with the public employees' unions indicate that the problem will persist. In the educational field, the growing school population and rising personnel and building costs in both the central city and the suburbs have sent the school district budgets into an upward spiral. This trend is dramatized by the 100 per cent increase in Milwaukee school levies over the last ten years.

Adding to the fiscal woes of the metropolitan polity, the resources upon which local government must rely are fractionated by the organizational division of public services across the Milwaukee area. Although basic economic changes have taken place in the region over the past four decades, they have not been accompanied by corresponding modifications in local governmental institutions and the methods of financing them. As the metropolis spread over the landscape, accelerated by technological and economic developments, the core municipality was compelled to assume a disproportionate share of the burden for the area's poor and disadvantaged members. At the same time, its ability to meet this responsibility was diminished by the dispersal of the metropolitan tax base to newer sites in the fringe localities.

Related to the out-migration of money-providing groups and the metropolitanization of taxable space in the central city—for every regional function from subsidized parking and convention complexes to university expansion—is the increased economic specialization among the more recently established communities in the four-county SMSA. The Milwaukee Metropolitan Study Commission, in a survey of the governmental problems of the area in the early 1960's, referred to this development in dispersal as "a high degree of internal homogeneity as to land use types."[1] The municipalities of the local metropolis, in other words, specialize as dormitory, factory, or even public utility suburbs. Moreover, just as some of them are identified with particular industrial and commercial activities, so are many others given over to the housing of socially differentiated groups. This high degree of both functional and social specialization inevitably increases the interdependence among the local units. The dormitory suburb of corporate managers or white collar workers, for example, is possible only because of the nearby industrial and blue collar communities. This fact of social and economic geography logically calls for a system of public finance that explicitly recognizes these relationships. But logic is ill served by the existing situation.

The problem for the less affluent communities, both in an income-need and diminishing growth sense, is that the main source of municipal and school revenue continues to be the property tax (see Appendix I). And, as the Citizens' Governmental Research Bureau points out, this tax is the least responsive of local revenue sources to growth or decline in the economy. Property taxes in Milwaukee county, when adjusted for changes in the value of the dollar, increased 23 per cent over the last five years, while the equalized property valuations grew only 5 per cent. The city of Milwaukee is in a particularly disadvantageous position in this respect. Not only is its property levy the highest in the local metropolitan area, it is also among the highest in the nation. Several studies, in fact, show that, in terms of ratio of general property taxes to personal income, it ranks second only to Boston.[2] Comparisons of this sort must, of course, be viewed with caution because of the multiple factors that should be taken into consideration but which defy accurate measurement, such as the range and quality of services provided. There is little question, however, that the property tax burden of Milwaukee city residents occupies a position near the top of the list, whether it be second or tenth.

Milwaukee's high property taxes are a result not alone of the rising costs of government and the demands for new social and other services—these are problems faced by all major municipalities—but also of the state's system of shared taxes. Wisconsin traditionally has left the financing of most local services, including welfare, to the municipalities and counties and has relied on a sharing formula to compensate for the relatively lower level of direct state financing and aids. The principal source for this purpose is the income tax, a straight percentage of which is returned to the localities (50 per cent to municipalities and 10 per cent to counties) based on the amount collected in each jurisdiction rather than upon need or even the number of people.[3] This practice penalizes the central city because the tax collected from those who work within its boundaries but live in the outlying communities is credited to the latter. The high-income suburbs, in particular, enjoy a decided advantage in this respect.

The real change that is often disregarded in consideration of fiscal formulas is that many taxpayers no longer live in the municipality from which they derive their livelihood. Thus, even if the central city maintains a good commercial and industrial climate within its territorial jurisdiction, its legal sources of revenue change appreciably less than those of the suburbs from which many businessmen and professionals commute each day. The higher-income residential areas, which shifted from the city of Milwaukee to the fringe areas beyond its northern and western boundaries, have as a consequence inverted the state system of revenue-sharing from the standpoint of need and resources. Correlative to the question of shared taxes, a recent fiscal study of the governments in Milwaukee county revealed that the amount of readjustments affected in the per capita base for the property tax has shown no major change for forty years, even though the capacity to finance local services from this source now ranges widely: from less than $6,300 of property valuation per person in one outlying community in the county to well over $40,000 in another.[4] The corresponding figure for the city of Milwaukee is approximately $6,500, while the suburban average is almost $10,000. These circumstances lead to the metropolitical proposition that, if any meaningful revenue adjustments or equalization are to be effected, they must be imposed from without.

This chapter examines the revenue and expenditure patterns of the city and county governments and of the three other major taxing units in the area: the Milwaukee school board, Technical College, and metropolitan sewer district. In the process, it shows the contrast with the general suburban pattern wherever possible. Finally, it provides a brief account of current efforts to achieve some reasonable measure of equality in the financing of local public services.

The Fiscal Panorama

Local government is no cheap commodity. Providing public services essential to the adequate functioning of a large urban agglomeration is both difficult and expensive. The task requires technical and administrative skills of a high order as well as political acumen, social sensitivity, and mature judgment. To the extent that any one of these qualities is lacking, the community itself pays the price in poor government, inefficient services, and general dissatisfaction. The investment that city dwellers and suburbanites make in their polity is a major determinant of the quality of urban life. The local budget, limited as it is in the total spectrum of public affairs, is a resource-allocating device of significance to the metropolis and its people.

The extent to which local government in Milwaukee county has become big business is indicated by the 1970 budgets of the forty-four taxing units within its boundaries. These aggregate $640 million (not including capital expenditures financed by long-term obligations), or an average of approximately $600 for every resident man, woman, and child. Central city services, including schools, account for the largest share (44 per cent). The county government is next in line, with one-third of the total, followed by the suburban municipalities and school districts (20 per cent) and the metropolitan sewerage district (3 per cent). These ratios have remained relatively constant in recent years, with only the county government showing a slight increase in the proportion of local public expenditures attributable to it. The import of these figures becomes clearer when the fiscal patterns of the various units are examined individually.

City of Milwaukee. Budget allocations, in much the same manner as employee distributions, serve to indicate the relative importance that a community places on its various public functions. They also provide a valid point of departure for ascertaining organizational commitments. When the expenditure pattern for municipal functions in Milwaukee is examined in this light, one feature becomes immediately evident: The changes in fiscal allotments that have occurred in recent years are represented primarily by increases within functional categories rather than reallocations among them. As Table 5.1 clearly shows, the proportion of expenditures for such traditional items as public safety, health, and recreation has remained virtually unchanged over the past five years. Public works has slightly declined in relative terms, while the percentage spent on general government has increased. This latter change, small as it may seem, reflects in part the city's efforts to gear itself up administratively in order to cope with an increasingly complex environment and carry out the newer social programs with which it has become involved, often against its own desires.[5]

TABLE 5.1
CITY OF MILWAUKEE FUNCTIONAL EXPENDITURES, 1966–70
(In Per Cent)

Functional Areas	Years				
	1966	1967	1968	1969	1970
Public Works	40.2	40.2	38.2	37.6	37.9
Public Safety	35.9	34.9	36.6	36.1	35.2
General Government	9.4	10.1	10.3	11.3	11.6
Health	6.4	6.3	6.3	6.0	6.2
Recreation and Culture	6.0	5.9	5.8	5.9	6.1
City Development	2.1	2.6	2.8	3.1	3.0
Total	100.0	100.0	100.0	100.0	100.0
Total Amounts (In Thousands)	$75,212	$80,771	$89,314	$93,109	$101,608

SOURCE: City of Milwaukee, *Budget* (for appropriate years).

Despite Milwaukee's growing resource investment in the less traditional areas, such as the poverty program and Model Cities, the bulk of its functional, or operating, budget continues to go to public works and police and fire protection—the long-recognized spheres of legitimate municipal concern.[6] These items consume almost three-fourths of its expenditures for general purposes. When the other outlays required for the normal housekeeping operations of the polity are also added, the remaining proportion available for human developmental programs is not large. The obvious implication is that, if any concerted attack is to be made on the community's social problems, the major portion of the funds will have to come from public authority outside city government.

When debt retirement payments, cash capital outlays, and employee retirement allocations are added to the functional expenditures, the total city budget for 1970 climbs to $146 million. In per capita terms, this amounts to slightly over $200 for every Milwaukee resident. The comparable figure for the eighteen suburban municipalities considered collectively is $145. In each case, the increase over the proceeding year exceeded 10 per cent, a rate substantially higher than the 6 per cent hike in the consumer price index and the average annual growth of 4 per cent in value added by manufacture and in retail sales. Wages and salaries consumed a large portion of the operating budgets, over 70 per cent, with supplies and services accounting for almost another 20 per cent.

Expenditures for capital improvements by the Milwaukee city government over the past five years have passed the $200 million mark. The community renewal program and special construction projects comprise over half of this total. The first has focused on neighborhood development and public housing; the second, on street paving, street lighting, and traffic control. Other major capital outlays include industrial site development, parking facilities, public buildings, and playgrounds. Sewer construction, undertaken on behalf of the sewerage district, and capital expenditures in connection with the city water utility are not included in the above total; both are budgeted independently.

Municipalities usually finance the bulk of their capital improvements by long-term obligations. It is interesting to note in this respect that Milwaukee, in keeping with its general posture, has long followed a conservative debt policy. The city's standard practice, and one that is seldom violated, is to finance a respectable portion of such improvements from current revenue. The six-year program of capital construction projected to 1975, for example, calls for tax levies to cover almost half of the cost, with general obligation bonds supplying the remainder.[7] Currently, the city's capital debt ($137 million) is only 41 per cent of the established statutory debt limit, and it has consistently remained below the 50 per cent mark. As a result of this policy, Milwaukee enjoys an "AAA" bond rating, the highest attainable in the United States, and the distinction of having a debt obligation well below those of most other cities of comparable size.

Turning to the revenue side of the coin, we find a picture not unlike that across the country. The big income producer, as indicated earlier, is the general property tax, although, consis-

tent with the national trend, its dominance in relative terms
has declined slightly in recent years. As Table 5.2 illustrates, the
proportion of the city's revenue from this source dropped from
50.2 per cent in 1966 to 46.5 per cent in 1970. On the whole,
however, the pattern has remained remarkably stable. State
aids and shared taxes produced 27.7 per cent of the total income
at the beginning of the period and 28.3 per cent at the end.
Similarly, service fees brought in 14.5 per cent in 1966 and 14.1
per cent in 1970.

TABLE 5.2
CITY OF MILWAUKEE REVENUE SOURCES, 1966–70
(In Per Cent)

Sources of Revenue	Years				
	1966	*1967*	*1968*	*1969*	*1970*
Property Tax	50.2	49.5	48.1	49.8	46.5
State Aids and Shared Taxes	27.7	27.5	28.9	28.2	28.3
Departmental Income, Service Fees, and Sundry Revenue	14.5	14.7	14.8	14.1	14.1
Tax Stabilization Fund Withdrawals	7.5	7.0	7.8	4.8	5.6
Grant and Aid Projects	—*	1.3	1.4	3.1	5.5
Total	100.0	100.0	100.0	100.0	100.0
Total Amounts (In Thousands)	$114,580	$124,350	$134,784	$142,833	$153,496

* Before 1967, Grant and aid projects were listed as part of departmental
earnings.
SOURCE: City of Milwaukee, *Budget* (for appropriate years).

In contrast to the Milwaukee city government, the suburban
units as a whole relied on the property tax for only 13 per cent
of their general municipal costs. And, whereas state aids and
shared taxes provided 28 per cent of the city's input for its
operating budget in 1970, sixteen of the eighteen suburban communities derived from 44 per cent to all of their revenue needs
for municipal purposes from the state.[8] Again, this situation is

in large part due to Wisconsin's system of revenue-sharing, which tends to help those most who need assistance least.

There have been many proposals for new forms of taxes in the city, including a municipal income tax, a piggy-back sales tax, and local automobile license fees. However, the drawbacks connected with each and the inability of the aldermen to reach agreement have militated against any serious effort to modify the local revenue structure. As a consequence, the city's main thrust has been directed outward: to the county government to assume certain service costs, to the state to change the tax redistribution formula and increase grants-in-aid, and to the federal government for additional grants and revenue-sharing.

Milwaukee County. Parallel to the city's, Milwaukee county government expenditures for general operating purposes amounted to $186 million in 1970.[9] When capital improvement outlays, debt retirement and interest, and miscellaneous appropriations are added, the total exceeds $218 million, or slightly over $200 for every county resident. To an even greater extent than in the case of the city budget, one functional area, public welfare, dominates the pattern. Its proportional share of the operating budget has increased sharply from 1967 until it now constitutes well over half the total (see Table 5.3). Welfare costs, for example, rose 44 per cent in 1970 over the previous year. Health outlays are second in importance (the county government operates a huge medical and institutional complex), comprising over one-fourth of the budget.

A combination of increased case loads due in part to the economic recession, a cut-back in state aid, and higher personnel costs is contributing to a situation that is becoming ever more critical. The time is rapidly approaching when the present arrangement of county-level welfare financing will have to be modified by either state assumption of greater responsibility or a system of complete federal funding. County officials favor the latter course and have sought to persuade the National Association of County Governments to support such a movement. Unless basic changes occur in the financing of this item, the county

TABLE 5.3

MILWAUKEE COUNTY GOVERNMENT FUNCTIONAL EXPENDITURES, 1966–70
(In Per Cent)

Functional Activities	Years				
	1966	1967	1968	1969	1970
Public Welfare	38.7	37.6	40.9	45.1	52.1
Health	33.5	33.6	31.4	28.6	25.8
Parks, Recreation, and Culture	10.8	11.0	10.3	9.4	7.6
Courts and Judiciary	5.5	5.9	5.8	5.6	4.5
Public Safety	4.0	4.5	4.2	4.0	3.4
Public Works	4.2	4.2	3.9	3.8	3.5
General Governmental Services	3.3	3.2	3.5	3.5	3.1
Total	100.0	100.0	100.0	100.0	100.0
Total Amounts (In Thousands)	$94,451	$102,337	$124,717	$149,273	$186,428

SOURCES: Milwaukee County, *Summary of Budget and Personnel* and *Financial Report* (for appropriate years).

will be compelled to curtail other services. This tendency is already apparent in the decreasing proportion allocated to the park system. Other functional areas will also begin to feel the effects of the growing welfare outlays in the absence of new financing arrangements.

The county's capital debt represented by general obligation bonds is now approximately $100 million. Like the city, it follows a conservative policy in its funding, deriving a substantial portion of its capital program costs each year from the tax levy. In 1970, for example, of the $14.3 million appropriated for capital improvements, almost $6 million was marked for payment out of current revenue. Its debt level at the present time stands at about 43 per cent of the legal limit. The largest category in the capital program during the last decade has been the allotments to expressway construction. Park expansion and development has also been a favorite item, although it is now suffering from the general fiscal bind that the county faces. In 1969, over $2 million was assigned for this purpose; in 1970, the allotment was less than half that of the previous year. Other areas of major commitment are public buildings (represented principally by the construction of the courthouse annex and a new safety building), hospitals, and airport development. The metropolitan nature of the county government can again be seen in the range of area-wide functions that these capital expenditures reflect.

The current revenue pattern for the county government resembles that of the city in its heavy reliance on the general property tax but differs from it substantially in other categories. As Table 5.4 shows, the county derived 42 per cent of its total revenue from the property levy, only a few percentage points less than the city. It received a higher proportion of its budget from federal aids than the latter (12 per cent to less than 3 per cent) and a smaller percentage from state aids and shared taxes (18 per cent to 28 per cent). The first difference is attributable mainly to the welfare funds that the county receives from the national government, and the second to the formula for shared taxes under which only 10 per cent of the state income levy is returned to the counties in contrast to 50 per cent to the muni-

TABLE 5.4

MILWAUKEE COUNTY GOVERNMENT REVENUE SOURCES, 1966–70
(In Per Cent)

Sources of Revenue	Years				
	1966	1967	1968	1969	1970
Property Tax	51.6	51.7	49.8	49.9	42.0
Departmental Income, Service Fees, and Sundry Revenue	18.2	19.0	21.0	21.6	27.9
State Aids	12.8	12.2	14.1	13.4	11.7
Federal Aids	9.3	8.6	7.0	7.9	11.9
State Shared Taxes	8.1	8.5	8.1	7.2	6.5
Total	100.0	100.0	100.0	100.0	100.0
Total Amounts (In Thousands)	$130,728	$136,052	$148,960	$178,250	$225,981

SOURCES: Milwaukee County, *Summary of Budget and Personnel* and *Financial Report* (for appropriate years).

cipalities. Another major difference occurs in the departmental income and service fees category, where the county proportion is 28 per cent and the city figure only half this amount. The income-producing nature of many of the county operations, such as the hospitals and other medical institutions, airports, golf courses, and marinas, accounts for this variance.

Public School System. The large share of local governmental outlays attributable to educational needs is reflected in the costs of the public schools. In 1970, the operating budget of the Milwaukee city system was $113 million, an increase of more than 75 per cent over the 1966 level. When capital costs are added, the total rises to $120 million.[10] This amount represents an outlay of approximately $140 for every resident citizen in per capita terms, and over $950 per student on an average daily membership (ADM) basis. The higher allocations to public education by the suburban communities are reflected in the 1970 budgets of the seventeen districts within the county. These totaled $77 million, an amount equivalent to $230 per resident, or almost $1,100 for each student on an ADM basis.

As Table 5.5 reveals, the Milwaukee system (and the same is true of the suburban districts) relies on the property tax for a substantially higher proportion of its revenue (72.5 per cent) than do any of the other major taxing units in the area. Of the current rate of $88 per $1,000 of assessed valuation paid by the owners of property within the city, $35 goes to the public schools and $3 to the Technical College, while the municipal government receives $26, the county $20, and the Sewerage Commission $4.[11] In the suburbs, on the other hand, 52 cents out of every dollar collected from the property levy is devoted to school purposes. The bulk of educational expenditures, moreover, represents instructional costs (over 71 per cent in the city system), an item that has climbed steadily in recent years as teacher demands have intensified. Payment of principal and interest on bonds also absorbs a much smaller but still significant portion of school budgets. In the city, the debt service charges amount to 6 per

TABLE 5.5

MILWAUKEE PUBLIC SCHOOL SYSTEM ESTIMATED REVENUES, 1970

Categories	Amounts	Per Cent
Property Tax Levy	$ 82,046,202	72.5
State Aid	16,246,275	14.3
County Tax	1,205,400	1.1
Utility and Highway Privilege Taxes	1,970,000	1.7
Tuition and Fees	611,500	0.5
School Lunch Receipts	3,200,000	2.8
NDEA and Vocational Education Aids	300,000	0.3
Unexpended Balance	7,322,798	6.5
Miscellaneous Receipts	325,400	0.3
Total Current Revenues	$113,227,575	100.0
Construction Fund Balance	540,400	
Sales of School Bonds	6,125,000	
Total Revenues*	$119,892,975	

* Does not include federally aided or state funded emergency programs.
SOURCE: Milwaukee Public Schools, *Facts . . . Figures (1969–1970)* (Superintendent's Annual Report), p. 20.

cent of the system's total expenditures, and in the suburban districts from 10 per cent to 21 per cent, the latter charges reflecting the greater expansion needs of the outlying areas.

Milwaukee Area Technical College. The recent realignment of the vocational, technical, and adult education facilities in the state, as noted previously, has expanded the former city-based unit into an area-wide district encompassing all of Milwaukee county and portions of three adjacent counties. Beyond an increase in the scope of its operations, the district will have a property tax base covering not only the city, as was the case before the expansion, but also the suburbs and outlying areas. Communities that previously were not in a vocational district paid the tuition to the city vocational school for those of their residents who desired such training. In the upper-middle-class and more affluent suburbs, the outlay for this purpose was minimal because few took advantage of it. With the enlargement of the district, these areas now find that they must help support the training of a school population of predominantly city residents.

The reorganization thus represents a small movement in the direction of securing greater equity in the metropolitan tax structure.

The current operating budget for the Milwaukee Area Technical College is $19.4 million, with capital outlays' constituting another $1.3 million. The college's revenue is derived from the property tax (56 per cent), state aids (20 per cent), fees and tuition (8 per cent), federal aids (5 per cent), class materials (4 per cent), and miscellaneous sources (7 per cent). Enlargement of the district, as well as mounting costs, has more than doubled its budget (in 1966 it was $8.3 million), and the increase is likely to be even more precipitous as the district expands its facilities and operations to cover the broader area it now encompasses. Salary and wage expenditures, in particular, have spiraled. Recent labor agreements for MATC personnel provided for a wage increase of 7 per cent, costing almost $1 million. This action necessitated a transfer of more than $300,000 from capital improvement funds to the personnel account and resulted in the delay or curtailment of several educational programs.[12]

Sewerage Commissions. For most residents of Milwaukee county, sewage disposal, like the traditional municipal services, is taken for granted. To those on the peripheral areas of the metropolis with poorly functioning septic tanks, the subject is of more concern. This facet of urban expansion, as discussed in a previous chapter, has been handled in a systematic fashion for Milwaukee county by the twin sewerage commissions: city and metropolitan. These operate as a unit under a single budget. The treatment plants and interceptor sewers within their jurisdiction represent an investment of approximately $175 million. During 1970, the commissions expended $17.5 million, with over half of this amount (51 per cent) used for debt service and the remainder for operating costs.

Slightly less than 60 per cent of the commissions' operating costs, exclusive of debt service, are financed by property tax levies prorated to the various municipalities in the district according to the quantity of sewage contributed by each (on this basis, Milwaukee city property-owners pay almost three-fourths of the levy). The remaining revenue is derived principally from the sale (some $3 million annually) of Milorganite, a commercial fertilizer produced at the treatment plant. The debt service is also financed from property taxes levied throughout the district by the county government, which issues the bonds for the commissions. This assessment, however, is on the basis not of quantity of sewage generated but of the equalized valuation of the property. When this item is included in the expenditures of the commissions, the proportion of their budget derived from property taxes jumps to almost 80 per cent. One might well argue, of course, that sewerage costs, unlike those of social services, are directly attributable to the property served and therefore should be financed by the property levy or, alternatively and even more appropriately, by a user's fee based on the quantity of sewage contributed.

Federal Aid. The growing involvement of the national government in the affairs of the local polity is now an accepted fact of life. One measure of the extent of this phenomenon is the amount of federal aid that communities receive. In Milwaukee county, the local units were recipients of nearly $59 million from this source in 1969 and over $70 million in 1970. This figure does not include other federal inputs into the area, represented by social security and retirement payments, defense contracts, veterans' benefits, federal agency expenditures, and similar items that total over $600 million annually. Not only the central city but the suburban units as well are drawing increasingly on the national treasury in the form of federal safe street act funds, 701 planning grants, school aids, open-space programs, and facilities grants for sewers and other capital improvements. Milwaukee suburbs have been slow in using this revenue source otherwise than for school purposes, but this situation is fast changing, particularly since their budgets have been rising at a more rapid rate than that of the central city.[13]

Figure 5.1 depicts the proportional distribution of federal funds to the Milwaukee governments and the Social Develop-

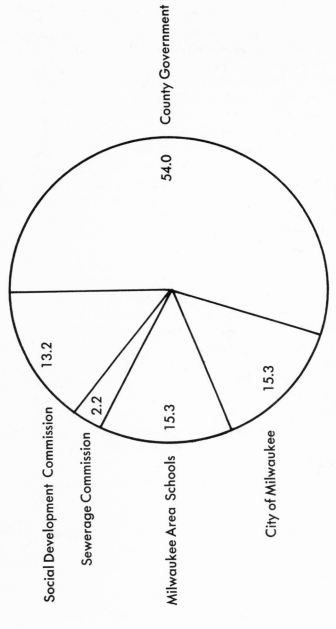

Social Development Commission   13.2

Sewerage Commission   2.2

Milwaukee Area Schools   15.3

City of Milwaukee   15.3

County Government   54.0

Source: Citizens' Governmental Research Bureau, *Bulletin* 58, no. 9 (Dec. 19, 1970).

FIGURE 5.1 ALLOCATIONS OF FEDERAL FUNDS RECEIVED BY
MILWAUKEE COUNTY GOVERNMENTS IN 1969 (IN PER CENT)

ment Commission, the local Community Action Program agency for the poverty program. Of the $59 million received, $42 million was for operating costs, with about 50 per cent of this total allocated to welfare, about 25 per cent to education, 14 per cent to adult manpower programs, and 5 per cent to inner-city community development. The remainder went to miscellaneous projects. The bulk of the $16 million received for capital improvements was assigned to expressway construction (41 per cent), housing and urban redevelopment (35 per cent), sewer facilities (16 per cent), parks (5 per cent), and airports (1 per cent).[14]

Wisconsin cities have tended to lag behind those in many other states in vigorously pursuing federal grants. Wisconsin has also been behind the national trend in which state governments are steadily assuming a larger share of the financing of services and programs formerly regarded as local responsibilities. Increased federal and state aid provides an obvious route for bringing some measure of relief from the heavy reliance on the property levy, which has now, perhaps more than ever before, become the bane of urban governments. A question frequently raised in this connection is whether federal assistance, as presently administered, is merely substitutive for local revenue or whether it has the effect of stimulating additional expenditures on those functions to which it is directed. The latter would appear to be the case in Milwaukee, where federal programs have elicited a greater allocation of local resources to the social problems field than would otherwise have been politically possible. In the final analysis, however, federal and state assistance offers only a partial solution to the fiscal woes of the nation's urban centers. Major surgery on the whole tax and redistribution system is badly needed; bandages can only temporarily stave off the inevitable.

The Quest for Fiscal Equity

What is now a classic problem in metropolitics nationwide—the great fiscal disparities among local units—assumes an extreme form in the case of Milwaukee because of the state's tax-sharing formulas, as we have just seen. Ironically, the same revenue policies that helped to put Wisconsin in the forefront of progressivism shortly after the turn of the century now place it near the rear in so far as the discriminatory effects of these policies on its major city are concerned. A study made for the Advisory Commission on Intergovernmental Relations in 1967 commented sharply on this situation:

> Wisconsin is known for sharing funds with local governments; yet this generosity is upside down from the standpoint of equalization: The rich industrial communities get $314 per capita, the high income suburbs get $161, and Milwaukee proper is low man with $88. It would be hard to devise a more perverse effect on local government financing—and the indirect result is intralocal balkanization and ferocious fiscal zoning.[15]

Although Milwaukee officials had frequently complained of the inequities of Wisconsin's tax redistribution policies, the city's campaign to revise state aid formulas did not get into full swing until the creation of the department of intergovernmental fiscal liaison in 1966. Through the new department, the mayor carried the plea for more aid to the state's legislative council, the interim arm of the General Assembly. The council, however, tossed the politically sensitive issue to the governor (at that time, Warren Knowles), and he in turn passed it along to a special Task Force on Local Government Finance and Organization, which the legislature created at his prompting. Headed by Curtis Tarr, who was then president of Lawrence University at Appleton, the committee was primarily charged with examining the state's revenue-sharing formulas in terms of adequacy and equity. For two years, the group labored diligently, holding many public meetings and listening to the testimony of many experts and public officials. During its deliberations, its staff prepared a series of forty-three research reports covering all aspects of the problem.

While there was general agreement among those who appeared before the task force that something should be done with the existing formulas, there was little consensus on what specific changes should be made. Many argued for a system of tax redistribution that would be based on local need, but how this need was to be defined drew a wide range of responses. One measure suggested was for the state to make up the excess over the statewide average spent by a municipality on a per capita basis for essential public services. Other witnesses, however, pointed out that spending variations depend on many factors other than a head count and that variables such as geography, income, tax effort, and population density can elude a straight need formula.

In the end, the task force recommended a new system in which all taxes that the state shared with local units—individual and corporate income, utilities, and liquor taxes and automobile registration fees—would be pooled (after deducting the state's share) in a single fund and distributed to the municipalities and counties.[16] Under the proposed formula, all Wisconsin communities would receive a flat return of $30 per person to compensate for the unavoidable costs of government generated by population alone because "people create the need for public services." This allocation would consume about half of the fund. The other half would be used for property tax relief, with the state's paying up to one-third of the municipal levy over and above $20 per $1,000 equalized valuation. As an integral part of the plan, the Tarr committee also proposed an increase in school aids that come from the state's general fund.[17]

The Tarr recommendations satisfied no one. They purport to reduce, but by no means eliminate, the disparities in local tax burdens, and they are not designed to bring about the massive aid being asked for by the fiscally beleaguered cities. The recommendations, however, represented a step in the direction of changing the current imbalance between local public service needs and the financial resources available to meet them. Despite the relatively moderate reforms called for, a bill incorporating the task force proposals was defeated in the 1969 legislative session. Suburban opposition, coupled with an extremely conservative and cost-conscious legislature, was the major factor contributing to the failure. Opponents argued that adoption of the suggested changes would cause a hike in all taxes and drive industry not only from central cities but from Wisconsin altogether. They also broadcast the ideas that any alternative to existing formulas would simply exchange old inequities for new ones and that the future and unpredictable impact of the task force's recommendations might be disastrous for some communities.

While the Tarr committee was conducting its work, Mayor Maier stepped up his efforts to prod Governor Knowles into pushing for major increases in state aid to the city, but, as the *Milwaukee Journal* headlined, "Maier Keeps Pleading, Knowles Keeps Studying."[18] Differences in constituencies and party affiliations added to the difficulties of the situation. The governor argued that the mayor's requests did not give weight to the problem of the underprivileged areas of Wisconsin, which do not have a large property tax base but still have many problems. Maier, on his part, pointed out that the state was discriminating fiscally against its most important population and economic center and that the governor was ignoring the wishes of the overwhelming majority of Milwaukeeans by refusing to call a special session of the legislature to consider the question of more financial aid (city residents had favored such action by a three-fourths vote in a special referendum engineered by the mayor as part of his strategy to put pressure on the governor). Knowles (a Republican) also opined that he could not recall that Maier (a Democrat) had pressed for redistribution and special legislative sessions during the Democratic administration of the previous governor. The mayor, in turn, charged that partisan considerations had much to do with Knowles's delaying tactics, noting that the deadline for releasing the Tarr report was extended until after the gubernatorial elections in 1968.[19]

When it became apparent that the frontal assaults on Madison would not succeed so long as Milwaukee remained the only aggressor, the mayor moved to form the Wisconsin Alliance of Cities for the purpose of joining strategies and lobbying the urban cause at the capital. The new coalition consisted of fifteen communities representing 35 per cent of the state's population. It was organized after the refusal of the long-established association of cities and villages, the League of Wisconsin Municipalities, to endorse a Milwaukee resolution calling for a special legislative session to consider tax relief. Two of the largest municipalities in the state—West Allis and Wauwatosa—both Milwaukee suburbs, refused to join the alliance, because of their "defensive relationship" against the central city.[20]

Later, when the Tarr proposals met defeat despite the efforts of the new alliance, Maier again moved to win additional allies by organizing a "have-not" conference of all committees throughout the state that would benefit from the tax reforms. Staff members of his intergovernmental fiscal liaison department visited almost five hundred municipalities to drum up support for the conference, which was held in early 1970. Through this device, the mayor is seeking to build up an urban-rural coalition to break the power of the suburban-rural bloc, which has successfully functioned in the legislature over the past several decades to the disadvantage of the central cities. Such a coalition of units with widely divergent needs and interests is obviously a tenuous one, but, because it is based on the common grievances related to revenue-sharing, it may be able to operate in this limited sphere with some measure of success. That it will be cohesive enough to bring about the basic reforms in the tax and revenue allocation system essential to the fiscal health and general well-being of Wisconsin's metropolitan communities is, however, highly dubious.

Notes

1. *An Analysis of Land-Use and Zoning in Milwaukee County, Wisconsin* (Milwaukee: Metropolitan Study Commission, 1958), p. 28.

2. According to a comparative study recently conducted by the Finance and Revenue Department of the District of Columbia, Milwaukeeans pay higher taxes (state and local combined) in proportion to their total personal income than residents of any of the other twenty-five largest cities. Although Mayor Maier has condemned the study as "next to worthless," most Milwaukee property-owners would be inclined to agree with its general tenor (*Milwaukee Journal*, Dec. 18, 1970).

3. See John Riew, "Fiscal Disparities in the Milwaukee, Wisconsin Metropolitan Area," in Advisory Commission on Intergovernmental Relations, *Fiscal Balance in the American Federal System,* vol. 2 (Washington, D.C.: U.S. Government Printing Office, Oct., 1967), pp. 278–324.

4. See in this connection, Donald J. Curran, "Social Change and Political Lag in Metropolitan Milwaukee," *American Journal of Economics and Sociology* 25 (July, 1966), pp. 238–39.

5. The proportions cited here and in Table 5.1 do not take into account those miscellaneous items that appear in the "special fund of the Common Council." This fund, which totaled $15.2 million in 1970, includes a miscellany of allocations covering everything from the Veterans Recognition Day Committee and the World Festival to unemployment compensation and group life insurance. It is also used to cover the allotments to the newer agencies, such as the Department of Intergovernmental Fiscal Liaison, Social Development Commission, and Model Cities Agency. In addition to the "special fund," there is also a "contingent fund" (currently $3.7 million), which enables the Common Council to assign resources to purposes it deems necessary during the course of the year. A large portion of this fund in recent years has been allocated to the police department for overtime resulting largely from civil disturbances.

6. Of the total public works budget of $38.5 million, street sanitation takes approximately 18 per cent, refuse collection and disposal 17 per cent, street and sewer maintenance 12 per cent, traffic engineering 11 per cent, bridges and public buildings 9 per cent, forestry 7 per cent, engineering 4 per cent, and municipal equipment 22 per cent. The budget of the police department is almost $24 million and that of the fire department slightly less than half that amount.

7. City of Milwaukee, *Capital Improvements Program for Milwaukee, 1970–1975.*

8. Citizens' Governmental Research Bureau *Bulletin* 58, no. 7 (July, 1970).

9. This total, as was the case with the city's figures, does not include sundry appropriations and grants totaling $6,604,076. Examples of categories included in this miscellaneous fund are the cost-of-living increase appropriation, the county share for the Milwaukee Convention and Visitors Bureau, and the Community Relations–Social Development Commission; the county's contribution to an art center expansion is also budgeted here.

10. The Board of Educaton also administers the city-wide recreation program and has a separate budget for that purpose. Estimated expenditures for 1970 were $3.5 million.

11. Property within the city of Milwaukee is currently assessed at 52 per cent of market value.

12. *Milwaukee Journal,* Jan. 7, 1971.

13. Suburban cities and villages within Milwaukee county received less than $20,000 in federal aid in 1969. However, this figure increased to an estimated $485,000 in 1970, and, in view of the applications now pending, it may exceed $1 million in 1971 or 1972.

14. The figures on federal aids are derived from a study conducted by the Citizens' Governmental Research Bureau and reported in its *Bulletin* (vol. 58, no. 9 [Dec. 19, 1970]).

15. John Riew, *op. cit.*, p. 278.

16. Curtis Tarr, *The Report of the Task Force on Local Government Finance and Organization in Wisconsin* (Madison, Wis.: Task Force on Local Government Finance and Organization, Jan., 1969).

17. The committee also recommended that a special fund of $10 million be established for the next biennium in the state department of public instruction to encourage new programs for the educationally disadvantaged throughout Wisconsin. The major portion of such an allotment would go to Milwaukee.

18. *Milwaukee Journal*, Aug. 18, 1968.

19. *Ibid.*

20. *Ibid.*, Feb. 23, 1969.

6

Race and Housing

The concerns of Milwaukee city officials have run the gamut of reform efforts: from altering administrative structures to changing popular attitudes and from internal economizing to pleas for more federal and state funds. Until recent years, the main press for reform came from good-government sources and taxpayers' associations, while the demands for enlarged services came from the traditional interest groups. Today, the lineup of players outside City Hall has increased, with the "problem people" (the clientele who historically were "acted upon") moving into the local political arena with new and "troublesome" strategies. At the same time, central city officials—now as "have-nots" also—are carrying their case in novel and continuing ways to a wider state and national audience. These developments from centers as disparate as the ghetto and City Hall pose new challenges and agendas for officials and residents alike.

The feeling persists among many Milwaukeeans that the city's problems are less serious and more amenable to solution than in most large urban centers. The notion also abounds that, while the city is not so small as to be insulated from the mainstream of national urban events, neither is it so large as to prevent its officials from staying in close touch with local needs and sensitivities. Accurate as these feelings may be, the problems of aging housing stock and of social needs within the core areas of the city and the indifference or hostility of the communities beyond its territorial jurisdiction spell trouble as intense, although not as extensive, as that faced by other large central municipalities within the northeastern quadrant of the nation. Metropolitan Milwaukee's local governments are far smaller in number than Chicago's 1,000 or New York's 1,400, but differences in incomes and attitudes reveal variances in wealth and commitments among publics that are probably as wide-ranging as elsewhere. All of this suggests that the roots of the city's problems lie in resources and attitudes that go much deeper than the question of governmental structure or leadership.

Differences in the size and boundary configurations of municipalities have become less decisive than the external forces affecting them, particularly as they relate to their environmental character, the mobility of their populations, and the state of their physical plant and services. The dispersal of people and resources throughout the area has led to serious inequities in the quality of municipal and school district functions and the incidence of paying for them. The Milwaukee mayor has on many occasions voiced his concern over the results of a dual migration that brings the rural poor into the city and encourages the middle class to flee to the suburbs.[1] As the situation stands today, the majority of area residents live in relative affluence and in a pattern of regional dispersion, while the minority poor find themselves locked in the deteriorating neighborhoods of the core.

This chapter concentrates on two issues—race relations and low-income housing—that serve to illustrate the response of the city and its institutions to the internal and external forces that impinge upon them. (A third major problem—the fiscal plight of the central city—was dealt with in Chapter 5). Focusing on these issues is arbitrary to the extent that they are essentially of "one piece," while a dozen or more other problems of major import also merit attention. Environmental pollution, student demonstrations, juvenile delinquency, drug addiction, crime, and transportation deficiencies, for example, are among the other difficulties that have brought additional shares of anxiety to civic-minded Milwaukeeans. None of these, however, have been more disruptive of community consensus or tranquillity than the interrelated issues of race and housing.

Race Relations

Milwaukee's ghetto, called the inner core, encompasses four square miles and more than 90,000 residents, about 68 per cent of whom are black. This area is distinguished from what geographer Harold Rose refers to as the city's "ghetto space," a more inclusive section of twelve square miles (extending north and west from the central business district) and 217,000 people, 20 per cent of whom are nonwhite.[2] According to Rose, the spread of the black population during at least the next decade will be confined largely to this latter portion of the community. Although many of the worst features of big-city slums are absent in Milwaukee, its ghetto is characterized by a rigid pattern of racial segregation, above-average unemployment and underemployment, inadequate housing, relatively high crime rates, and substandard schools. It is here also that a large proportion of the county's welfare recipients reside.

Before the 1960's, Milwaukee's black community had been generally quiescent and politically inactive, although there was a history of friction between the police and blacks.[3] Beyond token representation on various community boards and committees, blacks were almost totally excluded from the decision-making structure of the city.[4] The acceleration of the civil rights movement nationally in the early years of the 1960's, with its shift of emphasis from the courts to the streets, had its impact on Milwaukee as elsewhere. Both CORE and the NAACP began to become more active and aggressive and to turn to protest politics in efforts to further their demands. In 1965, a series of boycotts against twenty-eight public schools in the inner city was launched by the Milwaukee United School Integration Committee (MUSIC) to protest the racial imbalance that existed in the system.[5] Shortly thereafter, the NAACP Youth Council (the Commandos), organized and directed by Father James Groppi, emerged as the most militant protest group on the local scene. Among its early activities, it picketed the homes of public officials who belonged to the Eagles Club. This action led to a confrontation with angry whites in suburban Wauwatosa, an upper-middle–income community with strong conservative leanings.

The Commandos also centered national attention on Milwaukee and its racial problems when they conducted marches around the city for two hundred successive nights to dramatize their demands for an open housing ordinance. Countermarches by southside whites organized as the National Association for the Advancement of White People and the Citizens Council served only to highlight the controversy and increase the pressure for some resolution of the issue. By this time also, the marches had affected business in the downtown area, where sales fell off substantially and conventions were canceled. Downtown merchants worried about the economic impact, as well as civic leaders disturbed by the damage the marches were doing to Milwaukee's national image, publicly announced their support of an open housing ordinance and urged the Common Council to proceed with its enactment. Mayor Maier, who had consistently espoused a metropolitan open housing law, continued to oppose city action on the ground that it would only speed up the migration of white families to the suburbs.[6]

The open housing controversy provides an excellent illustration of how local officials temporize when they would like to resolve an issue because of its disruptive effects but are fearful of acting because of adverse reactions from their constituents. On four occasions between 1962 and 1967, the Common Council voted 18 to 1 against an open housing bill, the lone dissent coming from Vel Phillips, the only black member of the council during this period. With the growing pressures generated by the

Commando marches, the aldermen realized that they could no longer act in such a direct fashion but would have to use other means of dealing with the issue. The first tactic was to ask for an opinion from the city attorney as to whether the council could enact a stronger open housing law than that already adopted by the state. The city's legal arm willingly obliged by holding that the council could not act, because the state had pre-empted the field. This interpretation was disputed by Bronson La Follette, Wisconsin's attorney general, who ruled that municipalities had the power to pass stronger local codes if they so wished.

The aldermen next began to toy with the idea of putting the issue to the voters through a referendum. At the same time, the mayor submitted his options: a stronger state law; a county-wide law for all municipalities, to be enforced by the district attorney; or an open housing ordinance for the city, provided that similar legislation was adopted by a majority of the twenty-six suburban governments in the metropolitan area. Several proposals to prohibit racial discrimination in the sale and rental of homes were introduced in the County Board after the mayor's declaration of options. The board, however, wanted nothing to do with the controversial issue, holding that it was not empowered by the state to legislate on housing. In the meantime, various groups, such as the League of Women Voters, the Interdenominational Ministerial Alliance, and the Metropolitan Builders of Greater Milwaukee, began to carry their message of support to the suburban governments. And the majority leader in the State Senate, Republican Jerris Leonard, representing the well-to-do north shore suburban area, mailed to all mayors in the county an appeal urging the adoption of unrestricted open housing measures to "lay to rest the fear that fair housing ordinances would precipitate a mass exodus of Negroes to the suburbs."[7]

Maneuvering within the Common Council continued as pressure for action mounted. A committee of five aldermen and six civic leaders met in a closed session at a local hotel and worked out a proposal covering nondiscrimination in all realty sales but exempting certain types of rental property. Although the proposal was bottled up in the council's Judiciary and Legislative Committee, a recommendation did emerge from that body in late 1967 calling for passage of an open housing ordinance that duplicated the state law but that would be enforced by the city attorney. This passed by a 15-to-4 vote in an emotionally charged session. Even though the action made no change in the *status quo,* a south side group, the Citizens Civic Voice, filed a petition containing 27,000 signatures calling for a referendum on the measure. In a suit challenging the validity of such a referendum, the federal district court held that the submission of the open housing legislation to the electorate would be unconstitutional.

The embattled ordinance was not as significant as were all of the strategies and tactics that finally brought the city's elected officials to the point of passing it. Once the symbolic leap had taken place, moreover, the council later adopted, with little discussion, an amendment by Vel Phillips, which considerably strengthened the ordinance. By this time, the federal open housing law had been passed, the spring, 1968, municipal elections had been held, and most aldermen were convinced that such a law would have little effect on the actual housing situation. The issue once again served to make metropolitan residents more aware of the discontent and grievances of core area residents. It also sensitized local officials to the fact that they would have to pay greater attention to minority groups if domestic tranquillity was to be preserved.

The most serious outbreak the city has experienced occurred in July, 1967, in the Third Street shopping area of the inner core. Unlike most riots of recent years, the eruption was triggered off by no single incident. Unusually large numbers of teen-agers had gathered on street corners around the area during the afternoon (a Sunday), and, by early evening, some of the youths were stoning cars and breaking store windows. When the police appeared unable to disperse the crowds or contain the action, the mayor imposed a city-wide curfew and called in the National Guard. The situation was soon well in hand, although sporadic disturbances were recorded over a period of several nights. Three people were killed during the course of the action. Property damage was not extensive; eighty fires, mostly of a minor nature, were set off. Considerable dispute exists over the severity of the disturbance—whether it was a riot or rampage—and over the manner in which it was handled. Some charge that the city overreacted, but many others maintain that the quick and decisive action of the mayor prevented the outburst from accelerating into a major conflagration.

Surprised Milwaukeeans wondered how such an event could take place in their community.[8] The answers ranged widely from the notion that outsiders had instigated the violence to the belief that the eruption resulted from the community's unresponsiveness to the legitimate grievances of blacks. As an attitude survey conducted shortly after the disturbance revealed, a vast gulf exists between the perceptions of blacks and whites in this regard. The overwhelming majority of the former saw bad housing, racial discrimination, and police brutality as among the underlying causes of the disorders, while the latter were inclined to attribute the outbreak to factors associated with the breakdown of social control, to civil rights agitation, and to outsiders' coming into the community and stirring up trouble. Blacks saw the answer to decreasing the likelihood of future disturbances in proposals that seek to reduce the disparities and inequalities between the two races, while the majority of the whites looked to measures designed to control deviant behavior and violence through increased police powers.[9]

The myth of outside agitators was effectively dispelled by a study of the people who were arrested during the three days of disorders.[10] Contrary to popular beliefs, nearly all of the arrested who were charged with serious offenses, such as looting or damaging property, were Milwaukee residents of long standing.

About 80 per cent of them were under thirty years of age, and about half of them were unemployed or did not have a full-time job. A majority of them, when asked about the causes of the disturbances, stressed police-community relations and frustrations concerning employment and housing. The Milwaukee example, consistent with the findings in other cities that have experienced major disorders, further documents the intellectual bankruptcy of the "riffraff" theory and points to the tendency of white Americans to misread the symptoms of race-related poverty and discrimination.

Demonstrations in Milwaukee have not been confined to governmental agencies and public officials; they have also been directed against firms and unions in the private sector. Six inner-city stores, for example, operated by Kohl's Foods, a major merchandising chain in the area, were boycotted over the firing of a black assistant manager. The action was called off when the company agreed to train and upgrade its black employees. Allen-Bradley, Milwaukee's largest employer and taxpayer, was also picketed because of its hiring policies, which had resulted in only a handful of blacks and Latin Americans in a work force of over 6,800 employees. After prolonged resistance to both the demonstrators (led by Father Groppi) and the orders of the Office of Federal Contract Compliance (about one-fourth of Allen-Bradley's business is with the government), the company finally agreed to modify its employment practices to admit more minority group members.[11] Pressure has also been put on the unions and building contractors in efforts to get more nonwhites into the skilled trades.

The actual changes, in "pocketbook" terms, that these various protest actions have wrought in the private sector are as yet difficult to ascertain. Allen-Bradley has not opened its employment records to the Urban League, and the building trades unions move with deliberate respect for their traditional apprenticeship rules. What has occurred since the Allen-Bradley stronghold was first breached is an increase in corporate and federal governmental sensitivity to minority economics, on the one hand, and more aggressive persistence on the part of nonwhites in seeking enlarged employment opportunities, on the other.

This brief overview of protest activities during recent years serves to illustrate the extent of the racial problem in Milwaukee. The demonstrations, picketing, and civil disorders brought to the surface the latent prejudices of the community's white residents and provided further documentation of the Kerner Commission's charge of "white racism." Milwaukeeans, looking in the mirror of events, saw themselves to be little different from their counterparts in other urban areas. The image of *Gemütlichkeit,* of a city of friendly people, was shattered by the angry, shouting crowds of whites that confronted the protesters and by the 27,000 citizens who signed the referendum petition opposing even a weak open-housing ordinance.

Municipal Responses. The reactions of the local governmental establishment to racial problems in Milwaukee have taken several forms, including the creation of a human relations commission, the establishment of an intergovernmental social agency, and the utilization of various federal programs such as Model Cities. The Commission on Human Relations was formed immediately after the Detroit race riot in 1944. Although it has continued in existence (with some modifications) to the present day, it has never become an influential or effective instrumentality for promoting racial harmony. Dependent upon the Common Council for its operating budget, it has been circumscribed in its actions by the conservative views of most city officials toward race relations. On a number of occasions, for example, aldermen have strongly criticized commission members for taking stands favoring social legislation, such as open housing or fair employment ordinances, beneficial to nonwhites.[12]

Earlier mayors remained aloof from these clashes, but the present incumbent, consistent with his philosophy of administrative control, has at times spoken out against members with "crusading opinions" who were unwilling to support policy decisions emanating from the executive office. Largely as a result of these restrictions and the general unwillingness of public officials to have a strong agency in this politically sensitive field, the commission has not been able to establish effective ties with aggrieved groups or to serve as a meaningful link between City Hall and the minority communities. Its role, moreover, was further eclipsed by the creation of a new agency, the Social Development Commission (SDC), in 1963.

During the summer of 1959, several clashes occurred between blacks and police in the inner core, presaging the shape of events to come. Seriously concerned after witnessing one such incident involving a crowd's hostility toward two policemen making a street arrest, Mayor Zeidler appointed a Committee on Social Problems in the Inner Core, composed of a broad range of citizens.[13] When Mayor Maier assumed office the next year, the committee's report, in his words, sat "monolithically" on his desk while "powerful voices in the community" demanded that he do something about the inner core. His response was the creation of an agency specifically designed to deal with social problems, but one "cutting across boundaries of ethnic or class areas . . . and across arbitrary divisions of jurisdiction and responsibility."[14]

The new body, known as the Social Development Commission of Greater Milwaukee (now the Community Relations–Social Development Commission in Milwaukee County) consisted originally of ten members, two from each of the five sponsoring units: the city, county, Milwaukee School Board, Technical College board, and United Community Services. It was enlarged after 1967 to include seven representatives from the Community Action Program (CAP) Residents Council and two each from the Conference on Religion and Race and the County Labor Council. As is evident, the mayor's action to improve race relations did not aim at stronger municipal legislation but looked to a county-wide mechanism for this purpose. This move again was consistent with his over-all strategy of enlarging the jurisdictional sphere of responsibility for the social problems and needs of the central city. The creation of such an agency encompassing the major governmental units and the private welfare sector provided a unique but logical mechanism for area-wide social planning and coordination. As the Common Council resolution authorizing city involvement in the new body stated:

> The purpose of such a commission shall be to review on a continuing basis the action programs aimed at the solution of social, economic and cultural problems as they affect individuals in various parts of our city with particular emphasis on coordinating existing programs at a grass roots level so as to make them more effective and to recommend policy changes, additional programs, or changes in emphasis of existing programs to the respective governing bodies.[15]

The commission got off to a bad start. At an early meeting, one of the County Board appointees, Fred Lins, made several remarks derogatory to blacks.[16] These received wide press coverage, setting off a flurry of protests in the community and making the new agency a prime target for irate inner-city groups. Pressures were brought on the mayor and County Board chairman to remove the guilty member, but the former insisted that he had no authority to act, because the commission was an intergovernmental body and Lins an appointee of the county, while the latter simply refused to revoke the appointment. The incident created a negative image among inner-city activists and left them skeptical about the values and motives of an agency that was designed to ameliorate social problems but that refused to remove a "racist" from its membership.

When Congress passed the Economic Opportunity Act, the Social Development Commission became the local CAP agency. A long dispute over the question of how the poor were to be represented was finally resolved by providing that one-third of the commission's membership be selected by the CAP Residents' Council, an umbrella group representing community organizations in the target areas. In the subsequent months, the new members, often over the protest of the others, sought to direct the energy of the agency toward those activities and programs that would have high visibility and impact in the deprived neighborhoods. Issues such as open housing and police brutality received top priority, while social planning and coordination were pushed into the background. When commission members were later asked, as part of a survey funded by the Office of Economic Opportunity (OEO), what changes they would like to see in the operation and programs of the SDC, those representing the established agencies unanimously said "more social planning" and "less involvement in civil rights," while representatives of the poor mentioned "more innovation and creativity" and "more control by the deprived." A former staff member of the commission sums up the situation in this way:

> The Community Relations–Social Development Commission began as a social planning and coordinating agency and saw the Economic Opportunity Act [EOA] as a way to implement, through funding, its initial charge. But the Guidelines of EOA added a totally new dimension to the Commission—representation of the poor and the resultant political orientation. Theoretically, the social planning and community action functions should have blended well since the Commission . . . had already built into it the constituent agencies that could have made it an effective instrumentality for social change. But historically, this has not become a reality. The gap between the established agencies (stressing social planning and coordinated service delivery) and the representatives of the poor (emphasizing community organization and political power) is evidently too great to make such a coalition possible.[17]

Despite these dilemmas, the commission has been generally successful in balancing the demands of the public agencies and the representatives of the poor. Serving simultaneously as a spokesman for the disadvantaged and an arm of established power is a hazardous undertaking at best. Yet the commission has managed to retain the support, even though tenuous at times, of both elements, mainly by following a strategy similar to that described by Martin Rein and Frank Riesman: combining a program of modified clientele or consumer advocacy with efforts to assist the traditional agencies.[18] The federal funds at the disposal of the SDC as the local CAP agency have been critical in this regard. These have given the commission a large measure of fiscal independence from the local sponsoring units. Even more importantly, they have enabled it to give financial support to programs operated by the established institutions while, at the same time, funding new community-based projects and providing the poor with a platform from which to speak out about community issues. The intergovernmental nature of the SDC, moreover, has "kept the heat off" the constituent bodies even on the few occasions when it has approved projects considered "radical" or critcized local institutions, such as the police. Neither the city nor the mayor nor the other governmental units have at any time been forced to assume public responsibility for its actions.[19] Some officials would undoubtedly like to see it abolished, but they are powerless to act, because it serves as a conduit for bringing substantial federal funds into the community.

The SDC's activities have further narrowed the role of the city's Commission on Community Relations. In recent years, the latter has opened several "rumor control centers" and conducted a billboard campaign urging Milwaukeeans to overcome their racial biases. The public relations campaign was the result of recommendations made by a private research firm retained by the commission to study ways of eliminating prejudice against minority groups. Along with long-range programs of public relations through the use of mass media and other advertising, the report also recommended that pupils be bused out of inner core schools to achieve better racial balance and that a citizen's advisory council be created within the police department.[20] Both of these proposals relating to governmental practices have been conveniently ignored, as have others made by sources outside the community, including a report by the U.S. Commission on Civil Rights, which ranked Milwaukee the lowest of seven cities examined, for its failure to have a policy aimed at remedying racial isolation in its schools,[21] and a study by the national Academy for Educational Development, which sharply criticized the school board's policy of compensatory education as "tokenism."[22]

Model Cities Program. The Model Cities program provided the scenario for a climactic showdown between City Hall and those in the inner core who were insisting on a greater measure of power and participation in social programs than the former was willing to permit. Mayor Maier, as one of the leading spokesmen for the National League of Cities, had strongly supported the Demonstration Cities legislation and had received early assurances from the U.S. Department of Housing and Urban Development (HUD) that Milwaukee would be in a favorable position to obtain a grant if the bill were enacted. After its passage in May, 1967, the mayor had an application prepared by city departments and agencies but at the same time indicated that he foresaw major complications in obtaining a grant without full support from the county government. His strategy was apparently to emphasize the need for intergovernmental cooperation while playing down the actual content of the application.

Although the mayor's motives have been sharply questioned,[23] the strategy was again entirely consistent with his over-all objective of enlarging the sphere of responsibility for the city's social problems and was anticipatory of the objections likely to be raised against the program. Actually, Milwaukee missed out on the first round of grants when the Common Council, by an 11-to-8 vote, refused to endorse the application. Aldermen argued that they were not given enough time to study the proposal and that the mayor was asking for excessive power over another agency that would be accountable only to him. A year later, the council reversed itself and unanimously approved submission of a Model Cities application for planning funds, which differed little in content from the one it had previously rejected. Speculations as to the reasons for the about-face vary. The civil disturbances that occurred locally and nationally in the interim, the continued pushing by the news media, and the spring elections of 1968, which brought the defeat of several of the mayor's strongest critics on the council, were probably all influential factors in inducing the change.

The next stage in the Model Cities drama shifted from the council to the neighborhood, with the challenge to the mayor's control over the program now coming from community organizations within the target area. While HUD was reviewing the city's

application, Triple O (Organization of Organizations), one of
the more aggressive inner-city groups, launched its campaign of
opposition to the mayor and the proposed program. The major
issue was control, although objections were also raised over the
contents of the application and the boundaries of the area selected. Through door-to-door solicitations, press releases, mass
meetings, and letters to federal officials, Triple O charged that
Maier was seeking "complete dictatorial power" over the program. The latter in turn attacked Triple O as unrepresentative
of the model-neighborhood residents and called for an investiga-
tion of its spending of OEO funds.

When the president of Triple O challenged the proposed composition of a Policy Commission for the program because residents
would have only ten of the thirty seats, the mayor responded
that, as the only city-wide policy-maker in Milwaukee's municipal government, he had a responsibility to the electorate for the
board. Later, when HUD temporarily withheld the planning
funds, he modified his stance and announced that local residents
would constitute fourteen of a twenty-six-member body. Triple O
then endeavored to convince HUD officials that the split between
City Hall and the inner core was so complete that federal mediators should handle the elections of representatives to the Model
Neighborhood Resident Council, which would advise on planning and select the fourteen representatives to the policy commission. The federal responses at the public level remained
noncommittal throughout this contentious period, although it is
known that federal officials pressed the city to broaden resident
representation and participation in the program. At one point,
in fact, Maier accused the HUD regional office of creating the
controversial climate surrounding the Milwaukee Model Cities
program.[24]

After months of in-fighting, elections to the Residents' Council were finally held in August, 1969. Triple O had recruited a
slate of candidates, while supporters of the mayor, with assistance
from the city's community organization staff, backed another
list. The elections brought no decisive victory to either faction.

With only a 6 per cent turn-out of eligible voters, candidates sympathetic to the mayor won a small majority of the forty seats. This margin, together with Maier's power to appoint Model Cities staff, enabled him to remain in firm control of the program. Since that time, he has further consolidated his position, although his difficulties with opposition groups in the model neighborhood continue to be evident.

Planning for the first year's program began in August, 1969, after receipt of the initial funds from the federal government. A year of activity followed, involving committees of residents of the model area, technical advisory personnel, and numerous meetings. During the entire planning period, the Model Cities staff carefully structured the agenda and guided the proceedings toward the formulation of the program package, despite sharp clashes between the pro-Maier and anti-Maier factions on the Residents' Council. In fact, the badly divided council stopped debating individual project proposals toward the end and agreed to support whatever program the Policy Commission decided on. This again was a decisive victory for the mayor and a damaging setback for his opponents. Out of a total of 117 proposals submitted by public agencies and private organizations, 55 were selected by the Policy Committee as the first year's program. In August, 1970, one year after the planning process began, the mayor submitted the package to HUD officials. The program was approved by federal authorities several months later, after revisions were made by the city to satisfy objections of the HUD regional office, and, in late February, 1971, Milwaukee received a grant of $8.2 million to carry out the first year's operations.

One may question whether the long conflict between the mayor and the dissidents within the model area would have been less intense and less extensive had the former been willing to give residents a greater share of control over the program. At the same time, however, it is well to remember that local officials and Milwaukeeans in general had shown no great enthusiasm for, or active commitment to, Model Cities. Maier, as one observer points out, used his influence and political skills to keep

the program alive during difficult times; he worked on key aldermen for critical votes; he continually described Model Cities in
terms of his efforts to get outside funds to help solve the problems of the central city; he turned to Washington when he was
stymied by the HUD regional office; he carefully capitalized on
his support in the model area, mostly from black ministers and
small businessmen, to stress the argument that he was seeking to
improve the neighborhood while his opponents were interested
only in building a power base; and he came out on top in the
resident elections by carefully designing campaign strategies and
providing staff support for his candidates.[25]

From inception to deadline, the struggle between City Hall
and inner-city activists moved from issues over procedures (the
symbolic question of determining who is to be representative of
what) to matters of substance (how are the material rewards to
be allocated). Little, if any, compromise, much less any mutually
acceptable formula, was worked out between the opposing factions. Whatever magic there is in Model Cities inheres in federal
expectations. Ironically, in the case of Milwaukee, the "fresh
attack" at coordinating projects and resources for upgrading a
concentrated area of the inner city has served to exacerbate
internal divisions between the mayor and core area groups and
among the latter themselves. Much of the wrangling over what
is still expected to be a sound program has occurred because an
area and a constituency are involved where residents—particularly blacks—are suspicious of local government and resentful of
being told what to do with their lives.

Triple O's resistance and ultimate defeat in the power struggle over Model Cities dramatizes the extent of Maier's administrative control over the development of plans and projects, as
well as over the program in general. This control over all stages
assures that the outputs will be compatible with City Hall's goals
and views, and thereby obviates the necessity of resorting to the
final veto that federal authorities now assure local officialdom.
The last chapter in this play has not, however, been written.
With all the exigencies of urban interdependence, modern

mayors are expected to develop constituencies both within and without their corporate jurisdiction. The efforts of Milwaukee's chief executive to maneuver in this complex milieu received a bad setback by the "riot" and civil disturbances and the prolonged marches of the Commandos, which went on quite against his wishes. These events, in becoming problems over which the city government had little control, indicated that, although minority groups may be the most deprived and needful public in Milwaukee, they are determined to no longer be the least heeded constituency.

So long as the city's social and economic problems could be run on different tracks or held to symbolic rhetoric, the assumption prevailed that the material improvement of social needs would have to await development of the community's economic base and enlargement of outside funding or the transfer of responsibility to external agencies. With the new activism and growing self-consciousness of the deprived, this intended sequence of municipal priorities is being vigorously challenged. Model Cities appeared to offer one way out of the dilemma, but, for better or worse, depending on one's perspective, it has become the exclusive property of the city administration. Neither the Residents' Council nor neighborhood organizations are lined up solidly behind it. The program was tortuously shaped while core area factions on the council fought each other and intermittent sniping took place between the staff and the membership. Although the mayor continues to call the signals, the final outcome will probably be determined more by external pressures and the availability of outside resources than the internal maneuverings of the local participants. In fact, the resources already made available by the Model Cities grant have enabled him to build up an inner city constituency that serves to neutralize the activism of the dissidents.

The Housing Problem

Milwaukee is a community of homeowners, with one or two family units constituting 80 per cent of the housing stock. The earlier arrivals who had made good by the turn of the present century had built staunch Romanesque and Gothic mansions on Prospect Avenue just above Lake Michigan and on Highland Boulevard, which runs westerly through the center of the city. The former became Milwaukee's "silk stocking district," and the latter was known as "Sauerkraut Boulevard" in reference to the large number of German-Americans who lived there. Prospect Avenue today is lined with luxury apartments, while Highland Boulevard's fine homes have been replaced mostly by offices and apartment buildings. The working-class families of the immigration era had settled in single-family and duplex units on the southside and to the north of Highland. Still later, with the wave of black migrants, the 300-block area of working-class homes in the latter section became Milwaukee's inner core. As early as 1949, a survey of this section concluded that its housing was not the type "which all of us consider representative of the American standard of living."[26]

Milwaukeeans are right in denying that their community is confronted with the magnitude of slum life as reported in cities such as Chicago, Saint Louis, and Newark. But the problem of housing for low-income families has intensified in recent years as urban renewal projects and expressway construction have depleted the supply, while the number of needy families has increased. Milwaukee's efforts to house its citizens date back to 1922, when the city and county joined hands to construct 105 units, which were leased and eventually sold to their occupants. This coordinated effort was not to be duplicated in subsequent years, as the city was left to its own devices. In 1933 and again in 1937, Mayor Hoan appointed committees to document the city's housing needs for the purpose of seeking federal funds, which were then becoming available. The Common Council, however, ignored the reports and refused to participate in the initial national housing programs.

The shortage of dwelling units that plagued urban communities in the wake of World War II pushed the Milwaukee Common Council into action. A housing authority was established and the construction of homes for low-income families and veterans inaugurated. In the quarter century since that time, the authority has constructed or acquired approximately 2,500 units for needy families.[27] (It also continues to operate some 1,068 units for veterans, which it built with city funds in 1949 and 1950.) The demand for low-rent housing space in recent decades has always exceeded the supply of public and private dwellings available. Not only has Milwaukee consistently had a backlog of applicants, but its housing authority is one of the few in the nation that continues to operate in the black. General public housing, however, has met increasing opposition in the community, while that for the elderly has gained in favor. Since 1964, the city has built less than 300 units for needy families and over 2,100 for its senior citizens, with more now under construction. During this same period, several times that number of inner city homes have been torn down to make room for urban renewal projects and expressways.

Urban renewal, the companion thrust to public housing, got under way in Milwaukee in 1958 with the establishment of a city redevelopment authority. The creation of the agency had the strong backing of downtown business groups (and the building and construction trades) concerned with the loss of potential markets and the high cost of building in the CBD. The initial emphasis of the renewal program was to extend the commercial area into the adjacent deteriorating residential sections and stimulate the erection of moderate-to-upper–income apartments on the periphery. The first project, the clearance and redevelopment for commercial use of approximately seventeen acres south of the CBD took more than eight years before rebuilding began. (Acquisition of the land parcels was severely hampered by state law; this impediment was subsequently eliminated by constitutional amendment.) The Juneau Village apartment complex (East Side A) at the northern edge of the CBD met with greater success. Within four years after its authorization, the project was a paying reality with its semiluxury units and shopping center attracting middle- and upper-income residents and adding ap-

preciably to the city's tax base.[28] To date, three high-rise buildings containing 600 apartments have been completed, and another 125 town house units are under construction. In each of
these renewal cases, the persons dislocated were predominantly
whites: Italian families in the first instance and elderly pen-
sioners, along with some Puerto Rican families, in the latter.

In contrast to Juneau Village, the later Kilbourntown (K-3)
project located farther from the central business district and well
within the inner core has met a less kindly fate. Over 1,000
families, in this instance mostly blacks, and 100 small businesses
have been dislocated from the 104-acre area. The site remains
largely vacant five years after clearance began with slightly more
than 100 single-family units of low-cost housing thus far constructed. The slow pace of redevelopment prompted the *Journal*
to charge that "K-3 is a glaring example of how higher income
and more profitable projects are getting more attention than the
low income families desperately in need of good housing."[29] The
simple fact, however, is that developers are not interested in
building in inner core areas away from the central business
district—the Kilbourntown project has received very few realistic
bids—while current federal guidelines mandating dispersal and
small projects rule out extensive use of the site for public housing even if the city were so inclined.

The large-scale clearance activities for renewal and expressways, combined with the accumulation of delays in redevelopment, rising building costs, relocation problems, and the general
unpopularity of public housing, have served to aggravate more
than alleviate the housing problems of the poor, particularly
those with large families. The ghetto space, in Rose's terms, has
not only expanded; it has also become increasingly segregated.
And, as always, the disabilities of the various clearance programs
have fallen heaviest on the disadvantaged.

Milwaukee's mixed results with renewal, similar to the experiences nationally, have caused the emphasis to be shifted from
land clearance to conservation and rehabilitation in efforts to
save neighborhoods threatened by deterioration or blight. The

largest project in this respect is Midtown, an old section of the city still largely white, located about one mile west of the CBD. Of the 183 acres involved, 110 are scheduled for conservation and 73 for redevelopment. The project, approved by the Common Council in 1967, has moved slowly. No land acquisition has taken place for more than a year, with federal officials insisting that the city build more relocation housing before approval will be granted. The project has also been plagued by in-fighting among resident factions over control of the neighborhood organization that has spearheaded the battle against physical and social blight in the area. One group, representing largely the older residents and homeowners, contends that newcomers and transients, including students (Marquette University and other institutions are located nearby) have dominated the association. The latter faction, in turn, charges that City Hall is attempting to gain control through the older group. Underlying the controversy is the fear of some residents that young activists with divergent life styles want to convert the neighborhood into some kind of a commune.

One of the major techniques employed in the conservation and rehabilitation program is the enforcement of building and housing codes, a device ostensibly more practical for Milwaukee than for larger cities with more abandoned and dilapidated properties. Code enforcement had already been started in the 1950's, but in recent years it has been stepped up in the blighted areas with the aid of federal funds. Added emphasis was given to this approach some time back when it was discovered that more than 70 per cent of the dwelling units occupied by blacks in the inner core were absentee owned.

New Issues. The long battle over open housing, which came to an end in early 1968, has been succeeded by a new set of controversy-producing issues: tenant militancy and scattered dwelling sites for low-income families. The first has taken two forms: the objections of public housing occupants to the manner in which the projects are administered, and the protest strategies utilized by low-income families who are being displaced by expressway construction or other public and private development. The second is an outgrowth of current federal policy, which not only discourages large-scale housing projects but also insists that shelter be provided for the poor outside the ghetto areas.

Milwaukee's housing authority from its inception has been administered in an efficient and business-like manner. Looking upon its responsibility as that of professional management and not social work, it has moved swiftly to rid the projects of "troublemakers" and other undesirables. Its rigid concept of administration and its suspicion of social action programs left little room for tenant participation and involvement in the operation of the projects. Wholly unsympathetic to the new winds of "activism" that began to blow during the 1960's, its efforts at readjustment have emerged reluctantly and minimally. The pressures to change have come from both above and below: from federal officials who have insisted on tenant involvement and the provision of social services, and from the occupants themselves.

The Milwaukee Tenants Union, organized in the late 1960's with the help of staff members of Inner City Development Program (ICDP), an OEO-funded agency, has become the sharpest thorn in the side of the authority. With the argument that the housing administrators have failed to regard the tenants as a constituency, the union has promoted such protest tactics as sit-ins, court appeals for evicted residents, and picketing. It has also brought pressure on project managers to seek improvements in physical conditions and to institute additional social services.

More recently, the union, together with antipoverty lawyers, has attacked the authority for evicting tenants without a fair hearing. Under present procedures, occupants are notified verbally that they must vacate their units. They can then appeal the order to the management supervisor and ultimately to the housing board itself. The Tenants Union has called this procedure unconstitutional and has urged, without success, that the authority create an impartial hearing board. (New lease and grievance guidelines now under consideration by HUD would mandate such action.) The activities of the union and the federal pressures for tenant participation are resented as "interference with management prerogatives" by many of the old-line administrators in the Department of City Development. However, recognition of the need to establish better relations with public housing occupants has increased in the higher echelons of the agency and in the mayor's office. The deputy director of the department evidenced this new orientation when he stated, "We have become increasingly sensitive at the administrative level here to the rights of tenants."[30] The mayor also has moved to accommodate the new participational trends by appointing a tenant to the housing authority and by wooing factional leaders in the projects who are receptive to city hall overtures.

The Tenants Union has not confined its activities to the central city but has also effectively dramatized the shortage of low-income housing in Milwaukee county generally. This, in fact, has been its major thrust. It has carried its case to the suburbs by demonstrations and by appearances before local councils urging them to provide a fair share of low-income housing in their communities. Its major target, however, has been the County Expressway Commission. Among other things, it has demanded that the county replace every house taken for road-building on a one-to-one basis before any further construction takes place. Coming at a time when there is general public reaction in the area against freeway expansion, this demand has generated considerable sympathy. Largely as a result of the union's activities, the expressway commission has agreed to rent rather than demolish dwelling units it has acquired until such time as they must be removed for actual construction.

The driving force behind the Tenants Union has been Ted Seaver, a former ICDP staff member. Interestingly, Seaver is one of the few "protest activists" in the community who has been able to establish a working relationship or understanding with the mayor. Perhaps the principal reason for this *rapprochement* is the compatibility of the union's approach with Maier's overall strategy of dispersing responsibility for the city's social problems to other units of government. Seaver's actions, in effect, support this strategy by directing attention to the suburbs' failure to provide shelter for low-income families and by attacking the county for aggravating the housing situation. Although the union's actions in behalf of public housing tenants have irked some city officials, including the former director of the Department of City Development, who originally served as head of the Housing Authority, they have not alienated the mayor. Seaver is careful to avoid any criticism of the chief executive, and the latter in turn is apparently willing to tolerate some protest activity on the part of the union so long as it is kept in reasonable bounds and does not prove embarrassing to his administration. The mayor, in fact, helped mediate the situation which arose when the union seized several buildings in an abandoned Army Disciplinary Barracks and turned them over to sixteen families in need of shelter.

Scattered sites, the second major housing issue on the current agenda is a direct consequence of federal intervention. In 1967, HUD guidelines were amended to discourage the construction of further housing projects in "areas of racial concentration." It was felt that the distribution of low-income families within neighborhoods throughout the city could reduce service imbalances and enhance opportunities for the disadvantaged to live in an environment of human scale. Responding to the new policy, the Milwaukee Housing Authority proposed that the turnkey technique be employed to build some 400 units on municipally owned land located in various sections of the city, including the southside. In making this recommendation, the authority ignored a Common Council resolution that only 300 units for the elderly and no general housing for families be built south of the Menomonee River. The Chicago regional office of HUD made it clear that no more funds would be forthcoming for public housing, either for the elderly or families, unless turnkey construction of low-cost units on scattered sites was undertaken, a directive that Perrin described as "bureaucratic blackmail." Regional officials for some time had been disturbed by the housing situation in Milwaukee and had, in fact, re-stricted renewal activities pending the making of adequate pro-visions for sheltering the dislocated. This running battle be-tween HUD and the local agency over low-income housing still continues. The former insists that the city build approximately 1,200 new units in this category by the middle of 1972, while the latter contends that far less than this number is needed. Perrin has summed up the long-standing dispute by saying, "We're en-gaged in a statistical ball game with HUD on what our defi-ciency is in low-income housing."[31]

The issue of scattered sites, like that of open housing, was one the aldermen would have preferred to avoid. Those from the southside wanted housing for the elderly (their opposition to any housing program in their own bailiwicks had finally given way under pressure from older constituents) but not for families. Northside councilmen were cool to the location of any units in their districts, while those from the inner core areas argued that the best interests of Milwaukee's poor would be served by hav-ing no more projects in their wards. The mayor, as indicated in an earlier chapter, took no public position on the issue although he worked quietly to bring about its resolution. When pressed at a news conference to state whether or not he supported scat-tered sites for the southside, he parried the query by replying that his office was

concerned with the corporate limits of this municipality and not concerned with dividing our site questions into balkanized, regional divisions. [That tactic] is the game and rationale of our suburban-oriented editors who use one section of the town as an excuse of not facing the basic question: that one municipality is financing this public housing.[32]

Faced with the federal mandate to act or lose the funds, the Common Council finally agreed in April, 1970, to the construc-tion of 268 housing units on sixty-seven city-owned sites located in fifteen of Milwaukee's nineteen wards. (This number was later reduced to 247, when soil tests indicated that some of the sites were not suitable for homes.) Only sixty-three, or about one-fourth of the new units, are to be built on the southside. In taking this action, the council stipulated that it would not approve the building contracts unless it also endorsed the housing designs. This proviso was unprecedented because the council had on no previous occasion chosen to act as an architectural review board but had always relied on the Department of City Development to perform this function. The novelty of scattered-site development and the sensitivity of the aldermen to the reactions of their constituents prompted this precautionary measure.

To ensure final approval, the city development department's staff worked painstakingly to inform the aldermen of the plans. Each site was photographed so that the developers' designs and plans could be compared with the neighboring homes. A private briefing was conducted for every interested alderman, and assurances were given to southside residents that few, if any, black families would even want to apply for any of the units in that section of the city. These efforts, coupled with a warning from HUD's regional office that it considered scattered-site public housing "an essential component of the city's badly needed relocation resources"[33] brought the last necessary endorsement from the Common Council in November, 1970, and HUD approval four months later.

The Housing Inventory. Experiences drawn from the issue of low-income housing in Milwaukee and elsewhere are not restricted to the persistence of the problem over time. New federal programs have presented novel opportunities as well as difficult challenges to local officials; groups formerly powerless have emerged to pressure for changes in the direction of social policy; and breaches have occurred in some of the old barriers to enlargement of the opportunity structure for all segments of the community. In the process, national policy has become more attentive to the housing needs of low-income families and less sympathetic to renewal projects that are designed to boost the economic base of the city but which frequently fall heaviest on the disadvantaged. And local housing directors, who have often appeared more concerned with property management than with relieving deprivation, now find it necessary to modify their perspectives and procedures in order to survive.

Federal standards in housing and redevelopment have expanded significantly from the earlier "bricks-and-mortar" emphasis to a concern for citizen participation and social amelioration. The new requirements have created political problems for local officials and pushed them into actions that they otherwise would not have taken. Some local functionaries have welcomed or waited for such pressure, because it has given them cause for acting while at the same time minimizing political risks. A recent study of HUD local assistance programs by the National Academy of Public Administration concluded that Milwaukee falls within this category. According to the Academy's report, the city's housing authority prefers "the prod and protection thus afforded [by the federal government] to self-motivated action that would be contrary to the majority will as they perceive it."[34] Whether this assessment of Milwaukee is correct or not—the mayor vigorously denies it—the fact is that the city has traditionally been slow to take action in the social field. Without federal pressure, it is highly unlikely, for example, that the housing authority would have liberalized its rules to recognize resident councils and other tenant participation activities in the projects or that the Common Council would have approved the scattered site program.

In attempting to steer a viable course in this highly volatile field of low-income housing, the mayor has followed two broad strategies. On the one hand, he has sought to blunt the issue in order to make it less controversial and thereby increase the possibilities of negotiating some alleviating arrangements. On the other, using the zoning dispersal recommendations of the National Commission on Urban Problems (Douglas commission) as a fulcrum, he has endeavored to broaden the responsibility for the problem by calling for the allocation of more low-income residential sites outside the central city and chiding the suburban communities and the county and state governments for failing to assume their fair share of the burden. Both strategies have brought a measure of success, although not of sufficient magnitude to change materially the housing situation.[35] Nor is this situation likely to be substantially bettered, either in Milwaukee or other large central cities, until higher levels of government (1) allocate funds for this purpose in far greater amounts than they have thus far been willing to do and (2) determine to use their fiscal and legal powers to open up outlying areas to housing for the disadvantaged.

Notes

1. *Milwaukee Journal,* April 12, 1970.

2. Harold Rose, "The Development of an Urban Subsystem: The Case of the Negro Ghetto," *Annals of the American Association of Geographers* 60 (March, 1970), pp. 6–14. "Ghetto space" represents the area presently identified as the ghetto as well as the contiguous territory estimated to be sufficiently adequate to accommodate the new increase of Negro households over a ten-year period.

3. See Bernard Toliver and Joseph Hinden, "Research in Police Community Relations, Inner Core Area Milwaukee, 1959–60," (Unpublished paper, School of Social Work, University of Wisconsin, Madison, 1961).

4. Steven Pflanczer, "Negro Community Leadership in a Northern Metropolitan Center: A Study of Its Structure Under Conditions of Rapid Social Change" (Unpublished paper, Social Welfare Department, University of Wisconsin-Milwaukee, 1968).

5. H. James, "Milwaukee Argues Racial Problems," *Christian Science Monitor,* Oct. 26, 1965, p. 10.

6. In the mayor's words, such an ordinance "would reinforce the walls of segregation between city and suburbs, [making Milwaukee] the poorhouse, and providing another reason for flight from the central city." Statement of Mayor Maier on Open Housing Ordinance Given Before Common Council Judiciary Committee, Oct. 16, 1967.

7. This action by Leonard was later cited in support of his appointment as Assistant Attorney General in charge of civil rights cases in the Nixon Administration.

8. In a study of several hundred cities in the United States in 1967, John C. Maloney derived a scale of "riot proneness." Milwaukee ranked in the top 10 per cent on the scale. "A Study of Riot Proneness in American Cities" (Unpublished paper, Urban Journalism Center, Northwestern University, Evanston, Ill., 1967).

9. Jonathan J. Slesinger, *Community Opinions of the Summer 1967 Civil Disturbances in Milwaukee* (Milwaukee: University of Wisconsin-Milwaukee, Office of Applied Social Research, April, 1968).

10. Karl H. Flaming, *Who "Riots" and Why? Black and White Perspectives in Milwaukee* (Milwaukee: Milwaukee Urban League, Oct., 1968).

11. The Allen-Bradley case is discussed in Carole Southerland, "Public Policy Development: A Functional Analysis of Affirmative Action" (Master's thesis, Department of Political Science, University of Wisconsin-Milwaukee, 1970).

12. In this connection see John Nichols, "The Development of the Mayor's Commission on Human Relations in Milwaukee," (Master's thesis, University of Wisconsin-Madison, 1949). Also see Ron Snyder, "The Milwaukee Commission on Community Relations," (unpublished paper, University of Wisconsin-Milwaukee, 1968).

13. Mayor's Study Committee on Social Problems in the Inner Core of the City, *Final Report*, April 15, 1960.

14. Henry W. Maier, *Challenge to the Cities: An Approach to a Theory of Urban Leadership* (New York: Random House, 1966).

15. City of Milwaukee, *Code of Ordinances*, Section 2-309.

16. He was reported as saying, "Negroes look so much alike that you can't tell them apart" and "many of them have an IQ of nothing." (Maier, *op. cit.*, p. 59.)

17. Jenann Olsen, *Administrative Change in Milwaukee Municipal Government* (Master's thesis, Department of Urban Affairs, University of Wisconsin-Milwaukee, Dec., 1969), pp. 65–66. The analysis of the commission here relies heavily on Miss Olsen's study.

18. "A Strategy for Antipoverty Community Action Programs," *Social Work* 11 (April, 1966), p. 1.

19. Olsen, *op. cit.*, pp. 69–70.

20. Arthur Greenleigh and Associates, *A Plan to Reduce Prejudice and Discrimination in the Greater Milwaukee Area* (1967).

21. U.S. Civil Rights Commission, *Racial Isolation in the Public Schools* (Washington: U.S. Government Printing Office, 1967).

22. *Milwaukee Journal*, Sept. 17, 1967. The Milwaukee Police Department under Chief Breier has been adamant in its refusal to permit studies that relate in any way to its practices. It has refused, for example, to cooperate with the President's Advisory Commission on Civil Disorders, President Johnson's Crime Commission, and the International Association of Chiefs of Police. In the case of the first, the chief ordered members of the department not to cooperate with interviewers from the commission under penalty of dismissal from the force.

23. Former Mayor Zeidler, for example, charged that the issue of intergovernmental cooperation was a subterfuge and suggested that Maier wanted to avoid "the crucial problem of conforming with civil rights requirements of the law." (*Milwaukee Sentinel*, March 2, 1967).

24. *Milwaukee Sentinel*, March 8, 1969.

25. Olsen, *op. cit.*, p. 47.

26. *Milwaukee Housing Survey of 1949* (Milwaukee: Housing Authority of City of Milwaukee, Jan., 1949), p. 13.

27. The Federal Public Works Administration in 1937 built 518 of these units, which were turned over to the city in 1953.

28. Even in this case, however, the original developer has withdrawn from completing the later stages of the project. As a result, the city recently approved the construction of more moderately priced units on the remainder of the site. Apparently the large increase of high-rental apartments in the outer areas of the city and in suburbia, together with the civil disturbances of the last several years, has lessened the demand for units situated close to the CBD.

29. *Milwaukee Journal,* Feb. 27, 1970.

30. *Ibid.,* Nov. 16, 1970.

31. *Ibid.,* Jan. 17, 1971.

32. *Ibid.,* Feb. 12, 1970.

33. *Ibid.,* Nov. 15, 1970.

34. "Achieving More Effective Delivery of HUD Local Assistance Programs" (Washington: National Academy of Public Administration, 1969).

35. At the initiative of the county executive, the county government has now entered the housing field. The Board of Supervisors has created a housing and relocation committee and allocated $1 million for stimulating the construction of low- and moderate-income units by making use of all available federal programs. The county's efforts, however, have proceeded at a snail's pace, partly because of the difficulty of finding suitable sites and partly because of the resistance of suburban governments to the location of low-income housing within their territorial confines.

7

The Intergovernmental Complex

Relations with other governments and organizations have always been a vital component of Milwaukee's municipal administration. Today, these relationships have a significance that is more political than functional because of the scale and effects of other public entities and populations operating farther beyond the city's boundaries and because local taxable resources have not kept pace with the rise in demands for urban services. Like other large cities, Milwaukee is greatly affected not only by the actions of higher levels of government but also by the vertical coalitions of business interests, labor unions, and religious and ethnic groups, which transcend the local arena. In addition, the city is surrounded by suburbs, which, some critics maintain, take the best the central municipality has to offer and give little in return.

Employing a "diplomatic" or "national state" analogy to explain the competitive relations among municipalities, local governments in metropolitan areas may be viewed as contenders for resources and not just as service-providing bureaucracies. Legally, they are accepted as jurisdictional equals trying to augment their fiscal and other powers while maintaining their social distances by every means available, from mutual aid pacts to high court litigation. In this interplay of metropolitics, supramunicipal agencies and organizations, ranging from the Suburban League of Municipalities and the Wisconsin Alliance of Cities to the Wisconsin Department of Local Affairs and Development, the national Department of Housing and Urban Development, and the National League of Cities, have been drawn into the "negotiating" arena.

Local governments in metropolitan Milwaukee have a long history of intra-area controversies over such items as parks, water, sewers, health care, highway construction, and tax reform. Attempts to arrive at consensus over these matters have consistently been marked more by sentiments of separatism than cooperation. When efforts toward establishing a sewer authority (1921) and a county park system (1936) were finally realized, it was more because of increasing pollution and the shortage of public land than any feeling of common identity or any spirit of "reasoning together."[1] Similarly, the move to create a regional planning commission in the area made little headway until the governor actively intervened. When structural changes in government have come to Milwaukee, they have usually been responses to crisis situations or the results of state or federal leadership and subsidy.

Shifts in patterns of population settlement, from central city to suburban sprawl, have increased the number and variety of local jurisdictions and underlined the differences among them. These developments in turn have given rise to a dualism in operations or approaches among the governmental segments of the metropolitan complex. One set of orientations emphasizes the norms of grass-roots participation and community amenities; the other stresses activities and services that are program-centered rather than territorially defined, such as pollution control and transportation. The first is championed mainly by the suburbs, whose primary concern is the preservation of their life styles and social environment. The second is promoted by the professionals and technicians—highway engineers, regional planners, sewerage system administrators, conservationists—and on a selective basis by central city officials. These differences in approaches have diminished chances for social mediation or intergovernmental cooperation at the metropolitan level. They have also spawned new forms of nonregional transactions among the local units and generated new arguments for more functional programs to be handled by the county government.

The Central City "Octopus"

Most major core municipalities, as recent censuses show, are losing resident populations to their suburbs. Until the latest count, Milwaukee appeared to be bucking the trend, even though the rate of growth in the outlying suburbs was higher. The gains it has experienced in absolute numbers since World War II have enabled it to contain a population proportionately larger than that enjoyed by other big midwestern cities in relation to their periphery. This advantageous position, however, was due to the large-scale annexations Milwaukee accomplished during the 1950's and not to increases within its prewar boundaries. Now that further territorial expansion is no longer a possibility—the last unincorporated space in the county was acquired in 1962—the city's proportionate share of the metropolitan population will drop more sharply in future years, as will its share of taxable wealth (see Appendix J).

Efforts to redesign the local governmental system to accommodate growth have taken three forms: political integration, voluntary intergovernmental cooperation, and functional consolidation. The central city has generally pursued the first, the suburbs have consistently favored the second, and both have on occasions supported the last. Consolidation movements were started in Milwaukee county as early as 1870, when a bill was introduced in the state legislature to merge the city and county governments. These efforts continued intermittently in subsequent years and were accelerated after World War I, with no less than fifteen consolidation bills introduced in the legislature between 1919 to 1935.[2]

The depression years of the 1930's increased the tempo of the merger movement and led to the first comprehensive metropolitan study in the Milwaukee area by a joint city-county committee. An advisory referendum conducted in 1935 at the committee's request brought an over-all vote of 104,832 to 40,832 in favor of consolidation. All but two suburbs, however, voted overwhelmingly against the question, and, when the legislature by narrow margins refused to approve merger bills later that year, the last serious threat of political amalgamation in Milwaukee county came to an end.[3]

With the repeated failure of consolidation attempts, Milwaukee officials turned to annexation as a means of preserving the primacy of the central city and obtaining more *lebensraum*. In the late 1920's, the city established a department of annexation for the avowed purpose of promoting expansion. The strategy proved successful, with the city increasing its size from twenty-six to forty-four square miles in less than a decade. The second concerted drive came after World War II, when Milwaukee again embarked on an aggressive annexation program that doubled its territorial size by 1957. Two factors were influential in prompting these moves: the necessity of securing additional land for industrial expansion in order to maintain a sound tax base; and high suburban zoning and building requirements that restricted residential development for the small wage-earner. Frank Zeidler, who served as mayor during the period of the city's greatest annexation successes, was particularly sensitive to this latter factor. He felt that, unless Milwaukee expanded, low-income workers would be effectively barred from living in the outlying areas and crowded further into an already congested central city.[4]

The territorial onslaughts by Milwaukee were not without their costs. They stirred up considerable animosity among suburban officialdom and generated a series of countermoves in the adjacent and outlying areas. New incorporations were hastily accomplished and already existing suburban governments began annexing land in their own right. A law (since repealed), lowering municipal incorporation requirements, was steered through the legislature by a suburban attorney, enabling two large and almost wholly undeveloped townships at the southern extremity of the county to become "paper" cities and thereby immunize themselves against annexation. The most effective weapon the city had in its expansionist drive—its water supply—also came under attack. In 1956, the city of Wauwatosa started proceedings before the state Public Service Commission to compel Milwaukee to sell it water. The commission supported the suburban position, ruling that, by selling water to selected buyers outside its territory, the central city had constituted itself a metropolitan utility and therefore could not discriminate against Wauwatosa.[5]

In recent years, the city-suburban battles have shifted from service and annexation issues to social and economic fronts. Central city protagonists amass more evidence that suburban governments discriminate against have-nots and racial minorities by their "quality" land use policies. Mayor Maier, for example, repeatedly criticizes suburban zoning laws as "fundamental declarations of intent that Negro citizens are condemned to ghetto imprisonment."[6] He and other Milwaukee officials continually reiterate that the city maintains many well-managed and high-cost services that benefit the total area, yet neither the state nor county government makes any attempt to force suburban compensation. The common plaint is that outlying residents use Milwaukee's streets, libraries, museums, and hospitals but resist all efforts to share the costs of such facilities or to effect a more equitable redistribution of tax resources.

In 1968, the mayor estimated that central city taxpayers were subsidizing suburban dwellers and their governments to the tune of $12 million to $14 million annually. An elaborate report from the treasurer's office listed such items as employee benefits in traffic thoroughfares, downtown jobs, and state compensation aids; direct benefits in hospitals, museums, libraries, electricity rates, colleges and universities, and other nontaxed properties; and intangible benefits, including cultural events, departmental service spillovers, and the suburban ability to escape "poverty costs" (those attributable to the extra social services needed by disadvantaged newcomers situated in the core area).[7] Fortified with this bill of particulars, however dubious its validity, the mayor proposed a metropolitan social district to handle more uniformly and equitably the problems of poverty, delinquency, housing, and the elderly; and a single metropolitan school district to assure that core area schools would be as well financed as those in suburbia. "If," Maier averred, "parks, expressways and even animals in the zoo can be put on an areawide functional basis—why not people?"[8]

Just as suburban officials vigorously resisted Mayor Zeidler's annexation drives, so they now rankle at Maier's "psychological warfare" against them. Faced with this new type of challenge, their line of defense has taken several forms. One is to contend that the mayor's attacks on them are attempts to divert attention from the real problem: the inefficiency and ineptness with which the city manages its affairs. Another is to point out that benefits flow in two directions: many central city dwellers draw their paychecks from industries in outlying areas; many public institutions, including the county welfare and medical complex, are located outside the city; and patronization by suburbanites keeps downtown Milwaukee in business. A third is to argue that suburban dwellers, through charity drives, county property taxes that finance the welfare load, and federal and state grants that are paid for disproportionately by taxes collected outside the core city, actually bear the brunt of Milwaukee's social costs.

Considerable difficulty awaits anyone trying to identify the first offender or the most injured party in what has become the great American standoff between central cities and their suburbs. In metropolitan Milwaukee, the conflict is particularly bitter if the volume of charges and countercharges between the two protagonists is an accurate indicator. Like their counterparts in most large central city governments, Milwaukee officials feel that many of their noblest efforts are under the "siege" of suspicious and self-centered "localists" from suburban enclaves and their friends at the state capital. Yet, one might point out, it was Milwaukee's aggressive annexation tactics that served to draw the outlying municipalities closer together, even bringing some into being in the process.

Not surprisingly, the city of Milwaukee finds itself in a different and less maneuverable position today than formerly. It is still better off than most other midwestern core municipalities in such categories as land use potential, revenue base, physical plant, and population mix. It is not as well along as many of them in promoting the projects that its present and previous mayors—who have all carried on the fight with the suburbs—consider essential for the community's survival and development. The city finds itself badly handicapped in playing a leadership or brokerage role among governments in the area because of the many autonomous units with proportionately more money and talent available to them than the core municipality and with well-entrenched interests. It is also faced with the fact that contemporary intergovernmental relations include not only more suburbs and a stronger county administration but also neighborhood associations demanding their own measure of autonomy, aided by federal agencies sensitive to their wants.

The order of Milwaukee's projects has been shifted from "booster-type" priorities for territorial development and commercial enhancements to more urgent and no less cost-conscious issues of resource redistribution and social justice. But, because of the urban specters of population "flight and blight" and greater area diversity, the power to decide the more urgent policies has increasingly shifted from its hands to the suburban and county governments and, by cumulative default, to higher levels of public authority. The horizontally fragmented politics that pits Milwaukee against other local units further disperses powers to outside jurisdictions. Yet, throughout the course of these developments, the central city has remained "bloodied but unbowed," still sparking most of the program controversies in the area.

The Suburban Redoubt

Contrary to the popular image, the suburban municipalities in the Milwaukee area do not constitute a tightly knit and homogeneous group. In fact, the only real agreement of long standing among them is their almost reflexive opposition to any proposals that would enhance the power and influence of the central city at the expense of their own autonomy. Differing in size, socio-economic characteristics, and political orientations, they provide an excellent example of metropolitan decentralization and spatial specialization. Five of the eighteen suburbs in the county may be classified as industrial (manufacturing jobs in the community equal at least 50 per cent of the total number of employed residents); ten residential (manufacturing jobs are less than 10 per cent); and three mixed (manufacturing jobs are between 10 per cent to 50 per cent). Similar to the findings elsewhere, relations are closer and service agreements more common among those with similar social rank than among divergent types.[9]

Despite broad statutory authority for intergovernmental co-operative arrangements and suburban preachments about the advantages of the voluntaristic approach in metropolitan functioning, Milwaukee area units have made little use of such devices. A comprehensive survey conducted in 1960 found fewer than 125 agreements in effect, most of which involved minor matters such as several school districts' sharing a vocational teacher or the establishment of uniform traffic control regulations on a street dividing two municipalities. Over half the cases consisted of informal understandings among administrative officials covering the lending of equipment, exchange of purchasing information, and similar activities. The only significant instances of cooperative agreements were represented by the library and water contracts between the central city and outlying municipalities and the creation of a water utility by three north shore communities.[10] The minor role played by intergovernmental arrangements reflects in part the tendency of the suburban units, no matter what their size, to develop their own complement of services.

The official instrumentality for generating intracounty cooperation is the Intergovernmental Cooperation Council of Milwaukee County (ICC) organized in 1968. The initiating force behind its creation was the county executive, John Doyne, who looked upon it as a means of bringing the local units together and working out agreements on matters of concern to the area as a whole. He felt that such a mechanism was essential, given the divided nature of governmental power in the county, if there was to be any serious effort at formulating common responses to problems that were becoming more critical, such as transportation, waste disposal, and housing. Even with its voluntary character, however, it took Doyne more than five years to win acceptance for the council approach from all of the suburban units.

Despite repeated invitations to join, the city of Milwaukee has thus far spurned the overtures. It is the mayor's contention that it should not participate until voting on the council is allocated proportionate to population rather than on the existing basis of one for each unit regardless of its size. Such an arrangement, as the mayor well knows, is totally unacceptable to the other members since it would give the central city a clear majority. Suburban officials repeatedly refer to Milwaukee's refusal to join as a typical example of Maier's unwillingness to cooperate with the outlying governments while at the same time castigating them for failing to help the city. The mayor, on his part, sees small reward in such participation and is convinced that the suburbs will not give up any of their privileges willingly. As he apparently views the situation, "conflict politics" rather than consensualism or voluntarism is the more effective strategy for forcing concessions from a reluctant suburbia.

Conditions of regional interdependence are not manifested solely in horizontal transactions and relationships between the core city and the surrounding ring; they are also exhibited in interactions among the suburban units themselves. The newer municipalities, in fact, are drawing economic and residential development away from the older suburbs as well as from the central city. Most of the communities incorporated prior to World War II have little space left for development and, like Milwaukee, must contend with more daytime traffic, rising institutional costs, and a property tax "squeeze." The tax advantages they enjoyed earlier have steadily diminished as more service-demanding residents have moved into their confines and as newer enterprises have been developed farther out beyond the reach of annexation. Free from the problems of obsolescence and deterioration, the newer suburban municipalities in the outlying sections of Milwaukee county and the adjacent areas are in an increasingly advantageous position to lure modern shopping centers and "cleaner" industries while avoiding the problem of housing the workers.

Suburban differences, based on income and class levels, land use patterns, and stage of development, have already found reflection in the ICC. Even in the absence of the city of Milwaukee, disagreements and fractiousness over such issues as the location of a convention center, waste disposal, and a study of program budgeting and uniform municipal accounting, have plagued the council and minimized its potential effectiveness. What it has accomplished—it was able, for example, to effect an agreement on the consolidation of technical school districts as mandated by state law—has been due largely, to the efforts and negotiating skills of the county executive, who serves as its presiding officer.

Cracks in the "iron ring" around Milwaukee are beginning to appear, however, as the competition for tax resources and amenities intensifies. Although these breaches are still far from the point where they can transcend the united front of suburban officials vis-à-vis the central city, they nevertheless harbinger the formation of coalitions between the latter and various fringe area governments on selected issues. It is a well-known fact, for example, that the interests of the industrial and lower-income suburbs in tax redistribution reform are more akin to those of Milwaukee than to their wealthier counterparts in the fringe areas. In the face of increasing economic and tax pressures, the specter of central city domination is not likely to remain as effective a rallying cause for suburban unity as it has traditionally been.

The Regional Arena

We have already seen that over the course of time the Milwaukee county government has assumed many functions of a metropolitan nature, such as welfare, parks, expressways, airports, and hospitals. Its role in providing these area-wide services has not only lessened the need for special districts; it has also weakened the demand for metropolitan government. However, now that urbanization is spilling over significantly into the adjacent jurisdictions, the county's ability to serve as regional supplier and mediator is steadily diminishing. County Executive Doyne recently reflected this changing perspective in pointing out that there were now 168 taxing units in the Milwaukee SMSA. "How long," he asked, "can we afford to allow this kind of an archaic governmental structure to continue?"[11]

The only existing mechanism for regional coordination in the Milwaukee area is the Southeastern Wisconsin Regional Planning Commission (SEWRPC), which covers seven counties, including three SMSA's: Milwaukee, Kenosha, and Racine. Established in 1960, the commission is made up of twenty-one members, three from each county. One of the three is designated by the County Board and the remaining two by the governor (one of his appointees must be from a list submitted by the County Board). The agency's statutory charge is to develop a comprehensive plan for the physical development of the area. More recently, it has been designated by HUD to perform the review function (as provided in Section 204 of the Demonstration Cities and Metropolitan Development Act of 1966) of applications for federal facility grants submitted by local governments within the region. The commission is invested with power to assess the member counties for the costs of its operations, but its planning and functional authority is advisory only.

SEWRPC has assembled a highly competent staff of professionals and has produced a wide range of studies and plans. Its most successful accomplishment to date has been the preparation of a land use and transportation plan for the region. In addition, it has collected and disseminated large amounts of primary data covering such matters as soil conditions and stream pollution. It also assists local communities with their individual planning and zoning problems. Up to this point in its history, the commission has concentrated almost wholly on physical planning, believing that its influence and usefulness would be greatly reduced, if not destroyed, by entering into the social problem field. As its chairman recently explained, "there are those who would equate our effectiveness in physical plan implementation with our absence from the social, political, or economic involvement that surrounds the urban political systems which daily lurch from crisis to crisis."[12] That it can maintain this posture much longer is doubtful. It has already been compelled, for example, to undertake a housing study at the urging of the Milwaukee mayor, and federal authorities are becoming more insistent that social components be included in the planning process.

The commission has no implementing authority nor any legal power to compel adherence to its plans. It represents simply "an attempt to provide the areawide planning services necessary to solve areawide [physical] problems in southeastern Wisconsin on a voluntary, cooperative basis."[13] Lacking a regional government or operational body to which it can relate, the commission is not integrated into the political decision-making process except in a very peripheral fashion through the County Board members and the few other local officials who serve on it.

Despite these limitations, SEWRPC has unquestionably served a useful function. The transportation plan has been adopted by the seven county boards although local opposition to additional expressway construction and a slower-than-anticipated population growth are forcing reconsideration of some aspects of it. The various studies, data collections, and plans provide a basis on which local units can more rationally formulate their own developmental plans. The commission staff has established close working relationships with their counterparts—planners and engineers—in many of the local jurisdictions so that the regional position receives sympathetic consideration at least at the administrative level. On occasions also, the commission has been able to prevent flagrant violations of the land use plan, such as industrial or commercial encroachment in the environmental corridors and flood plains, by publicly protesting the action. The current national emphasis on environmental protection has strengthened the agency's influence in these matters.

In the last analysis, however, whatever significant success SEWRPC has enjoyed is attributable less to its ability to persuade local units than to the backing that state and federal agencies have given it. The state Department of Transportation, for example, has adopted the transportation plan and has clearly indicated that highway funds will be allocated in the region only for conforming projects. Similarly, the Section 204 review authority has given the agency a weapon to prevent or discourage the construction of facilities (for which federal funds are sought) that are incompatible with regional plans.

Useful as the commission is and excellent as its professional credentials are, its integrative possibilities remain limited. Lacking the recognition of the Association of Bay Area Governments (San Francisco) or the enforcement powers of the Metropolitan Council of the Twin Cities (Minneapolis-Saint Paul), it has emerged not as the regional spokesman or coordinator but as its gentle educator and persuader. Although there are signs that local officials have become more cognizant of the socio-economic and environmental interdependence among the individual political jurisdictions as a result of the commission's work, their commitment to the region, with some few exceptions, remains at the level of platitudes and rhetoric. They are quick to accept the advice of the regional planners when it is in the immediate interest of their locality to do so; they are equally quick to reject it when they are asked to sacrifice some short-term gain or advantage for the future well-being of the area as a whole. The burden of regional coordination or integration in the Milwaukee area thus remains on higher levels of public authority; only now these levels have more information and guidance at their disposal, thanks to the work of SEWRPC.

The State Level

The complex of relationships between Milwaukee and the state is revealed in the labyrinth of statutory and case law, the struggles between political leaders and party factions, and the daily contacts between city and state administrative personnel. State officials influence local policy in many tangible and intangible ways and, in turn, find their own thinking and actions shaped by the problems of the large-scale urban areas. Like most American metropolises, Milwaukee is much larger than the state's capital city and therefore has problems that many state politicians rarely if ever come in contact with. This fact was dramatized some time back by the comments of grave shock expressed by legislators from other parts of the state who had just completed a bus tour through Milwaukee's core area.

Much of the problem of poor city-state relations comes from disparities in performance of the latter in respect to territorial space and finances. In the case of the first, the ease of incorporation laws practically automated the creation of fringe area municipalities, thereby effectively thwarting annexation chances for older cities and contributing to metropolitan fragmentation. This disparity was reduced in Wisconsin only in 1959 by the establishment of sterner formation standards and a planning office for examining incorporation and annexation proposals to see if they are in the "public interest" (in terms of service capabilities and impact upon the remainder of the total community). And, in the area of finances, as we have previously seen, state tax-sharing formulas return a percentage of income revenue to the local government of the community in which the money is collected, a policy that gives proportionately more assistance to better-off suburbs than to the needy cities.

State and regional programs that transcend the boundaries and powers of the central city help explain Mayor Maier's functionalist preoccupation with economic development as well as his promotional efforts which range from his own intergovernmental fiscal liaison staff to his state-wide Wisconsin Alliance of Cities. Milwaukee's Department of City Development is designed, as part of its planning responsibility, to turn the direction of the region's economy inward toward the central city while the liaison staff and alliance of cities seek to bend state policies into assisting the city with more money. In this campaign, the mayor frequently clashed with the Republican governor, Warren Knowles, who served from 1966 to 1970.[14] Consistent again with his strategy of dispersing responsibility for the city's plight, he repeatedly attacked the governer for failing to support a program of massive fiscal aid for Milwaukee. He has also feuded with other state officials including Joseph Fagan, the former head of the Department of Industry, Labor, and Human Relations, referring to him as a "curbstone commissar." Fagan's critical statements about the city's handling of its racial problems particularly irked Maier.

The impasse between Milwaukee and the state, which has been prominent at the political level, is less evident at the administrative level. There is hardly a state agency or department that does not extend help to some segment of the city. The Department of Health and Social Services, the largest agency in state government, has many of its personnel located in the Milwaukee area. The Department of Industry, Labor and Human Relations assists in job placements for inner-city residents and its equal rights division brings initial enforcement proceedings against cases of discrimination in hiring. The Department of Local Affairs and Development, formed in 1967, has established an office in Milwaukee and has supervised the expenditure of $1 million allocated to inner-city groups for self-help projects. Many under-takings have been started with the assistance of state funds, in-cluding a Black Credit Union and finance counseling; day-care centers; and the Inner City Arts Council. Milwaukee officials have not greeted these efforts with enthusiasm but have tended to regard them as devices for giving minority groups new powers to use against city hall.

The 1969 legislative session brought two unprecedented ac-tions. For the first time in Wisconsin history, a governor ad-dressed a joint meeting of the two houses on urban problems, with an eloquent plea to continue the special programs under-taken in the Milwaukee ghetto. Also, for the first time, the Joint Finance Committee, under the control of ultraconservative Republicans, sharply reduced established welfare programs and virtually emasculated the urban budget of the Department of Local Affairs and Development. These actions, together with other cuts made in the governor's urban package and the legis-lature's refusal to enact the tax reform proposals vigorously sup-ported by Mayor Maier, were discouraging blows for those who looked to greater state involvement in the solution of the city's problems.[15]

Capping the lawmakers' obdurate stance was still another un-precedented act. Father James Groppi, who had long been a thorn in the side of Milwaukee officials, now turned on the state government, leading a "poor peoples' march" to Madison to protest the welfare cuts. Reports of how well or badly the march-ers were received as they passed through Wisconsin hamlets were newsworthy in themselves. But, when the welfare mothers and their supporting cadre arrived at the capitol building, they and several hundred students from the nearby campus of the University of Wisconsin forcibly occupied the floor of the As-sembly chamber. Although the demonstrators had at first vowed to stay in the capitol until the cuts were restored, they eventu-ally decided they had made their point and withdrew after eleven hours' occupancy. The shock, and then outrage, with which the legislators reacted to the invasion of their chamber destroyed all hopes of getting the cuts restored. In fact, one of their first acts was to approve a substantial increase in the capitol security force and allocate funds for covering the windows of the capitol building with unbreakable material.

Traditionally, the state legislature has used the lack of a united front from Milwaukee area representatives as a reason for not acting on urban program requests. This disunity runs deeper than the characteristic suburban-urban, or parallel political party cleavages, important as these are. Democratic legislators from the Milwaukee area are themselves divided ideologically as well as geographically. The majority of them stand in the New Deal image, highly solicitous of "bread-and-butter" labor union issues but cool to urban racial and social programs. However, the number of liberal young assemblymen from the central city has increased substantially in recent years, and members of this group are developing their own urban packages for introduction. Prospects that the city may fare better at the hands of the legislature increased in 1970 with the election of a Democratic governor from Madison and the party's capture of the lower house by a wide margin. Coupled with the victory, the bright and progressive young lawmakers may well give Milwaukee's representation a different and more attractive hue than it has had for some years.

Federal Relations

Diminishing degrees of local control over the problems of the contemporary urban community and the vagaries of state commitments to the resolution of these difficulties have increasingly brought the large cities to the doorsteps of federal agencies. Milwaukee officials, for some time, have been traveling to the nation's capital on the route already well-marked by their counterparts in New York, Chicago, New Haven, San Francisco, and elsewhere. Mayor Maier, as one of the country's leading urban spokesmen, has repeatedly called for a reordering of national priorities to save the major cities from disaster. The response has been sympathetic but partial at best. New urban-related programs continue to proliferate—some operating through the states, others directly with the local units—but the allocation of funds is far from equal to the intent.

The importance of outside assistance or intervention in the affairs of the modern urban polity was graphically demonstrated in Maier's thirty-nine-point program, which he issued shortly after the July, 1967, disorders in Milwaukee. Of the thirty-nine items calling for action, fourteen were to be performed by state authorities, nine by federal agencies, four by the county, and the remaining one-third by the city. The mayor's critics immediately cited this division of responsibilities as a typical example of "intergovernmental buck-passing." Yet the fact is that the listing was a reflection of the current dependence of urban communities on outside help for the solution of their problems. This reliance in turn is an outgrowth of the increasing complexity of the society as a whole.

In the Milwaukee area, as in similar SMSA's, functional programs supported by federal funds can be found in a wide variety of fields, including water and air pollution control, hospitals, urban renewal, public housing, education, preservation of open space, expressway construction, health and sanitation, job training, airport expansion, and harbor improvement. Earlier discussions have shown how the requirements of federal agencies have influenced the direction and management of local policies in several of these areas. The acceptance of federal supervision has not come easily for Milwaukee city policy-makers and administrators who have long been accustomed to conducting business in their own way. From the inception of the urban renewal program to the present time, for example, major disagreements between local officials and the regional office of HUD have been commonplace. (The same pattern is now manifesting itself in the Model Cities program.) The former complain of rigid guidelines and bureaucratic red tape, while the latter emphasizes that, if the Milwaukee agency would cooperate to a greater extent, the program would move along more smoothly and swiftly.

These differences are not limited to matters that may be politically sensitive, such as the directive for scattered housing sites; they also occur over management procedures and practices, and more recently over the question of resident involvement. What local officials would like are more noncategorical, or block, grants and less overseeing by federal authorities. What they are in effect getting are more centralized guidelines and policy controls along with the requirement for more decentralized citizen participation. The clashes are not likely to subside as federal bureaucrats with cosmopolitan perspectives attempt to oversee sturdy municipal officials with strong localist leanings.

Intergovernmental Relations in Perspective

The city of Milwaukee is significantly affected, but not overcome, by regional changes and national events. Its officials are more attentive than ever before to new opportunities from sources outside the region. At the same time, in addition to the more functional considerations of "growth and development," they are also more sensitive to integrational considerations within the metropolitan area because of the increasing burden of social costs and the inequities of the tax distribution system.[16] Suburban officials, on the other hand, continue to act more in defense of their turf and prerogatives than toward a united expression, with the rhetoric of "grass-roots democracy" and the "imperialism" of the central city still dominant. The county government occupies something of a middle position; although receptive to the notion of functional consolidation under its jurisdiction, it remains reluctant to take the initiative or assume leadership in any such movement for fear of alienating the suburbs.[17]

During the 1950's, Mayor Zeidler predicted that the suburbs would grow stronger, that more state help would be sought but found wanting, and that central cities would become administrative wards of the federal government.[18] His forecasts are extremely accurate as to the first two while the third still remains an open question. In the 1960's, Mayor Maier traded openly on the first prediction, walked a tightrope over the second, and worked assiduously to influence the third to the city's political and economic advantage. His concern with the last, however, is less one of fear that the federal government will supplant local power than, in his words,

> fear that the new rhetoric of the present Administration is going to mean a withdrawal of major concern for the problems of the central city, a kind of urban "Vietnamization" in which central city forces are left to fight the war themselves, only in this case without the Federal resources necessary to win the battle for survival.[19]

Certainly, a fundamental shift in the manner of policy determination—from a horizontal give-and-take among governments in the area to vertical relations with higher levels of public authority—has evolved in the Milwaukee metropolis over the last two decades. The chances of political consent by the suburbs to metropolitan government, which Milwaukee by force of numbers would dominate, were never great. The history of consolidation efforts indicates that major restructuring of the local governmental system has been a nonnegotiable item, thereby ruling out political integration with the region. In fact, the odds against such integration were forecast by the defensive propaganda and inaction of the suburban governments as well as by the concerns of Milwaukee mayors, who centered their efforts more on territorial conquest than on winning area voters over to a metropolitan system of regularized and institutionalized cooperation. Similarly, the odds against use of the county as the area-wide government can be traced to the older supervisors, who represent suburban areas, most often resist the programs of the county executive, and dominate the important committees of the board.

Suburban interests in metropolitan Milwaukee were the first to turn to outside forces, particularly the state legislature and state agencies, for help in solving their service problems (water supply and sewage disposal) and for defending themselves against the expansionist policies of the central city (easy incorporation and difficult annexation laws). The paradox is that the failure of the local governments in the area to work out any sort of

effective integration among themselves has left the fate of regional coordination at the mercy of outside forces over which
they have little control. The Southeastern Wisconsin Regional
Planning Commission, which was virtually superimposed on the
area by the state, stands as the only internal mechanism that
could play this role. However, its integrative capacity is of dubious value since it faces the ultimate obstacle of securing voluntary accession by the local units.

Operating in this intergovernmental mixture, Mayor Maier
appears to receive less opposition in metropolitan matters from
aldermen than County Executive Doyne from the Board of Supervisors. As a result, Maier has been able, like the national
chief executive, to shape the city's external relations or "foreign
policies" with relative freedom. His metropolitical strategy takes
several directions: the maintenance of a hard line against the
suburbs on the assumption that the gains to be derived from
cooperation would be meager in comparison to the costs of let-
ting them "off the hook" on such matters as exclusionary zoning
and tax-sharing; a commitment to "regionalize" or turn over to
the county certain programs, particularly those of a social nature
such as housing and relocation; and the vigorous presentation of
the city's plight to state and federal officials.

On all of these fronts, the mayor is usually able to choose the
time and place of battle. He does not negotiate openly with potentially hostile groups, such as the ICC or Triple O. He pro-
motes particular projects or goals with prepared persuasion,
whether it is to get the Regional Planning Commission to undertake an area housing inventory and analysis, to push the tax
reforms proposed by the Tarr commission, or to win Council
support for Model Cities.

As part of his over-all strategy, the mayor takes on both the
"paper curtain" of the press and the "iron ring" of the suburbs
through speeches before local and national groups, weekly press
conferences (portions of which are televised), and broadcasts over
what he likes to refer to as "Radio Free Milwaukee."[20] At times
he assumes the role of regional statesman, calling for a metropol-

itan school district and an area-wide social district, espousing low-cost housing in the suburbs, condemning the expressway-builders for displacing families without suitable relocation provisions, and urging major changes in public financing to relieve the growing burden of property taxes on homeowners. He is cool toward programs over which City Hall would have little control or experience possible embarrassment, such as former Governor Knowles's inner-city package. In effect, the state's lawmakers and its administrative agencies receive different signals from City Hall because the mayor is more interested in securing funds from the former than additional services from the latter.

Federal aid is welcomed and eagerly sought, although the mayor, as most municipal officials throughout the nation, would prefer to see block grants to the cities replace many of the categorical programs. Proposals, such as those for the dispersal of low-income housing made by the National Commission on Urban Problems, are also welcome since they draw further attention to suburban exclusiveness. Milwaukee officials recognize the many centers of resistance and the roadblocks to strengthening the city's position locally and nationally. Their strategies for moving against them have been developed under circumstances of regional fragmentation as well as higher governmental restraints. If the resulting actions appear strange or even illogical at times, it is perhaps because the metropolitical system that has evolved since the turn of the present century is itself out of place and contrary to good reason in the contemporary urban setting.

Notes

1. See R. D. Horvath, "The Sewage Disposal Controversy: A Study in Milwaukee Area Politics" (Thesis, Department of History, University of Wisconsin-Milwaukee, June, 1963); and Marvin Christian, "The Milwaukee Park Movement" (Thesis, Department of History, University of Wisconsin-Milwaukee, Aug., 1967).

2. A summary of bills pertaining to governmental consolidation in Milwaukee county is contained in a compilation by the Citizens' Governmental Research Bureau, dated October 6, 1947. For a well-documented study of governmental integration efforts in Milwaukee county, see Charles D. Goff, "The Politics of Governmental Integration in Metropolitan Milwaukee"

(Ph.D. diss., Department of Political Science, Northwestern University, 1952) 2 vols.

3. Reorganization efforts in Milwaukee county are also discussed in Henry J. Schmandt and William H. Standing, *The Milwaukee Metropolitan Study Commission* (Bloomington: Indiana University Press, 1965).

4. For a firsthand account of the tactics and rationale underlying Milwaukee's annexation efforts, see Frank Zeidler, "The Expansion of the City of Milwaukee from 1940 to 1960 and Some Related Matters" (unpublished manuscript in Milwaukee Public Library, n.d.).

5. The commission ruled that, because Milwaukee had been selling water to six suburbs, it "thereby assumed an obligation as a water public utility to provide such service to any municipal water utility." See David Gladfelter, "Water for Wauwatosa," in Richard Frost, ed., *Cases in State and Local Government* (Englewood Cliffs, N.J.: Prentice-Hall, 1961), pp. 280–91.

6. *Milwaukee Journal,* June 4, 1968.

7. Treasurer's Report to the Mayor, *Central City Benefits to Milwaukee Suburbs* (Milwaukee: Technical Committee for Fiscal Facts, 1968).

8. *Milwaukee Journal,* June 4, 1968.

9. As a study of Milwaukee suburbs shows, corresponding differences in the occupational status of council members reflect closely the socio-economic composition of their communities. Those who work within their own community—a growing phenomenon as industrial dispersion continues—tend to be more parochial in their civic decisions and less sympathetic to the problems of the central city than their counterparts who work in the latter jurisdiction. Henry J. Schmandt, "The City and the Ring: The Two-Way Street of Metropolitan Reorganization," *American Behavioral Scientist* (Nov., 1960), pp. 17–19.

10. Intergovernmental Cooperation Committee, *Final Report on Intergovernmental Cooperation in Milwaukee County* (Milwaukee: Metropolitan Study Commission, 1961).

11. *Milwaukee Journal,* Feb. 1, 1971.

12. George C. Berteau, address before Consortium Project on Regional Planning at University of Wisconsin-Waukesha, Nov. 5, 1970.

13. *Ibid.*

14. Knowles did not seek re-election in the November, 1970, gubernatorial contest. He was succeeded by Patrick Lucey, a Democrat, who pledged greater state concern for urban problems during his campaign.

15. The legislature's action precipitated the resignations of Douglas Weiford, director of the Department of Local Affairs and Development and Joseph Fagan, head of the Department of Industry, Labor and Human Relations, the two most important spokesmen for the governor's urban program. Both had been the target of conservative legislators because of their support of controversial programs of social rehabilitation.

16. In recent months, the Milwaukee Common Council president, Robert Jendusa, has advanced the notion of a metropolitan government in speeches before various civic groups. His proposal is to create a two-level regional gov-

ernment that would include Milwaukee county and the adjacent urbanized areas.

17. See, in this connection, Schmandt and Standing, *op. cit.*, p. 72.

18. Frank Zeidler, "Urbanism and Government 1957–1977," *Annals of the American Academy of Political and Social Science* 314 (Nov., 1957), pp. 77–81.

19. Letter from Henry Maier to the *New York Times*, March 17, 1970.

20. Donald Janson, "Milwaukee Mayor Fights Joint News Ownership," *New York Times*, May 4, 1969.

8

The Future

The last quarter of the twentieth century will be a crucial period, a watershed as it were, for the nation's major metropolises. The widely practiced policy of temporizing with the forces of change that have been building up in the large urban areas will no longer suffice to ward off serious breakdowns in the system. Either the cities and their peripheries—with state and federal cooperation—must act more resolutely and vigorously to accommodate the pressures of a postindustrial society or they will, at a minimum, suffer further erosion of their traditional roles and their highly vaunted autonomy. Their capacity to function effectively and adequately in a rapidly changing social and technical milieu will come under increasing challenge during the waning decades of the century. Whether the governments of the principal metropolitan centers will become mere administrative arms of the national bureaucracy; whether new forms of communities or cities will evolve in response to human needs; whether social change of the magnitude called for by contemporary developments is possible within the existing structure of urban society: these are among the questions that will be tested in the years ahead.

Milwaukee faces the future well equipped in some aspects and deficient in others. It possesses a strong economy, a skilled labor force, an honest and generally well-managed government, a sturdy and law-abiding citizenry, a relatively efficient physical plant, a pleasant living environment, and a potential for steady and sound growth. On the other side of the ledger, its provincialism, the ingrained feeling of moral superiority for its way of life, a disbelief that its social problems are either great or due to defects in its institutions and policies, and its inability to act decisively and with dispatch, no matter what the issue, are among the major disabilities that handicap it in facing the uncertain future. To these drawbacks must be added the deep political divisions between the central city and the periphery that not only militate against coordinated action by the metropolitan community as a whole but also result in costly intra-area strife and senseless competition. Weaknesses such as these are not, of course, peculiar to Milwaukee; they are present in varying degrees in most urban areas of comparable size. It is the extent to which many of them appear locally, as if the community were not able to shake off its small town origins, that helps to distinguish Wisconsin's largest SMSA from its counterparts elsewhere in the United States. Qualities of this nature would undoubtedly be advantageous in a simpler age; in the emerging world of the last decades of the twentieth century, they can be highly dysfunctional.

In Milwaukee, as elsewhere, the traditional belief that the self-interest of individual localities is the main issue at stake has been superseded in recent decades by two developments: the proliferation of a new set of "haves" in separately incorporated suburbs, practicing their own exclusionary zoning and gatekeeping functions and shaping their own growth and land use patterns independent of the rest of the urban complex; and the rise of a new set of politicized "have-nots" in the inner sections of the central city, fashioning their own power bases and their own tactics and goals. Taken together, these two broad trends constitute the pivotal nodes around which controversy has been waged and political strategies devised in the Milwaukee complex. They also provide a starting point or basis for extending the analysis beyond the time limits of the present to the likely direction in which the local metropolis will be forced to travel in the immediate years ahead.

The Face of the Community

The visitor of today who returns to Milwaukee in the year 2000 will not find Frank Lloyd Wright's Broadacres City nor Oscar Niemeyer's Brasilia. No major transformation in its physical shape or design is likely to greet him. Although he may be surprised at some of the changes in its appearance and functions, he will have no difficulty in recognizing the community as the one he knew in 1970. Certain trends in the interim can reasonably be anticipated. The central city will continue to be "renewed"—as indeed it has for more than a century—with obsolescent structures and facilities being replaced and technological innovations accommodated. Growth in the area will not be diverted into satellite communities separated from the principal urban concentrations by open space or greenbelts, nor into strip cities extending along radial corridors that emanate from Milwaukee and the core cities of the two other SMSA's, Racine and Kenosha, in the seven-county region. Instead, existing trends will in general continue, with the most intense development taking place at the outer edges of Milwaukee county and the adjoining areas of the surrounding counties. This movement to the periphery has already been facilitated by the more than 150 miles of freeways constructed in the region since the late 1950's and by the steady growth of industry and commerce in the outlying communities.

The land use and transportation plan adopted by the Southeastern Wisconsin Regional Planning Commission provides a blueprint for the likely course of the area's physical development over the next several decades. It explicitly calls for the outward expansion of existing urban settlements and the continuance of growth in concentric rings around the peripheries of the three major centers: Milwaukee, Racine, and Kenosha.[1] Known as the "controlled existing trend plan," it places heavy emphasis on the effect of the land market in determining the location, intensity, and character of future development. In doing so, however, it seeks to alter what it refers to as the "historic growth trends" by restricting concentrated development to areas having suitable soils and readily available sanitary sewer service.

Under the commission's plan, which has been formally adopted by all but one of the counties, 75 per cent of all new urban residential development in the region up to 1990 would be located within twenty miles of the Milwaukee CBD. The housing would be largely single-family, concentrated into 150 new cellular or neighborhood units. Medium densities would prevail, although approximately one-fifth of the residential land would be developed at low densities (one-half to five acres) and 4 per cent at high densities for apartment construction. The plan is obviously a response to political realities since neither the corridor nor satellite alternatives were acceptable to the governmental units of the area. As such, it constitutes no radical departure from prevalent growth patterns but simply attempts to order them more rationally. On the basis of the plan and the expressed views of local officials, it is reasonably certain that the physical face of the metropolis, at least for the next several decades, will essentially retain its present character although its urbanized parameters will be more extended.

The most visible physical changes, aside from mere expansion or "more of the same," will take place within the inner city, where redevelopment efforts, both public and private, have already resulted in significant land use alterations. The population decline of over 3 per cent that Milwaukee city experienced during the last decade will be more than recovered by 1980. Residential displacement by public projects will lessen, and this, coupled with the development of the city's last annexation conquest and its present renewal sites, will reverse the tide of the last ten years. Housing stock in the inner sections will generally improve although shortages will persist and the very worst neighborhoods will continue to deteriorate.[2] Programs such as Model Cities, urban renewal, and conservation and rehabilitation will bring further changes in the cityscape, but anyone who envisions a NASA-like or quantum developmental approach to Milwaukee, or for that matter to any of the nation's other major population settlements, is in for a bitter disappointment.

Freeway construction, which has taken a high toll of the city's building stock and is now threatening some suburban neighborhoods, will be substantially curbed in the present decade once the projects already well under way are completed. Many of the additions to the system now on the drawing board or in the early stages of development will be abandoned as opposition from environmentalists and affected residents mounts in intensity. Greater emphasis will be placed on mass transit and efficient utilization of the street system in efforts to cope with the continued increase in the number of private vehicles in operation. Fortunately, congestion at the level now experienced in many large cities, such as Chicago and New York, is still a long way off for Milwaukee. In fact, the problem of moving people and goods swiftly and efficiently remains soluble and within the area's capabilities. Political fragmentation and the lack of state intervention, however, militate against vigorous action toward this end.

The creation of a metropolitan or regional transportation authority (or the assumption of this responsibility by the county government) is imminent, because the privately owned transit company, one of the last in the nation to survive, is now badly faltering. But, whether an automobile-oriented community, such as Milwaukee, will be willing to make the commitments essential to achieving a rational and balanced transportation system remains highly questionable. What is likely to happen for some time is that the citizenry will continue to bemoan the "evils" of expressway construction yet be unwilling to take the steps necessary to provide a viable alternative.

The Socio-economic Profile

From 1960 to 1970, the rate of growth for the Milwaukee SMSA as a whole was significantly less than anticipated. Population projections and estimates by various agencies had indicated an increase of well over 200,000.[3] The actual census count, however, showed a gain of less than 125,000 for the four-county area. Predictions of growth in the outlying areas were fairly accurate, but the 100,000 increase projected for Milwaukee county turned out to be only slightly over 18,000. Lower birth rates and a substantial decline in in-migration in recent years were among the critical factors accounting for the wide variance between the forecasts and the actual head count. Milwaukee county, in fact, experienced a dramatic reversal. During the 1950's, it recorded approximately 15,000 net in-migrants; in the 1960's it had 104,000 net out-migrants. In the surrounding counties, the rate of in-migration also showed some decline, falling 37,000 short of offsetting Milwaukee's out-migration.

Although disturbing to some public officials and a blow to the civic "boosters" for whom bigger means better, Milwaukee area's growth during the last ten years can be viewed as more of a blessing than a cause of alarm. For, if the pace of the last decade continues into the immediate future, it would permit the region to manage its expansion in a more orderly and humane fashion than will be possible in those SMSA's where growth is more explosive. Current projections of 250,000 for the four-county area during the present decade will have to be revised downward in view of the developments reflected in the latest census figures. The rate of increase should nonetheless be sufficiently large to maintain the viability and strength of the metropolitan community as well as its progressive thrust. Milwaukee's place among the top SMSA's in population size may drop a notch or two in the coming decades, but, aside from hurt pride, little will be lost. The more important question in this regard relates not to numbers but to the distribution of the increase within the area. The continued poor showing of the central city and county in the growth category could be a cause of serious concern and require a major reassessment of their position within the region. However, as noted earlier, all indications point to a rectification of this situation before the end of the decade.

Industrially, the Milwaukee SMSA will remain predominantly a capital-goods producer oriented toward an export market. No dramatic changes are likely to be seen in this sector of the community's life. Milwaukee industry can hardly be characterized as avant-garde in either its behavior or perspectives. It seems destined to remain for some time in the traditional mold, with its operations solid, capable, and efficient, but with few startling innovations emanating from its ranks. The size of the labor force relative to the total population will decrease in the decades ahead as longer periods of education on the one end of the life cycle and earlier retirements on the other reduce the average span of working years. Along with this development, the percentage of workers engaged in manufacturing will decline, while the proportion of those in the service categories will rise. This trend, which has been observed nationally since the end of World War II, is characteristic of a society that is enjoying a high rate of productivity and rising standards of living.

Milwaukee's central business district will continue to serve as the commercial and financial, as well as the governmental and cultural, hub of the metropolis, although some changes in its character and functions are inevitable. Shopping will decline in relative importance but will still remain an integral component of the downtown economy. The space devoted to office use will increase significantly, even though the lion's share of new industrial growth will take place in the peripheral areas of the metropolis. All indications, including the substantial amount of office-building that has taken place in recent years (thirty new major structures were built in the last decade after a long period of inactivity), point to the growing importance of the downtown area as a transactional and decision-making center for southeastern Wisconsin. The completion of the civic plaza in the near future, including a new convention complex and additional hotel accommodations, will further stimulate the activity base of the area. Similarly, the increasing number of new cultural facilities and recreational components, together with beautification of the Milwaukee river banks, will add to the CBD's capacity to attract people. While all of these developments will not be wholly accomplished during the 1970's, they will be well under way.

It is useless to speculate on the consequences that technological changes might have on the character of Milwaukee's economy or on its physical pattern. New break-throughs in the manner of processing raw materials, disposing or recycling waste, transporting people and goods, delivering health services, and constructing housing could radically alter present arrangements and trends. However, because of the existing investments in plants, buildings, equipment, expressways, and other costly capital facilities, along with the organizational structure and vested interests of both business and labor, any sudden transformation of the community's economic system is highly unlikely. Major changes are certain to occur, but, like the process of growing old, they will be incremental and cumulative, not precipitous or total.

Socially, the composition of the area, like its economic structure, will undergo modification, but no drastic changes are in sight during the 1970's. Despite talk of the central city's becoming exclusively the home of the poor and of racial minorities, this fate is not in Milwaukee's immediate future. Urban renewal, rehabilitation, the Model Cities program, apartment construction in the inner city, the development of the northwest extremities (acquired by annexation in 1962) for primarily middle- and upper-middle–income families, and the relative stability of the working-class southside are all factors that militate against conversion of the common image into reality. Migration of low-income families and ethnic minorities into the area has declined in recent years; and, while the proportion of blacks in the inner city will continue to grow, no prospect of a black majority is in the offing, as is the case in Saint Louis, Cleveland, Detroit, and several other large core municipalities.

There is little reason, moreover, to believe that either the social structure or social geography of the area will be transformed
during the next decade or even beyond. The mosaic of subcom-
munities segregated by income, class, and race will remain
largely in the present pattern, with the central city shouldering
a disproportionate share of responsibility for the economically
and socially disadvantaged segments of the metropolitan population and the outlying communities attracting a large percentage of white families in the lower-middle to upper-income levels.
Apartheid will continue to predominate, although penetration
of suburbia by nonwhites will become more common. This penetration, however, will not achieve significant proportions in the
absence of strong federal and state policies promoting the movement of racial minorities into the peripheral areas.

The lot of Milwaukee's minority groups will generally be bettered in the coming decades, but the process will be agonizingly
slow and far below that which justice and societal well-being
mandate. What progress is accomplished will be largely the result of the insistent demands of black and brown leaders and
federal and state pressures rather than any clear-cut commitment
or determination on the part of the local white citizenry—
central-city dwellers and suburbanites alike—to correct the existing inequities and move decisively toward the elimination of
institutionalized racism in the community. Milwaukee is little
different in this respect from other northern and eastern metropolises; like them, it is incapable of reaching a consensus
internally on the steps to be taken to ameliorate its social and
racial problems. Only intervention from higher levels of public
authority will push it along this path.

Milwaukee's share of the national income is unlikely to show
any major change in the next decade or two. Per-capita and
median family income will remain relatively high in comparison
to most other metropolitan areas, and the extremes of poverty
and wealth will be less prevalent. Although poverty in the community will be far from eliminated by 1980, the proportion of
those in this category will gradually decline as the educational

level and occupational training of all groups rise and as national income redistribution policies (such as family assistance, rent supplements, and increased Social Security benefits) expand. And, as these developments occur, a higher percentage of the central city population will be accorded greater freedom of choice in housing, life style, and place of residence. However, even aside from the question of relative deprivation, a significant minority of Milwaukeeans will still remain outside the mainstream of the society's affluence and its reward structure. This minority will be confined almost wholly to the inner city and will continue to be a potentially explosive factor. That this situation is permitted to persist attests to the nation's lack of commitment to the eradication of poverty and discrimination and to the intellectual bankruptcy of many of its social policies. Metropolitan communities such as Milwaukee are caught in this vortex to which they themselves have been major contributors.

The Governmental System

The governmental issues of metropolitan significance have long since shifted from questions of territorial consolidation to more functional considerations or accommodations. The integration of area-wide services rather than political merger has become the byword of those who are seeking a more geographically inclusive government for the Milwaukee metropolis. Civic reformers and some central-city and county officials are talking in these terms, although no common plans or strategies for achieving such a goal have evolved. Despite numerous pronouncements and the active interest of such groups as the Wisconsin Metropolitan Alliance,[4] the movement for reorganizing the existing political structure has remained at the level of abstraction and public rhetoric. Suburban governments continue to be united in their opposition to any basic alteration of the political *status quo,* and no groundswell of citizen support for metropolitan reform has evolved.

The issue, however, is by no means dead. Governor Lucey, in April, 1971, appointed a Study Committee on Metropolitan

Problems to examine, in his words, "the nonsystem of patchwork governments." In charging the committee, the governor warned that state intervention in the governance of urban localities would increase unless metropolitan areas clean their own house. As he put it, "If localities achieve an orderly organization which permits an equitable taxing procedure, the encroachment of the state in local affairs will then be abated."[5] The last state-created study commission, a decade back, led to no significant changes, but the situation at the beginning of the 1970's may be more propitious to action. Since the earlier effort, Milwaukee has faced a series of social and racial crises, the problem of transportation has worsened, and public attention has been directed to the critical need of protecting the environment. A movement for some form of metropolitan restructuring might well capitalize on these developments.

As the situation presently stands, Mayor Maier follows a strategy of survival in the politics of the Milwaukee urban complex. Fully cognizant of the central city's inability to cope effectively with its social problems on its own, he seeks consistently to lay a large portion of the blame and burden at the doorsteps of other governmental units and agencies. Thus, he vigorously attacks the suburbs and the state government for "abdicating" their obligations to the inner city; he proposes a metropolitan social district to handle the costly and politically sensitive issues; and he calls on the national government to enlarge materially its urban aid programs. Suburban officials, in response, fight a rear-guard action, charging the Milwaukee city government with creating its own "mess" and with trying to intimidate the outlying municipalities into assuming responsibilities that their residents are already meeting through county, state, and federal taxes, as well as through private means.

County executive Doyne, hampered by a rival leadership faction within the Board of Supervisors, has not moved to enlarge the substantive role of county government in any significant fashion but has devoted his efforts mainly developing a modern administrative structure to improve the execution of its existing functions and responsibilities. Externally, his one major attempt to play an area-wide coordinating role through creation of the Intergovernmental Cooperation Council has been impeded by the failure of the central city to join, on the one hand, and the reluctance of the suburban governments to act in concert, on the other. His relationship with the mayor has not been close although he has at no time publicly challenged the city's head even when basic differences over policy have arisen.[6] The latter, in turn, while often critical of county government actions, has excluded the county executive from among the targets of his strategy. So long as the present incumbents remain in office, this "arm's length" *modus vivendi* will likely continue. Given different occupants in the future, the two positions could become strong competitors for political leadership in the Milwaukee community.

Operating within this general milieu, the Regional Planning Commission walks a tightrope between the needs of area-wide planning and coordination and the sensitivities of its constituents' units. HUD officials, however, are now demanding that the agency devote more attention to social issues and play a more active part in policy promotion and stimulation. For example, they recently withheld funds for a comprehensive housing study until the commission agreed to include a crash planning program of housing for low-income families. It is becoming increasingly apparent that the regional body's powers and responsibilities will have to be enlarged and its general reluctance to move beyond its physical planning function overcome if it is to play the role that federal officials are demanding. If such changes are not made, this role will pass by default to either the state or some new regional or metropolitan authority.

When we move outside the metropolitan system, the picture is mixed. The state government, with some exceptions, has traditionally slighted the needs of the inner city and taken little affirmative action to assist in the solution of its basic problems. The present governor and an increasing number of legislators have evidenced signs of reversing this "hands-off" policy, but the

fiscal bind that faces the state will prevent any large-scale intervention in this regard, at least in the immediate future. At the
federal level, authorities had until recently exhibited little inclination to utilize their sanctioning powers in the aid programs
to promote meaningful cooperation among the local entities or
open up locational opportunities for the disadvantaged beyond
the confines of the central city. Now, however, there are growing
indications—HUD's action in the housing study is an example—
that the national bureaucracy is determined to play a more influential role in the affairs of the metropolis. This trend is not
likely to diminish despite the Nixon Administration's talk of
returning power to the states and localities.

Because of current trends and the existing predispositions of
the various participants involved in the process of governing
the Milwaukee metropolis, several sets of developments appear
within the range of strong possibilities for the next decade. An
associate of the mayor indicated two of these when he said,
"Cities must do something about their internal structures. Any
businessman who found himself with as little authority and as
much responsibility as the typical mayor would go berserk in a
week. Also, we may have reached the point where metropolitan
government should be imposed from the top."[7]

The events of recent months lend added emphasis to the first
point. Although Mayor Maier has managed to overcome the disabilities of his weak structural position, the increasing difficulty
he is experiencing will compel him to renew efforts to strengthen
the formal powers of his office. Maier, in fact, is now facing a
serious threat to the strong political and administrative position
he has managed to achieve over the past ten years. The threat,
moreover, comes from within city government, not from outside.
In his efforts to secure confirmation of Kenneth Fry to the direc-
torship of the Department of City Development, he for the first
time abandoned his cautious and conciliatory approach to the
Common Council and openly challenged it. The appointment
provided a convenient issue on which those members who are
outside the leadership faction supportive of the mayor could

unite. Although Maier was successful in this case, it is too early to say whether he can maintain the position of influence he has so assiduously cultivated or whether the council will regain its traditional primacy. The answer may have to await the 1972 municipal elections. The mayor has indicated that he will work for the defeat of those aldermen who were active in their opposition to the Fry nomination. This, however, is a dangerous strategy, in light of the political culture of Milwaukee.

In the larger arena, concerted efforts to achieve some form of metropolitan government for the urbanized portion of the Milwaukee SMSA are certain. Regardless of whether any basic reorganization of the existing system materializes during the 1970's, action toward this end will not be lacking. It may take the form of enlarging the jurisdictional sphere of the county government to include additional functions of an area-wide character, such as waste disposal, relocation services for those families displaced from their homes by renewal and other types of public projects, acquisition and operation of the mass transit facilities, construction of low-income housing, and acquisition of the public museum and central library. It may likewise involve strengthening of the regional planning commission to give it limited control over urban expansion, including the power to veto, or at least temporarily suspend, acts of local units that contravene basic aspects of areal development plans. And should a new metropolitan governing authority fail to evolve, this agency may also move toward the assumption of operative authority in several fields of regional scope—pollution control, for example—à la the Metropolitan Council of the Twin Cities.

Along with the centripetal tendencies, there will also be a growing movement for the decentralization of certain functions within the core city, as they are already in suburbia. This will be particularly true in the case of education, where the demand for neighborhood control over the schools will compel a reluctant response from those in charge of the system. The pressures for area-wide concentration of certain powers and the demand for greater neighborhood autonomy represented by these trends are not necessarily contradictory but may well presage the future evolution of the metropolitan governmental structure. By moving toward a territorially inclusive authority with jurisdiction over the principal maintenance functions, such as transportation, water supply, sewage disposal, and conservation, the devolution of certain life-style powers to the neighborhood or subcommunity becomes possible. In this way, the necessities for large-scale administration may be balanced by the virtues of small-scale control over matters of peculiar concern to locality residents.

These various developments will be accompanied by changes in the method of financing local governments. Cities everywhere are feeling the painful squeeze of an outmoded and grossly inequitable fiscal system. As of this writing, for example, Detroit is laying off hundreds of public workers, Cleveland has closed its police academy and dismissed its current class of cadets, and the New York City school system is cutting 6500 teachers and other personnel from its payroll in order to meet a $40 million budget deficit. Similar instances can be cited across the country. Direct federal sharing with the cities, aside from the existing categorical grants, is in the offing as is other remedial action. In Wisconsin, the state will modify its revenue-sharing policies to eliminate the worst inequities and give Milwaukee a measure of relief for the high social costs it must bear as the core element of the metropolis. Educational costs will gradually be assumed by the state although the administration of the schools will remain in the hands of local boards. The financing of public welfare is likely to be taken over entirely by the national government as the cries of the localities for assistance mount. These developments, together with some form of guaranteed income plan for American families, will ease the property tax burden for Milwaukeeans and lessen the intra-area competition for industry and resources.

The state government, in addition to revising tax policies, will also begin to play a more active role in the affairs of Wisconsin's metropolitan communities. Through its departments and agencies, such as Local Affairs and Development, Natural Resources, and Transportation, it will become more insistent on coordinated growth policies and practices in the urban areas and less sympathetic to local units that persist in ignoring regional plans. It will also take modest steps to assure better shelter for low-income families through such devices as state-chartered and subsidized developmental corporations, and will move with greater firmness to reduce the more flagrant forms of discrimination against racial minorities in the fields of employment, education, and housing.

Unpromising as the present situation may appear for effecting basic changes in the governmental system of the area, the problem of adapting the structure to the emerging needs of the Milwaukee community will not disappear with the passage of time. The informal and voluntaristic arrangements among local units and the early consolidation of several key functions at the county level have served the community reasonably well, but their inadequacy to cope with the new social, economic, and environmental issues of urban life is becoming increasingly evident. The issues of race, housing, relocation, transportation, exclusionary zoning, competition for industry, and conservation of open space, among others, are simply not amenable to the decision-making structure and processes of the existing system. These are the problem areas, moreover, that will grow in magnitude and intensity in the immediate decades ahead.

The cumulative forces of demand and change observed throughout this volume show that conditions determining the quality of life in Milwaukee, as in other large metropolitan areas, are neither subject to effective control by a community power structure nor finally resolved in the pluralistic arena of the local polity. External factors now intrude with increasing intensity to set the community's dimensions of control over its destiny. Although these exogenous forces are not likely to lead to any radical departure from present growth patterns in the region nor to reconstruction of the existing system of fragmented government, local pressures for more functions, more amenities, more equity, and more responsiveness will continue to generate further outside intervention. The strategies and change variables that have evolved in this general milieu are summarized in the following observations. If not culminating in an urban theory, the wider directions they represent at least indicate the new paradoxes upon which any conceptualization of the local or metropolitan political system must now be based.

1. Because suburbanization has made the restructuring of local governments and the significant redistribution of state revenues virtually nonnegotiable items, central city officials have increasingly tended to adopt a style of conflict politics (the "have-not" cities agenda is an example) rather than one of co-operation in their efforts to secure intra-area and state aid.

2. Strategies for civic advancement devised by central city officials tend to run on different tracks: more economic development within the core municipality to offset suburban competition and more sharing of social responsibilities and projects with governments outside its jurisdiction.

3. Changes in the economic and social setting that confront city officials are also two-directional in nature: more centralization of policy directives for developmental programs (the scattered-sites requirement of HUD, for example) and more decentralization of control over the administration of such programs (resident participation in community action projects and Model Cities are instances of this trend).

4. The preference of local public officials, including regional planning commissioners, to emphasize physical development rather than social reform has prompted "have-nots" within the central city to act outside the local political arena (on HUD and other federal agencies, and on downtown businessmen who fear disruption).

5. The growing activism or politicization of minority groups in the inner core, along with the zero-sum game played by central city and suburban officials, draw state and national functionaries increasingly into the metropolitan arena as mediators and stimulators, resulting in new rewards and new rules for local actors.

The Unanswered Question

It is easy to speculate about the future but difficult to predict it. We can conjure up visions of domed cities, moving sidewalks, intracity air travel, and computerized factories dominating the urban landscape. Or we can temper our imagination, eschew the prophetic and global, and concern ourselves with relatively short-run futures. Most predictions by social scientists are extrapolations of past trends, but even this procedure is highly tenuous, as the events of recent years have demonstrated. The creative powers of man and the idiosyncracies of his behavior constantly conspire to produce the unexpected and embarrass the forecaster. The urban analyst can be reasonably certain of developments within small stretches of time and with relation to particular limited spheres of community functioning. Beyond this, it would be naïve to place too much faith in the predictive capacities of urban planners and specialists.

We need not be reminded that American society has entered a period of enormous change in which long-established institutions and traditions are being vigorously challenged. The big question that remains for the major metropolitan areas is whether the moderate modifications of their governmental structures and the incremental measures being taken to ameliorate the social ills of their constituencies will be sufficient to keep the urban system functional in the face of these challenges. The answer in the case of Milwaukee is probably "yes"—at least for the next decade. Beyond that, the prognosis becomes more dubious. The storm warnings have already been raised. Much depends on how well they are heeded and acted upon, both nationally and locally. The stakes of urban society are far too high for temporizing.

Notes

1. Southeastern Wisconsin Regional Planning Commission, *Recommended Regional Land Use and Transportation Plans 1990* (Waukesha, Wis.: Nov., 1966).
2. Lawrence S. Katz, director of the Federal Housing Administration in

Wisconsin, estimates that housing shortages in Milwaukee can be overcome in ten years but only if the state government takes an active role (*Milwaukee Journal*, Dec. 20, 1970).

3. See Southeastern Wisconsin Regional Planning Commission, *1968 Annual Report* (Waukesha, Wis., April, 1969), pp. 28–29.

4. The Wisconsin Metropolitan Alliance is a small group of Milwaukee area residents, including several public officials, who organized in 1969 to promote restructuring of the metropolitan political system. Their activities thus far have been limited largely to studying possible alternatives. The individual responsible for the creation of the alliance, however, has been appointed by the governor to head the new metropolitan study committee.

5. *Milwaukee Sentinel*, May 4, 1971.

6. The most recent example of this occurred in connection with the question of waste disposal. After extensive study and negotiation, the county government prepared to enter into a contract with a private firm for the county-wide handling of waste. Execution of the contract depended on the concurrence of Milwaukee city and the major suburban municipalities. Most of the latter indicated their willingness, but the mayor withheld city approval, contending that the costs were too high. Later, after much maneuvering, the city unilaterally contracted with another firm. Many of the County Board members publicly expressed resentment at the mayor's action, but the county executive, although obviously perturbed, did not challenge him.

7. Kenneth Fry, "Central Cities Fight Back," *Nation's Business* (Sept., 1969), p. 62.

Appendix A

Milwaukee Area Population, 1900–1970

Year	Milwaukee City	Milwaukee County	SMSA[a]
1900	285,315	330,017	405,199
1910	373,857	433,187	511,194
1920	457,147	539,449	624,109
1930	578,249	725,263	821,566
1940	587,472	766,885	877,044
1950	637,392	871,047	1,014,211
1960	741,324	1,036,041	1,278,856
1970	717,099	1,054,063	1,403,688

[a] Adjusted to include four counties presently in SMSA.

Appendix B

Selected Population Characteristics, City of Milwaukee

Year	Per Cent Foreign Born	Per Cent Non-White	Median School Year Completed	Median Family Income
1900	31	0.2	n.a.	n.a.
1910	30	0.3	n.a.	n.a.
1920	24	0.5	n.a.	n.a.
1930	19	1.3	n.a.	n.a.
1940	14	1.5	8.3	n.a.
1950	10	3.6	9.1	$3,800
1960	8	8.9	10.5	$6,664
1970	7[a]	14.7	11.0[a]	$8,600[a]

[a] Estimated.

Appendix C

Milwaukee Mayors, 1876–1971[a]

Date	Name	Party Affiliation
1876	A. R. R. Butler	Democrat
1878	John Black	Democrat
1880	Thomas H. Brown	Republican
1882	John M. Stowell	Democrat
1884–88	Emil Wallber	Republican
1888	Thomas H. Brown	Republican
1890	George W. Peck	Democrat
1892	Peter J. Somers	Democrat
1894	John C. Koch	Republican
1896	W. G. Rauschenberger	Republican
1898–1906	David S. Rose	Democrat
1906	Sherburn M. Becker	Republican
1908	David S. Rose	Democrat
1910	Emil Seidel	Socialist
1912–16	Gerhard Bading	Fusion
1916–40	Daniel W. Hoan	(Socialist)[b]
1940	Carl F. Zeidler	(Republican)
1944	John L. Bohn	(Republican)
1948–1960	Frank P. Zeidler	(Socialist)
1960–	Henry W. Maier	(Democrat)

[a] The mayoralty term was two years during the period 1876 and 1920 and four years thereafter.

[b] Known party affiliation. Partisan elections were abolished by state law in 1912.

Appendix D

Per Cent Voting Democratic for President, U.S. Senator, and Governor, Milwaukee County, 1946–70

Year	Milwaukee City President	U.S. Senator	Governor	Milwaukee County Suburbs President	U.S. Senator	Governor
1946	—	46	50	—	37	37
1948	61	—	56	47	—	44
1950	—	59	58	—	45	43
1952	52	63	54	40	54	43
1954	—	—	60	—	—	46
1956	47	53	60	35	38	46
1958	—	68	66	—	54	51
1960	62	—	63	49	—	51
1962	—	66	63	—	51	47
1964	70	67	63	57	53	48
1966	—	—	60	—	—	44
1968	56	72	59	44	61	40
1970	—	80	71	—	69	53

SOURCE: Sarah C. Ettenheim, *How Milwaukee Voted* (Milwaukee: Institute of Governmental Affairs, University of Wisconsin, 1970).

Appendix E

Governments in Milwaukee County (Cities)

City	Year Incorporated	1970[a] Population	Area Square Miles	Number on Council	Term of Office (Years)	Elected Executives[d]
First Class (over 150,000)						
Milwaukee	1846	717,099	95.8	19	4	MKLT
Second Class (39,000–150,000)						
West Allis	1906	71,723	11.6	10	4	MACLT
Wauwatosa	1897	58,676	13.0	16	4c	MLT
Third Class (10,000–39,000)						
South Milwaukee	1897	23,297	4.8	8	2	MCLT
Cudahy	1906	22,078	4.7	10	2	MCLT
Greenfield	1957	24,424	12.6	4	4e	M
Glendale	1950	13,436	5.5	6	2e	MCLT
Fourth Class (under 10,000)						
Saint Francis[b]	1951	10,489	2.9	6	2	MCLT
Franklin[b]	1956	12,247	34.6	4	2	M
Oak Creek[b]	1955	13,901	28.2	6	2	MCT

[a] U.S. Census of Population, 1970.

[b] State law provides that, in order for a city to change from one class to another, it must qualify in population and adopt an ordinance specifying the change. *Wis. Stat.* 62.05(2). Saint Francis, Franklin, and Oak Creek qualify in size to be third class cities, but they have not taken the formal steps necessary for the change.

[c] Aldermen serve overlapping terms.

[d] M = Mayor, A = Assessor, C = Clerk, K = Controller, L = Attorney, T = Treasurer.

Appendix F

Governments in Milwaukee County (Villages)

Village	Year Incorporated	1970 Population	Area Square Miles	Number on Board[a]	Term of Office (Years)[b]	Elected Executives[c]
Whitefish Bay	1892	17,394	2.1	7	3	ACL
Shorewood	1900	15,576	1.6	7	3	None
Brown Deer	1955	12,622	4.2	7	3	T
Fox Point	1926	7,937	2.8	7	3	None
Greendale	1938	15,089	5.2	7	2	None
Hales Corners	1952	7,771	3.1	7	3	None
West Milwaukee	1906	4,405	1.1	7	2	ACT
Bayside	1953	4,461	2.3	7	3	None
River Hills	1930	1,561	5.5	7	3	CT

a Village president and six trustees.
b Members of village governing boards serve overlapping terms.
c A = Assessor, C = Clerk, L = Attorney, T = Treasurer.
d Part of Bayside is in Ozaukee County.
SOURCES: *Wisconsin Blue Book, 1970* (Wisconsin: State of Wisconsin, 1970) pp. 692–700; *Municipal Year Book, 1970* (Washington, D.C.: The International City Management Association, 1970) pp. 578–653.

Appendix G

Boards, Commissions, and Committees in
Milwaukee City Government

Key

Adv.—Advisory
C.—Confirmed by Common Council
Co.—Coordinating body
Years—Terms of office;
I.T.—Independent taxing body
M.—Appointments by mayor
Mem.—Members

No C.—No confirmation by Common
  Council
P.D.—Policy-determining body
Pres. C.C.—Appointments by presi-
  dent of Common Council
Q.J.—Quasi-judicial body
Salary—As indicated
S.E.—Special events

Annuity and Benefit Fund, Retirement Board of Firemen's
  P.D.—7 mem.; 1 by M., 4 years; 3 by firemen, 3 years;
    2 by annuitants, 2 years; city treasurer or deputy—no salary
Annuity and Benefit Fund, Retirement Board of Policemen's
  P.D.—7 mem.; 1 by M., 4 years; 3 by policemen, 3 years;
    2 by annuitants, 2 years; city treasurer or deputy—no salary
Annuity and Pension Board, Employees' Retirement System
  P.D.—7 mem.; 3 by pres. C.C., 3 years; 3 by employees, 3 years;
    city comptroller (ex officio)—no salary
Annuity and Retirement Fund Trustees, Public School Teachers'
  P.D.—10 mem.; 4 by school bd., 2 years; 4 by teachers, 2 years;
    pres. of school bd. and city treasurer (ex officio)—no salary
Appeals, Board of (Zoning)
  Q.J.—5 mem.; M.—C.—3 years—$1,320 per year, chm., $1,980 per year
Art Center Board
(city representatives)
  P.D.—M.—C.—1 year—no salary.
Art Commission
  Adv.—9 mem.; 1 alderman by pres. C.C.; 4 by the 2 ex-officio members
    and council member—2 M.—4 years—no salary
Assessment, Board of
  Q.J.—5 mem.—M.—C.—5 years—$1,650 per year
Auditorium-Arena Board
(city representatives, ex officio)
  (Auditorium Company Representatives—elected by stockholders—1 year)
  P.D.—no salary

229

Building Code Committee
 P.D.—12 mem.—M.—C.—5 years—(alderman—4 years)—no salary
Capital Improvements Committee
 Co.—3 mem.—no salary
Central Safety Committee
 Adv.—28 mem.—Appointed by department heads—no salary
Christmas Tree Commission, Municipal
 S.E.—7 mem.—M.—No C.—3 years—no salary
City Plan Commission
 P.D.—7 mem.—M.—C.—3 years—$660 per year
City Records Committee
 P.D.—5 mem.—no salary
City Service Commission
 P.D.—5 mem.—M.—No C.—5 years—$1,320 per year ($1,650 per year for
  Pres.)
Community Relations, Commission on
 Adv.—9 mem.—M.—C.—3 years—no salary
Crime Prevention Commission, Metropolitan
(city representatives)
 Adv.—M.—no C.—3 years—no salary
Debt, Commissioners of Public
 P.D.—3 mem.—M.—C.—3 years—no salary
Development Advisory Committee, Citizens'
 Adv.—15 mem.—M.—C.—terms, various—no salary
Election Commissioners, Board of
 P.D.—3 mem.—M.—No C.—4 years—$1,650 per year
Electrical License and Examining Board
 Adv.—5 mem.—M.—C.—3 years—$660 per year
Estimates, Board of
(members on board in ex-officio capacity)
 P.D.—11 mem.—no salary
Examining Committee for Stationary Engineers and Firemen
 Adv.—3 mem.—M.—C.—2 years—$660 per year
Fire and Police Commissioners, Board of
 P.D.—5 mem.—M.—C.—5 years—$1,320 per year
Fourth of July Commission
 S.E.—20 mem.—M.—No C.—3 years—($1,200 per year for Secy.)
Harbor Commissioners, Board of
 P.D.—5 Mem.—M.—C.—3 years—No salary
Housing Authority
 P.D.—5 mem.—M.—C.—5 years—no salary
Library Board of Trustees
 P.D.—9 mem.—M.—No C.—4 years—no salary
Motion Picture Commission
 Adv.—9 mem.—M.—No C.—4 years—($1,200 per year for Exec. Secy.)
Museum Board of Trustees
 P.D.—9 mem.—M. No C.—4 years—no salary
Parking Commission
 Adv.—7 mem.—M.—C.—3 years—no salary
Purchases, Central Board of

(Members on the board in ex-officio capacity)
  P.D.—7 mem.—no salary
Redevelopment Authority
  P.D.—7 mem.—M.—C.—5 years—no salary
Review, Board of
  Q.J.—5 mem.—M.—C.—5 years—$3,180 per year
Safety Commission
  Adv.—18 mem.—M.—C.—3 years—no salary
School Directors, Board of
  I.T.—Elected by the people—15 mem.—6 years—$600 per year
Sewerage Commission, City
  I.T.—5 mem.—M.—C.—5 years—$600 per year
Sewerage Commission of Milwaukee County, Metropolitan
  I.T.—3 mem.—Appointed by the governor—6 years—no salary
Standards and Appeals, Board of
  Q.J.—9 mem.—M.—C.—5 years—no salary
Symphony Orchestra Board
(3 city representatives)
  P.D.—M.—C.—no salary
United Nations Day, Committee for the Observance of
  S.E.—30 mem.—M.—C.—3 years—no salary
Vocational and Adult Education, Board of
  I.T.—appointed by school board—5 mem.—4 years—no salary

Appendix H

Department Heads and Assistants in Milwaukee City Government

Department	Title	Appointment Method	Term
Mayor	Mayor	Elective	4 yrs.
	Chief Administrator to Mayor	Exempt	
	Administrative Assistant III	"	
	Staff Assistant to the Mayor	"	
Common Council	Alderman	Elective	4 yrs.
City Clerk	City Clerk	Common Council	4 yrs.
	Deputy City Clerk	Appointive	
	Information Secretary to the Common Council	Exempt	
	Labor Negotiator	Civil Service	
	Labor Economist	" "	
City Attorney	City Attorney	Elective	4 yrs.
	Deputy City Attorney	Appointive	
City Comptroller	Comptroller	Elective	4 yrs.
	Deputy City Comptroller	Appointive	
City Treasurer	City Treasurer	Elective	4 yrs.
	Deputy City Treasurer	Appointive	
Board of Assessments	Acting Secretary, Board of Assessments	Civil Service	
Budget, Bureau of	Budget Supervisor	Civil Service	
	Assistant Budget Supervisor	" "	
Building Inspection and Safety Engineering	Inspector of Buildings	By Mayor (with confirmation)	4 yrs.'
	Deputy Inspector of Buildings	Civil Service	
Central Board of Purchases	City Purchasing Agent	Exempt (appointed by Board)	
	Deputy City Purchasing Agent	Civil Service	

Department	*Title*	*Appointment* Method Term
City Development, Department of	Director of City Development	By Mayor (with 2 yrs.' confirmation)
	Assistant Director of City Development	Exempt
City Service Commission	City Personnel Director	Civil Service
	Assistant City Personnel Director	" "
Civil Defense Administration	Director of Civil Defense	Mayor serves as Director
	Assistant to the Director of Civil Defense	By Mayor (without confirmation)
Election Commission	Executive Secretary, Board of Election Commissioners	Civil Service
Employees' Retirement System	Executive Director, Employees' Retirement System	Exempt
	Assistant Executive Director Employees' Retirement System	Civil Service
Fire Department	Chief Engineer	Fire & Police Commission
	First Assistant Chief Engineer	Fire & Police Commission
Harbor Commission	Municipal Port Director	Civil Service
	Deputy Municipal Port Director	" "
Health Department	Commissioner of Health	By Mayor (with 4 yrs.' confirmation)
	Deputy Commissioner of Health	Appointive
Intergovernmental Fiscal Liaison	Director of Liaison	Civil Service 3 yrs. (appointed by Mayor with confirmation)
	Fiscal Director	Civil Service 3 yrs. (appointed by Mayor with confirmation)
Library, Public	City Librarian	Civil Service
	Assistant City Librarian	" "
	Municipal Reference Librarian	" "
Milwaukee Commission on Community Relations	Secretary, Milwaukee Commission on Community Relations	Civil Service
Museum, Public	Museum Director	Civil Service
	Assistant Museum Director	" "
Police Department	Chief of Police	Fire & Police Commission

Department	Title	Appointment Method	Term
	Inspector of Police	Fire & Police Commission	
Director-Safety	Managing Director-Safety	Civil Service (appointed by Mayor)	
	Assistant Managing Director	Civil Service	
Tax	Tax Commissioner	By Mayor (with 3 yrs.' confirmation)	
	Deputy Tax Commissioner	Appointive	
Department of Public Works			
General Office	Commissioner of Public Works	By Mayor (with 2 yrs.' confirmation)	
	Deputy Commissioner of Public Works	Appointive	
Bridges and Public Buildings	Superintendent of Bridges and Public Buildings	Civil Service	
	Assistant Superintendent of Bridges and Public Buildings	" "	
Engineers	City Engineer	By Mayor (with 3 yrs.' confirmation)	
	Assistant City Engineer	Civil Service	
Forestry	City Forester	Civil Service	
	Assistant City Forester	" "	
Garbage Collection and Disposal	Superintendent of Garbage Collection and Disposal	Civil Service	
	Assistant Superintendent of Garbage Coll. & Disposal	" "	
Municipal Equipment	Automotive Equipment Superintendent	Civil Service	
	Assistant Automotive Equipment Superintendent	" "	
Plumbing Inspection	Superintendent of Plumbing Inspection	Civil Service	
	Assistant Superintendent of Plumbing Inspection	" "	
Street Sanitation	Superintendent of Street Sanitation	Civil Service	
	Assistant Superintendent of Street Sanitation	" "	
Street and Sewer Maintenance	Superintendent of Street and Sewer Maintenance	Civil Service	

Department	Title	Appointment Method	Term
	Assistant Superintendent of Sewer Maintenance	"	"
	Assistant Superintendent of Street Maintenance	"	"
Traffic Engineering and Electrical Services	Traffic Engineer and Superintendent of Electrical Services	Civil Service	
	Assistant Superintendent of Traffic Engineering and Electrical Services	"	"
Water	Superintendent of Water Works	Civil Service	
	Assistant Superintendent of Water Works	"	"

Appendix I

Revenue Sources to Finance 1970 Budgets of the Twenty-nine Milwaukee County General Governments[a]

| Governments | Total 1970 Budgets (1) | Per Cent Increase over 1969 (2) | 1970 Per Person Budget (3) | Per Cent of 1970 Budgets Financed by: | | | | |
				Property Taxes (4)	Shared Taxes (5)	State Aids (6)	Taxes and Aids (5)+(6)	Other Revenues (7)
County of Milwaukee	$156,106,176	18.3	$137	40.3	8.7	15.9	24.6	35.1
City of Milwaukee	145,987,180	10.4	185	46.3	26.6	3.1	29.7	24.0
18, Suburbs	48,950,576	11.5	138	30.6	51.1	4.2	55.3	14.1
Central Area								
Wauwatosa	8,977,587	8.3	143	24.3	53.4	4.8	58.2	17.5
West Allis	11,334,628	12.4	144	53.6	35.1	3.9	39.0	7.4
West Milwaukee	1,984,195	19.3	354	62.9	35.1	1.0	36.1	1.0
Southside								
Cudahy	2,840,331	12.6	123	39.7	40.9	3.3	44.2	16.1
Franklin	1,049,750	15.7	86	16.5	47.2	12.1	59.3	24.2
Greendale	1,282,426	20.9	86	24.0	51.6	7.1	58.7	17.3
Greenfield	2,089,306	23.2	80	13.6	44.8	7.1	51.9	34.5
Hales Corners	849,390	6.9	110	17.7	46.0	6.5	52.5	29.8
Oak Creek	3,631,941	14.2	249	0.0c	104.1	3.5	107.6	3.5
Saint Francis	1,081,088	11.4	89	27.6	54.7	3.5	58.2	14.2
South Milwaukee	2,711,660	10.0	115	36.4	45.0	4.3	49.3	14.3
Northside								
Bayside	799,306	8.6	183	13.8	58.4	4.5	62.9	23.3
Brown Deer	1,319,930	8.7	119	31.1	45.8	5.5	51.3	17.6
Fox Point	1,349,509	–9.4b	165	4.6	77.2	4.3	81.5	13.9
Glendale	2,168,632	17.2	171	11.5	72.9	4.2	77.1	11.4
River Hills	617,021	13.6	403	10.6	66.5	4.9	71.4	18.0
Shorewood	2,459,487	9.5	147	33.4	51.6	1.7	53.3	13.3
Whitefish Bay	2,404,389	9.5	128	16.6	55.1	2.6	57.7	25.7

a Budgets exclude: schools, water utilities, special assessments, bond issues, long-term loans, metropolitan sewerage operation charges.

b Due primarily to the retirement of the $311,250 Fox Point capital debt in 1969.

c Oak Creek levies no municipal property tax. Shared taxes alone generate 4 per cent *more* in revenues than is needed to balance the municipal budget.

SOURCES: Citizens' Governmental Research Bureau *Bulletin* 58, no. 5 (May 30, 1970); County of Milwaukee, *Summary of 1970 Budget and Personnel*, pp. vii, xiii.

Appendix J

*Equalized Assessed Valuation of Taxable Property in
Milwaukee City and County, 1949–70*[a]

Year	Milwaukee City (in thousands)	Total Milwaukee County (in thousands)	Per Cent of Total Within City
1949	$1,618,281	$2,375,561	68.1
1951	2,128,074	3,128,017	68.0
1953	2,746,820	4,044,371	67.9
1955	3,029,567	4,446,132	68.1
1957	3,466,457	5,195,742	66.7
1959	3,645,716	5,590,881	65.2
1961	3,756,093	5,885,077	63.8
1963	3,856,595	6,119,908	63.0
1965	4,014,665	6,467,723	62.1
1967	4,350,040	7,157,772	60.8
1969	4,657,427	7,940,429	58.7
1970	5,027,261	8,613,746	58.4

[a] Equalized assessed valuation is an approximation of full market value and is determined annually by the Bureau of Property Taxation, Wisconsin Department of Revenue.

Index